Democratization and Struggles against Injustice

Collective Studies in Knowledge and Society

Series Editor: James H. Collier is Associate Professor of Science and Technology in Society at Virginia Tech, USA.

This is an interdisciplinary series published in collaboration with the Social Epistemology Review and Reply Collective. It addresses questions arising from understanding knowledge as constituted by, and constitutive of, existing, dynamic and governable social relations.

Titles in the Series

The Future of Social Epistemology: A Collective Vision, Edited by James H. Collier

Social Epistemology and Technology: Toward Public Self-Awareness Regarding Technological Mediation, Edited by Frank Scalambrino

Socrates Tenured: The Institutions of 21st Century Philosophy, Adam Briggle and Robert Frodeman

Social Epistemology and Epistemic Agency, Edited by Patrick J. Reider

Democratic Problem-Solving: Dialogues in Social Epistemology, Justin Cruickshank and Raphael Sassower

The Kuhnian Image of Science: Time for a Decisive Transformation?, Edited by Moti Mizrahi

Taking Conspiracy Theories Seriously, Edited by M. R. X. Dentith

Overcoming Epistemic Injustice: Social and Psychological Perspectives, Edited by Benjamin R. Sherman and Stacey Goguen

Heraclitus Redux: Technological Infrastructures and Scientific Change, Joseph C. Pitt

Epistemic Paternalism: Conceptions, Justifications and Implications, Edited by Guy Axtell and Amiel Bernal

Philosophy in the Age of Science? Inquiries into Philosophical Progress, Method, and Societal Relevance, Edited by Wouter Floria Kalf, Michael Klenk, Jeroen Hopster, and Julia Hermann

Minority Report: Dissent and Diversity in Science, William T. Lynch

Democratization and Struggles against Injustice: A Pragmatist Approach to the Epistemic Practices of Social Movements, Justo Serrano Zamora

Democratization and Struggles against Injustice

A Pragmatist Approach to the Epistemic Practices of Social Movements

Justo Serrano Zamora

ROWMAN & LITTLEFIELD

London • New York

Rowman & Littlefield
4501 Forbes Boulevard, Suite 200, Lanham, Maryland 20706, USA
With additional offices in Boulder, New York, Toronto (Canada), and Plymouth (UK)
www.rowman.com

British Library Cataloguing in Publication Data

A catalogue record for this book is available from the British Library

ISBN: HB 978-1-53815-154-9

Library of Congress Cataloging-in-Publication Data

Names: Serrano Zamora, Justo, 1983- author.
Title: Democratization and struggles against injustice : a pragmatist approach to the
    epistemic practices of social movements / Justo Serrano Zamora.
Description: Lanham : Rowman & Littlefield, [2021] | Series: Collective studies in
    knowledge and society | Includes bibliographical references and index. | Summary:
    "This book provides a unique experimentalist approach to social movements that
    accounts both for the democratizing potential and the counter-hegemonic power of
    the epistemic practices of mobilized citizens"—Provided by publisher.
Identifiers: LCCN 2021003151 (print) | LCCN 2021003152 (ebook) |
    ISBN 9781538151549 (cloth) | ISBN 9781538151570 (ebook)
Subjects: LCSH: Social movements—Philosophy. | Democracy—Philosophy. |
    Democratization.
Classification: LCC HM881 .S49 2021 (print) | LCC HM881 (ebook) |
    DDC 303.48/4—dc23
LC record available at https://lccn.loc.gov/2021003151
LC ebook record available at https://lccn.loc.gov/2021003152

Contents

Contents

Acknowledgments

Bringing about this project has been a fascinating adventure from which I have learned a lot. Luckily, I have not been alone. I would like to thank, first, Axel Honneth and Roberto Frega for their invaluable support and engagement with my work. Arvi Särkelä, Gianfranco Casuso and Kurt Mertel have been both my friends and my closest intellectual partners during my writing process. I have had the chance to discuss parts of my book in many different contexts. Here I can just offer an incomplete list: the Institut für Sozialforschung (Frankfurt am Main); my defense committee at the Faculty of Philosophy of the Frankfurt University; Peter Niesen's colloquium at the TU Darmstadt; Fedinand Sutterlüty's colloquium as well as Axel Honneth's colloquium at the University of Frankfurt; Lisa Herzog's colloquium at the Hochschule für Politik in Munich; the CEMS-EHESS in Paris, and the seminars Roberto Frega and I have taught at the EHESS. I have also presented and discussed my work in several workshops and conferences, including John Dewey and Critical Philosophies (University College Dublin, 2017), Dewey Through Generations Panel (Washington D.C, 2016), The Future of Critique and Emancipatory Practice (EUI, Florence, 2015) and Razones: Libertad, naturaleza y posibilidad (Universidad Católica de Lima, 2015).

I also would like to thank Regina Kreide, Carolin Amlinger, Kristina Lepold, Christopher Zurn, Cornelia Schendzielorz, Stefanie Hürtgen, Benjamin Möller, Julia Masurkewiz, William Callison, Stephan Voswikel, Gregory Fernando Pappas, Sebastián Tobón, Daniel Cefai, Roberto Gronda, Dennis Ohm-Fickler, Matteo Santarelli, Martin Oppelt, Hervé Deswattenne, Federica Gregoratto, Andreas Antic, Jakob Moggia, Elior Kramer, Matin Oppelt, Tullio Viola, Peter Wagner, Edgar Strahle, Hannes Kuch, Cristina Popescu, Miquel Seguró and Sam Sadian for critical engaging with my work at different stages of my writing process. I also would like to thank to those who helped me along my journey and who gave me the courage I needed to carry on this project. Finally, I would like to express my gratitude to the Bischöftliche Studienförderung Cusanuswerk for their financial and intellectual support.

I dedicate this book to my mother and to the memory of my father.

Introduction

From Massive Evictions to Deepening Democracy

The 2008 financial crisis had very concrete effects on people's lives around the globe. In Spain, global financial instability was combined with the deficits of the domestic economy. In a country with high levels of mortgage debt, massive unemployment, and the impassivity of public institutions, thousands of families were condemned to leave their homes without any alternative left but seeking shelter with their relatives or sleeping in the street. The *Plataforma de Afectados por la Hipoteca (PAH)* was born in 2009 as a civil-societal response to this ongoing episode of massive evictions. The work of the members of the PAH—mostly activists and regular citizens directly affected by eviction announcements—went beyond effectively stopping hundreds of evictions and giving public visibility to this urgent problem at a time when big media outlets were silencing the devastating effects of the economic crisis. The PAH created solidarity networks, it developed new strategies of action, it organized innovative forms of political protests, and it promoted legal reforms aiming at protecting vulnerable individuals. Among its major achievements, the members of the PAH were successful in articulating the experiences of those directly affected by evictions as bearing some form of social injustice. Hence, they no longer talked about the economic "crisis," they started considering it a social "fraud." The PAH managed to build an oppositional consciousness (Mansbridge 2001a, 2001b), opposing those hegemonic views that attributed individual responsibility to the victims of the economic crisis (Mir 2016).

But there is one further achievement that deserves special attention from the side of all those interested in democracy and its actual fate. Seen as both a condition for the building of a consciousness of injustice and the efficiency of their collective actions, the members of the PAH placed special emphasis on implementing innovative forms of discussion and decision-making that fostered inclusion and horizontal participation. They organized assemblies, working groups, informal discussions, workshops, and so on, in ways that created symmetric relations between experts in legal and economic issues, activists, and those lay citizens directly affected by evictions (Colau & Alemany 2013). By doing this, they promoted the inclusion of a variety of perspectives and generated processes of individual and collective learning about topics such as self-organization, interaction with media, care, consumer rights, and the use of legal terminology. As a prominent example, the PAH promoted the political participation of social groups that were previously excluded from political life, such as Latin American women migrants, who played a decisive role in collective organization and political practice (Suarez 2017). All these democratic innovations were in continuity with the political cultures of activists struggling for housing rights many years before the financial crisis and involved a reactualization of old practical repertoires.[1] However, it should be underlined that the members of the PAH came to see in these practical innovations and reactualizations an essential condition for their success in generating collective knowledge, organizing protest, understanding injustice, promoting solidarity and effective action in the course of their struggles. In this way, participants in the movement came to relate their perception of collective victory to the very capacity of the PAH to generate deep forms of democratic practice in ways that challenged current political practices: "¡Sí, se puede!"[2] was their motto. And they immediately added: "but only if we collectively organize in a deeply democratic way."

After the activities of the PAH irrupted into public debate in the aftermath of the global financial crisis, these innovative forms of understanding democratic practice became one major reference for the protesters who reassembled in the squares of many Spanish cities. Those protests gave birth to what came to be called the *15M* or the *indignados* movement. The new, radical interpretations given by the PAH to the democratic nature of effective political action were echoed by those who demanded a *"Democracia Real YA"*; a "Real Democracy Now;" giving rise to a creative exchange of political experiences and democratic innovations.[3] What had been born in a collective effort to identify, articulate the problem of massive evictions as yielding an "injustice," and to implement just solutions significantly contributed to the transformation and implementation of current understandings of political action. It contributed to making citizens reconsider how

---

[1] See Martí (2017) for the influence of Spanish republicanism in the *Indignados* movement.
[2] Colau & Alemany (2013).
[3] See Martí (2017).

a "real" democracy would look like, expanding thereby the limits of their political imagination.[4]

The PAH is only one example among many others in which the struggle against injustice has gone hand in hand with the generation of new forms of collective organization, forms that challenge hegemonic understandings of democracy and democratic practices that reduce the latter to "electoral processes to form governments" (De Sousa Santos 2009: xxxvi). In the long list of such movements, we should also count feminist movements,[5] LGTBIQ+ rights struggles,[6] anticolonialist struggles,[7] workers' movements,[8] as well as movements for alternative globalization(s)[9] and for climate justice.[10] Not only well-established movements with a long tradition have promoted democratization, also geographically and temporally localized struggles like students' protests for better education,[11] antiausterity movements,[12] neighborhood organizations,[13] internal worker struggles in economically strategic sectors,[14] public struggle against the silencing of crimes committed by Latin American dictatorships,[15] just to name a few well-studied cases, have contributed to challenge hegemonic understandings of democracy. In online political life, new forms of contestation such as the *Me Too* movement have emerged, linked to the new role played by information technologies, promoting new forms of understanding political practice in the digital age.[16]

---

[4] Polletta (2004) has shown how many social movements consciously adopt internal democratic organization for reasons of political effectiveness. The question of political effectiveness is certainly part of any epistemic approach to social movements since it involves success in finding and implementing solutions to social problems. In this book I will focus on the normative dimension of problem definitions and problem solutions. In other words, it is not only about being effective but also about effectively identifying injustices and promoting just social relations.

[5] For how feminism has contributed to a deepening of democracy, see Mansbridge (1998).

[6] See De la Dehesa (2010).

[7] See Von Eschen (1997).

[8] See, for example, Castoriadis (2013a) and (2013b). Karl Marx makes in *The Civil War in France* (2009) the following remarks regarding how the proletarian class sees in the *commune* of Paris the best political way to realize economic liberation: "The multiplicity of interpretations to which the Commune has been subjected, and the multiplicity of interests which construed it in their favor, show that it was a thoroughly expansive political form, while all the previous forms of government had been emphatically repressive. Its true secret was this: It was essentially a working class government, the product of the struggle of the producing against the appropriating class, the political form at last discovered under which to work out the economical emancipation of labor." (41) On proletarian publics see Negt & Kluge (1972).

[9] Della Porta (2009) and Maeckelbergh (2009).

[10] See Jamison (2011, 152). See also Demirovic (1989).

[11] See Guzman-Concha (2012).

[12] See della Porta (2013), Graeber (2013).

[13] See Cefai (2001).

[14] See, for example, Ghis Malfilatre (2017a) and (2017b).

[15] See Almeida & Johnston (2006), Casals & Perry (2020).

[16] For a study of the political role of contentious politics in the digital age, see Celikates (2015). Particularly interesting reflections about how social movements redefine political practice in the age of internet against the background of Habermas's notion of public sphere can be found in

The deepening of democratic practice promoted by these social struggles has adopted very different forms and continues to do so. In some cases, social movements have reconsidered the scope of those who should legitimately participate in practices of collective discussion and decision-making, thereby challenging hegemonic norms of inclusion. In other cases—and often simultaneously—innovations have concerned the procedures and methods put at work in political action.[17] In the same line, the deepening of democracy has involved the discussion about it to be considered a politically relevant or public issue, thereby expanding the "scope of questions" (Landemore 2013: 14) that are to be decided by democratic means.[18] Other movements have in their turn questioned the distribution of political power among formal political institutions and informal civil societal organizations.[19] Very often, these struggles have had a direct impact on political life by promoting the introduction of new democratic institutional arrangements and innovative forms of political practice. In other cases, the influence of these struggles on our democratic life has been less obvious but not less effective in providing new critical standards for challenging democratic practices and institutions. They have also promoted the emergence of new political cultures which are replicated, borrowed, adapted, and deepened in other mobilizations.[20]

This book aims at providing theoretical underpinning to the idea that, very often, the deepening[21] of democratic practice enacted by social movements can be directly attributed to the effort to identify, properly articulate, and promote solutions to social injustices. In other words, the need to collectively articulate grievances, to formulate justice claims, to make problems visible to the public and to oneself, to formulate solutions and organize effective (and just) collective action, in short, the building of an oppositional consciousness through "epistemic practices," has substantially contributed to deepening our common understandings of what it means to participate in political life. My thesis is both an empirical hypothesis and a theoretical claim. On the one hand, it aims

Dahlgren (2005). For a Deweyan approach to Global Acces to Knowledge Movement in the digital age, see Antic (2016).

[17] See Cefaï (2001, 2007, 2016), Cefaï & Lafaye (2001), Bohman (1998) and Della Porta (2009).
[18] See Della Porta (2017).
[19] See Della Porta (2009).
[20] See Mansbridge (2001a). Regarding communication and mutual influences among movements, see Tilly and Wood (2016: 14–15).
[21] Étienne Balibar and De Sousa Santos speak of a "democratization of democracy" (Balibar 2014: viii, De Sousa Santos 2005), Peter Wagner uses the expression "building democratic agency" (2016: 140), while Archon Fung and Erik-Olin Wright talk in terms of "deepening democracy" (2003). In the present study I use the latter expression in order to point to a main theoretical premise underlying my work, namely, that the developments involving the extension of inclusion, of the range and nature of "democratic" practices, and of "public topics" can be understood as realizing more adequate interpretations of political freedom and equality as the two basic democratic principles. I will also use the expression "democratic progress" to refer to this process.

to account for the fact that struggles against injustice have, due precisely to their orientation against injustice and toward justice, in many cases substantially contributed to change our understanding of democracy in deeper ways. On the other hand, it aims at theoretically substantiating this hypothesis by arguing that *the epistemic conditions for generating a collective consciousness against injustice have a democratizing potential.* Certainly, the conditions for building an oppositional consciousness do not only concern the epistemic practices of the oppressed. As Jane Mansbridge puts it, among other things:

> Oppositional consciousness requires ideal resources—ideas available in the culture that can be built upon to create legitimacy, a perception of injustice, righteous anger, solidarity, and a belief in the group's power. It requires emotional involvement and commitment. It also requires institutional resources. (Mansbridge 2001a: 7)[22]

Furthermore, an *epistemic* path to democratization is not the only way in which the deepening of democratic practice can be actually promoted by social movements. On the contrary, it needs to be seen as complementary to and, in many cases, simultaneous with other dynamics of democratization. Thus, we can identify at least another major path, namely, the one drawn by people's need for political recognition and inclusion in the political sphere.[23] As Axel Honneth (2014b) would put it, this path is fundamentally based on the capacity of individuals to reinterpret the norms and values that are embodied in social practices as well as on their fundamental need to be recognized as members of the political community. Hence, political practices and institutions embody—though only in limited form—political norms and values such as maximal inclusion and political equality. More often than not, these institutions and practices embody specific interpretations of those norms that exclude certain social groups from equal political participation. At some point, excluded groups learn, in virtue of their need for recognition, to see themselves as legitimate members of the political community and reclaim new interpretations of those values and norms so that they can be recognized as legitimate participants in political life. In contrast to this first recognition-based dynamics of political transformation, the second dynamics this book focuses on is based on the epistemic function of democratic practice as an autonomous democratizing force.

---

[22] As we will see later, not all these elements are to be seen as external to epistemic practice. Hence, political emotions such as anger or solidarity do not only have themselves a cognitive content but represent enabling conditions for epistemic practice. See Santarelli & Serrano Zamora (2020), Cojocaru (2018), and Queré (2012).

[23] See Honneth (2004). This certainly does not imply that we can identify more factors of political transformation such as aesthetic ones. Note, however, that both the moral and epistemic dynamics I aim at exploring have an essential aesthetic dimension.

In other words, in the present book I argue that next to the need for recognition and inclusion in democratic practices (and often complementing
it), an independent motivational source for changing our way of practicing
democracy concerns the capacity of democratic practices and institutions to
effectively identify and fight unjust social relations and promote justice. I
call these dynamics "epistemic" because they concern the capacity of institutions and practices to identify, define, and effectively solve social problems.
As the example of the PAH shows, the democratic quality of institutions
and practices is often reinforced and advanced not only because citizens
believe that current practices do not fully embody what they see as the
adequate realization of intrinsic democratic values. However important this
first motivation might be, citizens still may want to reinforce and advance
democracy because they see in it the necessary condition for achieving a
more just society.

In my view, pointing to the democratic contribution deriving from people's
efforts against injustice and toward a more just society represents a fundamental step for grasping to its full extent the political potential of many
emancipatory social movements. Hence, the present project emerges out of
the concern that, with a few exceptions, current accounts of social movements
have systematically overseen this epistemic dynamics of democratization. On
the one hand, in the literature on democracy and social movements we find
epistemic approaches to social movements that see them as merely "providers" of valuable information. These approaches have tended to conceive of
the contribution of social movements to democracy in terms of the *situated
perspectives* members of oppressed groups may convey in public discussion. Deliberative democrats like Iris Marion Young (2001) or John Dryzek
(2002) have put an emphasis on the positive epistemic effects of including
the points of view of the oppressed in democratic decision-making, based on
the idea that they enrich the amount of available perspectives in deliberation.
By enriching deliberation, at least certain forms of injustice can be effectively
identified and overcome.[24] By focusing on the *content* of perspectives and
demands rather than on the innovative potential of collective *practices*, however, theorists have tended to neglect the extent to which struggles are able to
challenge and transform the very practices in which those contents are collectively elaborated. This represents a serious challenge for democratic theory
since the political role we can attribute to social movements and the ways
in which we should conceive their significance for the political debates very

---

[24] As I will show, Young's position cannot be reduced to a "content-based account," since her work
also offers valuable insights regarding the kind of practice-based account I aim to elaborate in the
present study.

much depend on if we conceive them as mere providers of information or as coinquirers in the identification and resolution of our common problems.

On the other hand, we also find nonepistemic approaches to the democratic contribution of social movements. These approaches have certainly pointed to the capacity of many movements to promote innovative democratic forms and fostering inclusion, transforming the terms and procedures of political participation, also in digital times (Della Porta 2013). However, any approach that disconnects this democratizing capacity entirely from the movements' efforts to identify, define, and find solutions to social injustices has to confront a major difficulty. Hence, if we understand their democratizing powers to be exclusively the result of people's struggle for better forms of democracy that recognize them as political subjects on equal stand, our analysis loses sight of an autonomous source of democratic innovation that has a democratizing potential on its own. Hence, we may need to explain why some social group (undocumented immigrants, women, workers, slaves) has historically come to participate in political life (through their struggles) not because they struggled for political inclusion but because they wanted certain problems to be acknowledged and solved. Furthermore, this need to confront problems might have brought certain groups to participate in political life even when this was unthinkable from the hegemonic normative point of view of their society. Epistemic motivations have the potential to challenge hegemonic understandings of political values and norms and to expand the limits of our political imagination, a potential that cannot be explained only by people's struggle for political recognition.

I have referred to the epistemic dimension of political practices in social movements as including the identification and articulation of social injustices as well as the search for just social relations.[25] This view involves certain background assumptions regarding the characterization of the epistemic role of political practices and institutions in general. These assumptions are objects of discussion in the debate about the epistemic features of democracy, which has been driven by authors like Joshua Cohen, David Estlund, Elizabeth Anderson, and Fabienne Peter. Hence, one of the aims of this book is to explore the potential of the debates on epistemic democracy for the study of social movements, and particularly, the productivity of a pragmatist, John

---

[25] Note that this might involve not only movement's projects for institutional transformations in society at large. By "fighting injustice and promoting just relations" I also refer to more immediate problems regarding internal organization of the movement. So, for example, movements have to organize digital communication in a way that all (also those who are not familiarized with digital technologies) can equally participate. In fact, most of the apparently "technical problems" regarding the organization of a movement also have a normative component: they distribute resources more or less equally, they realize values better or worse, and so on. In this sense, being effective in the resolution of problems means, in our context, resolving them both in their strictly technical and moral dimensions.

Dewey-based approach. A few preliminary points may be necessary to understand the specific position I aim at defending within these debates.

First of all, in line with its focus on justice (and the fight against injustice) as the goal of social movements, the present account takes distance from what Fabienne Peter calls a "pure epistemic proceduralist" approach to democracy (Peter 2009). According to her view, the epistemic value of democratic procedures or practices is not to be measured according to the quality of political outcomes, but rather to the capacity of procedures to realize epistemic values. These values are intrinsic to epistemic practice itself, and include the value of epistemic fairness and inclusion. In contrast to this pure epistemic proceduralist approach, the view I aim at defending here does pivot on the question about the quality of the outcomes of democratic practice: democratization and the further deepening of existing democratic forms must be seen as requirements of people's efforts to "getting it right" in questions affecting them, whereby by "getting it right" I mean contributing to identify, properly articulate and, in the best case, solve a social problem. Surely, this view relies on the assumption that an outcome-based epistemic justification of democracy can be at the basis of the epistemic path to democratization this book aims at accounting for. It also represents a necessary step if our aim is to substantiate the idea of a connection between the democratization power of social movements and their pursuit of just social relations.

At the same time, the present account also takes distance from those approaches which assume that the epistemic value of any democratic procedures is to be measured according to their capacity to generate decisions that come close to a predetermined outcome, that is, a standard of correctness which is fully independent of the process that generates them.[26] In the present account, the epistemic dimension of democratic practice refers to its capacity to identify, articulate, and solve social problems that are at the same time "at once given and made" (Jaeggi 2018: 142). This is an idea that will be explored in detail in subsequent chapters even if some previous clarification may help to avoid misunderstandings.

By affirming that the kinds of problems social movements deal with are "at once given and made" I point to Dewey's idea according to which experimental inquiry represents the process of progressive determination of a partially indeterminate situation.[27] Experimental inquiry starts with the identification of some "determinate" aspects that vaguely point to the normative problematicity of certain social relations and structures. The process of inquiry involves the articulation of the situation as a definite problem. A problem is however only fully defined when its definition has empirically proved to be apt for its

---

[26] See, for example, Cohen (1986) and Estlund (2008).
[27] See LW: 12, Ch. VI.

solution, which is to be seen as the final stage of the determination process of the vague situation. Concerning collective processes of identification and articulation of injustice, the model proposed here assumes that the determination of a situation as unjust is a partly constructive process through which "unjust" situations are properly described and normatively evaluated. But in this process available notions of (in)justice are mobilized and may be actually transformed. Accordingly, the present book defends an epistemic account of democratic practice that assumes that the last word about justice must be left to the very process of its *articulation*. This thesis is certainly not incompatible with the affirmation that problems of justice have an objective dimension. However, as I aim to show, it certainly means a displacement from David Estlund's (2008) idea that the results of democratic practice can be measured from the perspective of a fully independent standard of correctness.

As I mentioned, the aim of this book is to provide a theoretical underpinning to the observation that social movements, in their attempts to identify, define, and solve social problems, often develop promising democratizing potentials. Based on the observation that in some historically available cases, social movements have effectively promoted democratization in their attempts to fight injustice, its goal is to explore a plausible explanation for it. In my view, this explanation can be provided by drawing on Dewey's notion of experimental inquiry. As I will show in later chapters, this is mainly due to two main features of experimental inquiry. First of all, from the background of a society marked by ideological hegemony that often veils the existence of hierarchies and power relations, the adoption of some form of experimental inquiry seems to be, other conditions given, positive (and maybe necessary) for unveiling those power relations. In other words, I want to show that the generation of an oppositional consciousness among those suffering from domination under conditions of hegemonic ideologies depends, other conditions given, on adopting an experimentalist attitude toward the experiences of individuals who suffer from domination. At the same time, experimentalism represents a form of collective inquiry that has by itself a democratizing force. Hence, adopting an experimental attitude in matters of social injustice involves developing strategies that deepen inclusion and participatory equality and which are understood by experimentalists as conditions for their own epistemic success.

In any case, the attempt to connect democratization and the fight against injustice through the notion of experimental inquiry represents a theoretical exercise that needs to be taken as an empirical hypothesis[28] to be tested. My aim is not to deny that other "methods" of inquiry can play a similar role[29]

---

[28] See, for a similar distinction, Landemore (2017).

[29] An interesting alternative to Dewey's experimentalist "method" is Th. W. Adorno's notion of "dialectical thinking" as a form of nonreified thinking (see Adorno 2017). Adorno's view seems

nor to deny that other nonepistemic factors may have been more decisive in the process. At the same time, I do not assume that all social movements succeed in generating an oppositional culture[30] or in generating more democratic forms of organization and decision-making. However, in line with authors like Jürgen Habermas, who sees in the adoption of democratic procedures the condition for the generation of concrete, just decisions (Habermas 1998a), my view is consistent with the thesis that any restriction in the democratic quality of a social movement must have, at least in long term, negative effects regarding the "normative quality" of their claims and decisions. In other words, we have good reasons to doubt about ability of movements that organize in nondemocratic, authoritarian ways to fully grasp the injustice of situations and to promote just social relations. Hence, exclusion of perspectives that follows, in more or less subtle ways, from authoritarian organization makes the necessary contrast, elaboration, and enrichment of our political claims particularly difficult if not impossible. Furthermore, even if an authoritarian movement may come to defend a just general cause, lack of inclusion within the movement sets reasonable doubt on the movement's capacity to give adequate concretion to its claims. Conversely, this view also sets reasonable doubt on the honesty of those movements who reclaim democracy as their preferred method of political organization while at the same time claiming for the restriction of rights of minorities. It would be certainly interesting to investigate if these kinds of movements are actually democratic, or if, on the contrary, they hide forms of authoritarian rule that permeate people's habits and character. By connecting democratization and the struggle against injustice, the book hopes to stimulate this sort of empirical explorations.

ARGUMENT AND STRUCTURE OF THE BOOK

The present study is divided into three parts. Part I aims at correcting what I consider to be a major deficit in current deliberative accounts, namely,

---

to be an interesting point of departure for an explanation of the necessary epistemic conditions for the emergence of an oppositional consciousness in social movements. Hence, for Adorno, dialectical thinking represents a method of inquiry that is able to unveil social wrongs. Even if this exploration cannot be pursued in the context of this book chapter 5 I will come back to Adorno's view of reified and nonreified thinking and show that Dewey's experimentalist view of inquiry is nonreified. To this extent, it represents a promising point of departure for describing how social movements are able to unveil injustices that would otherwise remain hidden. More generally, on the possibility of a dialogue between Critical Theory and Deweyan pragmatism where the notion inquiry plays a central role, see Kadlec (2007), Frega (2014, 2015a, 2015b, 2016), Testa (2017), and Särkelä and Serrano (2017).

[30] See Mansbridge (2001a).

the partial or full disregard of the epistemic dimension of democracy as the generator of innovative transformations and deepening of existing understandings of democracy. Part II aims to develop central insights for a theory of the epistemic practices in social movements. It explores the connection between their struggle against injustice and their capacity for advancing democracy. In order to account for this connection, it draws on John Dewey's notion of experimental inquiry. Part III explores in more detail some of these insights, focusing on the value of the experimentalist approach for approaching current debates on epistemic democracy and social movements. Before turning to chapter 1, let me first present the structure of the book in more detail.

Part I is meant to outline the democracy-theoretical context that is at the background of my epistemic approach to social movements. Hence, I take the latter to represent what many Deweyans would call "democratic publics," (Frega 2019), that is, collectives driven by specific social concerns that not only participate in democratic political life in a broad sense but also which often put at work democratic practices as part of their internal organization. From this perspective, I believe that the current discussions on epistemic democracy can have a say on the way we approach social movements, particularly, on the way political and epistemic concerns are articulated within social movements. My central thesis is that, through an exploration of Dewey's theory of democracy, we can gain a fruitful insight about the way in which social movements are able to challenge and deepen well-established understandings of democracy. In order to develop this idea, I follow the following steps. Chapter 1 starts with a discussion on democracy's two main values: democracy's intrinsic value—its capacity to embody fundamental democratic values such as self-determination and its derivative norms such as inclusion and equality in political participation—and its epistemic value, understood as the capacity to identify, define, and resolve problems of injustice. While some authors identify a necessary tension between both values and develop different normative strategies to come to terms with it, ranging from a full rejection of one of the values to the assumption of a hierarchical relation between both, other authors defend a compatibilist view that sees in the adequate institutionalization of democracy the condition for the generation of better and more just decisions. Among the latter, however, we can hardly find any view that is able to account for the capacity of democracy's epistemic value to stimulate changes in the specific interpretations that we give to democracy's intrinsic values in our everyday political practices.

Exceptionally, Fabienne Peter (2009) offers valuable insights on this epistemic dynamics of democratic deepening. According to Peter, we can gain "better" interpretations of democracy's intrinsic value and its derivative norms if we consider that democratic practices are also epistemic practices, aiming at the production of knowledge about how to cope with the problems of our social world. This is so because the norms that govern our epistemic practices have the potential of stimulating a change in the specific interpretations we usually give, for example, to the norm of political inclusion. After considering Peter's view in more detail, the chapter points to some of the advantages of proposing a version of Peter's approach that is based on the work of John Dewey (this Deweyan version is fully developed in chapter 3).

In chapters 2 and 3, my exploration is pursued through the critical examination of two different accounts of democratic practice: those of Axel Honneth and John Dewey. Despite the central difference lying between their approaches to democracy's epistemic value, the two authors provide insights regarding a dynamic view of democratic practice that allows us to speak in terms of democratic deepening. Hence, both for Honneth and Dewey, the possibility of deepening democracy must be rather understood as arising from improvements in the concrete interpretations given to the norms of (social) freedom immanent to political practice. However, even if Honneth's approach provides a plausible understanding of the normative dynamics lying behind the political learning processes that have historically taken place in modern democratic societies, only Dewey is able to fully account for the role democracy's epistemic dimension has played in that dynamics. In line with this idea, Dewey's theory of democratic transformation is presented as able to include Honneth's valuable normative approach and to expand it from an epistemic perspective, such that we can arrive at a more comprehensive understanding of the transformative potential of democracy.

Having brought to the fore the epistemic value of democracy as an autonomous motor of political transformation with radical potential, part II turns to the question about the particular contribution social movements can make to political life in their role as collective inquirers into social problems. As I have previously mentioned, this epistemic approach does not intend to deny the political potentials of other dimensions, particularly the normative and aesthetic dimension of mobilization. Moreover, it is necessary to prevent readers who are not familiarized with John Dewey's work from a strictly scientistic understanding of the idea of inquiry as well as of the epistemological vocabulary that will be deployed along this book. As it is shown in parts II and III, inquiry is essentially an articulative and expressive practice, one that can take very different forms, and in which affects, creativity, and imagination are deeply involved. So, practices such as those of the PAH but also what in second-wave feminism came to be called "consciousness-raising meetings" as well as a variety of other practices that, even if less visible, play a central role in the everyday of mobilization are taken to be instantiations of epistemic practices or methods of collective inquiry.

Thus, Dewey's notion of inquiry seems, due precisely to this rich understanding, a perfect candidate for accounting for those social practices that have in the articulation of experiences of injustice and the generation, implementation, and test of social alternatives that are at the core of our analysis. Hence, in order to account for the link I have previously identified between the collective struggle against injustice and pursuit of justice and the deepening of democratic practices, the present account focuses on what I call the "epistemic practices" or "practices of inquiry" of struggling collectives. I call epistemic to those practices directly or indirectly involved in the identification and definition of social problems such as that of injustice or domination as well as the formulation, implementation, and testing of possible solutions. Aware of the power dynamics in which practices of inquiry are embedded, social struggles are approached from the perspective of their capacity to generate innovative methodologies that are able to challenge *hegemonic* practices of public inquiry. In other words, they are considered in their role as *counter-hegemonic methodological innovators*.

But this is not the only contribution a Deweyan, inquiry-based approach to social struggles can make to current discussions. In fact, even if they do not use the same terminology proposed here, authors have already pointed to the capacity of social movements to generate practices that are able to articulate counter-hegemonic perspectives. This is precisely the case again of Miranda Fricker's analysis of consciousness-raising as inclusive forms of collective organization and communication that were able to generate new notions such as that of "sexual harassment" and "post-natal depression," which were able to account for the situated experiences of women thereby contributing to the overcoming of what Fricker calls "hermeneutical injustice" (Fricker 2007: 147–165). From this background, the aim of part II is to go a step further in the analysis of the counter-hegemonic power of epistemic practices by focusing both on the inclusive/exclusive effects of innovative communicative settings and the very "logical" structure of the inquiries that are put at work in these settings. Undertaking a logical analysis in Deweyan terms means[31] focusing on the capacity of movements as counter-hegemonic methodological innovators to challenge and transform the basic epistemic operations that take place in any public inquiry.

In general, we might say that these basic operations concern the relation between facts and ideas that is constitutive for any inquiry (LW 12, Longino 2002). In the view I aim at developing, it is precisely the transformations

---

[31] About the possibility and the interest of providing a logical perspective into political analysis, even from a different perspective as the one developed here, see Aya (2006).

concerning the relation between (operations with) facts and (with) ideas what can be at the root of what I have called the counter-hegemonic power of the inquiries of social movements. Hence, we observe very often that, even when epistemically positive conditions such as the promotion of cognitive self-esteem—which is, according to Fricker, at the origin of the counter-hegemonic power of consciousness-raising—are given, inquirers may still fail to articulate experiences in ways that can come to be experienced as adequately accounting for their own social experience. By pointing to the logical analysis of those collective inquiries, my aim is not only to point to the deep level in which inquiries may be distorted, but also to the kind of epistemic operations that may promote the emergence of an oppositional consciousness.

In order to develop this line of thought, part II focuses on social movements, taking them in their double potential as producers of counter-hegemonic views and as generators of deep democratic practices. In a first step, chapter 4 develops the idea that social movements often put at work epistemic practices that are able to generate counter-hegemonic knowledge, be it about how do describe social reality, about how to evaluate it as just or unjust or both. Accordingly, movements should be seen as collective inquirers making a specific epistemic contribution to democratic life that goes beyond providing a "different" perspective on social reality. While this is certainly important, movements also develop counter-hegemonic methods of collective inquiry. They are methodological innovators. In order to develop this idea, I explore and show the limits of the work of three existing epistemic approaches to social movements—that of James Bohman, Iris Marion Young, and Elizabeth Anderson. I also examine the existing literature on social practices and "knowledge practices" that is at the background of the present view.

After having shown that social movements should be taken as counter-hegemonic methodological innovators, chapter 5 develops the central argument of the book. It fledges out the idea that a Deweyan, experimentalist approach contributes to a better understanding of social movements' epistemic life and their dual counter-hegemonic potential: as generators of counter-hegemonic view and, simultaneously, as promoters of counter-hegemonic understandings of democracy. Based on Dewey's theory of inquiry, it develops an experimentalist approach that focuses on two main features: the "fluidity" of between the basic operations of inquiry that is enacted in experimental inquiries, and the articulative nature of experimental inquiry. As I will show in discussion with T. W. Adorno's notion of reified thinking, these two features, fluidity and articulation, essentially contribute to enhancing for the group's counter-hegemonic power, that is, for its capacity to generate alternative views of the world that are able to unmask existing power relations. At the same time, Dewey's experimentalism will be also shown to promote "deep" forms of democratic cooperation since they represent the condition for the epistemic success of counter-hegemonic inquires. From this background, chapter 6 approaches several well-studied cases of epistemic practices such as consciousness-raising groups during the second-wave feminist movements, testimonial practices in South- and Central-America, and the *conricerca* of Italian factory workers as examples of experimental, counter-hegemonic epistemic practices with democratizing potential.

Finally, part III explores some relevant implications of Dewey's notion of experimental inquiry, and more particularly, its articulative nature, for any epistemic approach to social movements. First of all, chapter 7 comes back to consciousness-raising in order to explore the theoretical prospects of the experimentalist approach in discussion with Miranda Fricker's analysis. Hence, for Fricker, consciousness-raising meetings were able to overcome epistemic injustices by promoting the cognitive confidence of the participants. According to my view, cognitive confidence is not a sufficient conditions for generating counter-hegemonic notions such as "sexual harassment" or "post-natal depression." This is only possible if those groups are also able to make their epistemic habits more experimental so that notions and personal experiences can be reconnected in a process of collective self-appropriation. Finally, drawing on Dewey's *Lectures in China* (1973, 2015), chapter 8 examines the internal developments and learning processes within social movements, understood as processes of articulation where experimental inquiry plays a major role. I develop the idea that the generation of experimental practices depends on factors such as the possibility for groups to participate in social life. Hence, by withholding social groups from any form of social participation, society deprives their members from the possibility of adopting an experimental attitude toward social reality. Hence, groups only become experimental if they can relate toward reality in a way that it can be taken both as a resource and as an obstacle for social action. As I show, this idea can be useful for developing a critical approach to the conditions that enable/block the development of experimentalism in social movements.

Part I

THE EPISTEMIC PATH TO DEMOCRATIZATION

Chapter 1

The Two Values of Democracy

In his contribution to the commemorative volume dedicated to Habermas, *Die Öffentlichkeit der Vernünft, die Vernünft der Öffentlichkeit* (2001), Bernhard Peters makes a central distinction concerning for the normative evaluation of democratic practices and institutions. While citizens, through their participation in democratic practices of public deliberation, can be said to realize values such as freedom, autonomy, equality, and mutual respect, they can also be seen as contributing to the quality—which may be further qualified as "rationality," "correctness," "justice," and so on—of the outcomes of political processes as well as of other cognitive elements—ideas, methods, problem-solutions—that are mobilized within them. In the first sense, democratic practices and institutions can be said to have an intrinsic value, while in the second sense, they have an instrumental or epistemic one.

The previous characterization may give the impression that we can either choose to justify democratic practices and institutions as legitimate from the perspective of the values they embody or to justify them by appealing to the epistemic quality of those practices and of the outcomes that result from them. We do in fact find political philosophies that assign relevance only to one of both possibilities. Thomas Christiano has discussed these views under the label of "monism." Among most political philosophers and democratic theorists, however, we find mixed approaches that combine both forms of justification. These combined or mixed models of democratic justification can be very different, ranging from those who assume a relation of potential incompatibility between both to those who argue for their compatibility. It is the aim of this chapter to provide a brief outline of the different positions to be found in current debates in epistemic democracy. At the same time, my goal is to point to the particular view that I aim at developing in the coming chapters, namely, the idea that intrinsic and epistemic values should be seen as standing in a relation of hermeneutical interaction, whereby the latter play an essential role in reinforcing and advancing the practical development of the former. The aim of this section is not to provide a systematic justification of this view, but rather to outline a general overview that serves to locate and make more precise the idea that intrinsic and epistemic justifications of democracy can interact with each other.

Among theories of democracy we can distinguish between two major positions regarding the relation between the two kinds of values: incompatibilist and compatibilist views. Incompatibilist theories hold that the practical and institutional requirements involved in the realization of each of the two kinds of values, intrinsic and epistemic, are in potential contradiction with each other. For incompatibilists, we cannot expect that democratic decision-making processes, no matter how inclusive and equal, will always be able to provide better outcomes than less inclusive or equal ones. Thus, in order to reach better outcomes, decision-making processes may sometimes need to limit the implementation of criteria of inclusion or of any procedural requirements derived from intrinsic democratic values. In other words, they may need to exclude certain groups or individuals from decision-making or to limit the equal participation of citizens, favoring the voice of those who are presumably better prepared for solving social problems. Facing this tension between both kinds of values, two groups of incompatibilist positions can be found in the literature as well as their monistic versions. On the one hand, we find those who defend the epistemic value of democracy over its intrinsic value in justifying and shaping democratic practices and institutions; on the other hand, those who give normative priority to their intrinsic value.

Moderate expertocrats are those incompatibilists who prioritize democracy's epistemic value over its intrinsic one. Moderate expertocrats are ready to limit the institutionalization of democracy's intrinsic values, for example, the scope of those who can legitimately participate in decision-making according to intrinsic principles, if such limitations involve an epistemic gain. These authors accept that democratic intrinsic values are valid and represent independent arguments for democracy. Thus, they argue that a mixed model combining both kinds of values is indeed desirable since intrinsic arguments play an important role in sustaining democratic institutions and practices. Their point is that a limitation in the practical realization of intrinsic values is desirable if this reduction contributes to reaching better outcomes or more efficient forms of collective problem-solving.

But expertocracy has also a nonmixed version, one that rejects the independent value of intrinsic arguments for democracy. Fabienne Peter describes this monist position, which she calls "epistemicism," in the following terms:

> According to epistemicists, political equality only has epistemic value—the value of political equality depends on its contribution to good outcomes overall, but does not, as in proceduralism, form an irreducible component of legitimacy. [. . .] If political equality does not contribute to better outcomes, it is not necessary for political legitimacy. (Peter 2009: 62)

This is the case, for example, of Richard J. Arneson, for whom "[s]ystems of governance should be assessed by their consequences; any individual has a moral right to exercise political power just to the extent that the granting of this right is productive of best consequences overall" (Arneson 2004: 40). For "epistemicists" or, in my words "monist expertocrats," the normative weight of intrinsic values such as political equality and maximal inclusion for shaping democratic practices and institutions is only derivative: they are only relevant to the extent to which they contribute to enhancing the quality of collective decision-making. In any case, taking intrinsic values as independent or derivative, epistocrats, moderate or monists, hold that the final shape taken by political institutions and practices—for example, the scope of those who can participate or the exact procedures a decision-making process should take—should be determined by epistemic criteria. To the extent that they assume that epistemic criteria of inclusion and epistemic procedures may be in tension with those deriving from intrinsic values, they advocate for restrictions in the realization of the latter.

For their part, incompatibilist democrats also claim that the realization of democratic principles may be detrimental to the quality of the outcomes of political processes of decision-making. However, contrary to defenders of expertocracy, they hold to the higher worth of democratic values. Even if democratic practices and institutions show to be incapable of solving public problems, or worse at doing so than other political systems, incompatibilist democrats still hold that the realization of political values is superior to the epistemic use of politics. For this reason, democratic practices and institutions should be shaped according to intrinsic criteria. As in the case of moderate and radical epistocrats, among democratic incompatibilists are those who deny to democracy any epistemic value at all—monists—and those who formulate a mixed model combining both intrinsic and epistemic values—moderate.

Monist democratic incompatibilists deny the possibility to justify democracy from an epistemic point of view, or even the desirability of doing so. Hannah Arendt's approach to democracy is in line with an understanding of democracy for which only counts its intrinsic value, while any attempt to consider democracy from the point of view of its epistemic use—like, for example, for its capacity to achieve more just social relations—represents a danger compromising the very possibility of realizing democratic values. We should also include under this label those approaches that Peter counts under the category of "Pure Proceduralism":

> What is commonly called Pure Proceduralism is the view that only the dimension of political equality or political fairness, is relevant for democratic legitimacy. According to conceptions of this kind, outcomes are legitimate as long as they are the result of an appropriately constrained process of democratic decision-making. This places all the normative weight on procedural values. (Peter 2009: 66)

Peter illustrates this view with Christiano's approach to democracy, which he characterizes in the following terms:

> [D]emocratic discussion, deliberation, and decision-making under certain conditions are what make the outcomes legitimate for each person . . . [W]hatever the results of discussions, deliberations, and decision-making . . . they are legitimate. The results are made legitimate by being the results of the procedure. (Christiano 1996: 35)

Outcomes are to be seen as legitimate only in virtue of the criteria and procedures followed in decision-making. This means that, for monist democratic incompatibilists, concerns about the quality of the outcomes cannot, in any case, play a normative role in shaping democratic institutions and practices. This must be left exclusively to intrinsic criteria.

In their turn, moderate democratic incompatibilists hold a mixed model of justification according to which democracy's epistemic value needs to be taken into account in normative reflection about democracy. However, due to the relative incompatibility of democracy's internal and epistemic values, they think of their relation in terms of a hierarchy in which democracy's internal value is prioritized while not leaving democracy's epistemic dimension fully out of the picture. This is the case of some of the defenders of epistemic democracy such as David Estlund in his classical book *Democratic Authority* (2008). For Estlund an epistocratic regime—that is, a regime where only those who know better are able to take decisions for the rest—may sometimes perform better than a democratic regime in finding the best solutions for social problems. Parting from this incompatibilist premise, he proposes the following strategy of democratic justification:

[I]t first demands that a procedure [of decision making] be 'recognizably democratic' [i.e. that it realizes democratic values and its derivative norms, JSZ], but
then adds to that the demand that, insofar as there is a choice among alternative
democratic decision-making procedures with different truth-tracking potential,
to implement the one that best tracks correct outcomes. (Peter 2009: 11)

On the other side of the spectrum we find an opposite understanding of
the relation between democracy's intrinsic and epistemic value, one that
denies a potential contradiction between the practical and institutional
requirements linked to both kinds of values. Compatibilist positions hold
that the concrete procedures of a decision-making process that derive
from intrinsic democratic norms such as equality enhance the quality of
democracy's epistemic function. According to compatibilist authors such
as Helène Landemore or Elizabeth Anderson, enhancing the quality of
the outcomes and processes of democratic decision-making requires the
practical and institutional implementations of intrinsic principles such as
maximal inclusion and political equality. Importantly, authors holding a
compatibilist view are willing to accept that political agents may de facto
come to see themselves forced to abandon democratic values in order to
identify and solve what they take to be their collective problems. However,
these authors believe that the democratically restrictive conclusions of
epistemic agents are wrong, precisely for epistemic reasons. Hence, by
restricting equal and inclusive public discussion about social problems,
agents deprive themselves of the use of otherwise available cognitive
resources and methods that may prove to be necessary for fulfilling the
concrete epistemic tasks of political processes. Fabienne Peter formulates
this view in a clarifying way:

Suppose the outcome of collective decision-making is sexist. It endorses a policy proposal that claims to increase the common good or social justice but rests
on sexist premises about family life. Now, a fair procedure should ensure that
everybody is able to participate in the process as an equal. It should enable all
those affected by and opposed to sexism to effectively challenge these premises
Longino's criterion of uptake of criticism that I discussed above underlines this
demand. If the procedure is genuinely fair, one would thus not expect a sexist
proposal to go through. Conversely, if a sexist proposal goes through, is this
not likely to be the result of unfair procedures, in which women may have been
nominally treated as equals, but not effectively so? I find it difficult to see how
a deliberative process can be called fair if deliberation over policy alternatives
leaves unchallenged background assumptions that undermine the equal standing
of all participants. (Peter 2009: 132)

For the compatibilist view, then, any gain in realizing intrinsic democratic values must have in its turn a positive epistemic effect, and any restriction must have a negative one. Conversely, any attempt at enhancing the quality of the outcomes of a political decision-making process must be compatible with the realization of intrinsic democratic values and sometimes even require a "deeper" interpretation of those values (see below). From this point of view, the inclusion of previously politically excluded minorities into the sphere of legitimate political practice must be seen as an enrichment of the resources available for taking good collective decisions. It goes the same way with political equality, which for compatibilists represents an epistemic requirement for enhancing the epistemic quality of the decision-making process and its results.

The two authors that are at the center of the coming analysis, Axel Honneth and John Dewey, provide different versions of this compatibilist approach to democratic justification. More importantly, they substantially differ in the way they conceive of the relation between both kinds of values. On the one hand, Honneth has provided a compatibilist model that, while affirming some kind of overlap between both kinds of democratic justification, keeps them essentially independent from each other. Intrinsic values, on the one hand, and epistemic values, on the other hand, seem to converge regarding the norms regulating the scope and the interactions of those participating in political life. However, they remain independent of each other. In fact, Honneth's aim is to show that, while democratic procedures and inclusion criteria can be independently justified via the mobilization of intrinsic values, the former also have a positive epistemic relevance.

In contrast to the idea of an overlap or convergence of both forms of justification defended by Honneth, Dewey provides what I will call an integrative approach to the relation between intrinsic and epistemic elements. The kind of phenomena that I have in mind with the term "integration" is can be already found in Fabienne Peter's "pure epistemic deliberative" model of democratic justification. In *Democratic Legitimacy* (2009) Peter aims at providing what she calls a "third epistemology of democracy," one that differs from two of the most extended models of epistemic democracy, that of David Estlund and that of John Dewey. Peter rejects both accounts due what she takes to be their problematic consequentialist, outcome-based premises. She identifies in Estlund's work a problematic veristic understanding of democracy that is based on the idea of a "procedure-independent standard of correctness." Due to this basic assumption, Estlund's model is unable to fully account for the "potentially productive value of epistemic diversity" (Peter 2009: 3) and conflict. Hence, "[b]ecause of the normative weight [Estlund's account] attaches to correctness, it will tend to cast persisting dissent in terms of an opposition between what counts as the correct view and what must be an expression of error" (Peter 2009: 3). On the other hand, Peter sees in Dewey's problem-solving approach a danger for democracy's reasonable pluralism. Even if Dewey, in virtue of his rejection of a veristic epistemology of the kind held by Estlund, is able to include epistemic diversity and conflict, his focus on the effective resolution of practical problems is unable to accommodate to the fact of reasonable pluralism by assuming that that there is something like a determinate solution to certain problems. Hence, reasonable pluralism involves that there may be problems that have no solution, since people's views about different ways to solve a problem may reasonably differ.

In order to avoid the problems related to each of these views, Peter provides a view based on a procedural epistemology which "focuses exclusively on the intrinsic merits of intellectual practices to judge their epistemic worth or property" (Peter 2009: 122). According to this proceduralist epistemology, the "epistemic value [of epistemic practice, J.S.Z.] resides in the process itself, and not in its outcome" (Peter 2009: 123). Peter draws her procedural epistemology from Helen Longino's feminist epistemological reflections. According to Peter, Longino has provided an epistemological account that is able to dissociate the normativity inherent to knowledge-producing practices "from a procedure-independent standard for what counts as a good outcome" (Peter 2009: 123). For Longino, the norms guiding epistemic practice depend on a view on science as a practice consisting in "critically engaging with each other in transparent and non-authoritarian ways" (Peter 2009: 124). They represent norms of epistemic fairness. Longino mentions four basic elements of this epistemic normativity: open criticism of original research, uptake of criticism, public standards of evaluation, and equality of intellectual authority (Peter 2009: 123–124). These normative criteria are meant to guide what Longino conceives of as the two basic set of operations of scientific inquiry: fact-gathering and operations of analysis. In the present context, it is central for Peter's argument that the norms specific to scientific practice are not derived from the goal of generating an outcome that is somehow external to the very process from which it results. On the contrary, they rely on a vision of epistemic normativity that is reconstructed by Helen Longino in her analysis of the norms guiding scientific practices.

This nonconsequentialist approach to science and to democratic decision-making is certainly different from the Deweyan approach I aim at developing in this book. Hence, in my Deweyan account, the normativity inherent to epistemic practices of science is to be derived from the historical accumulation of experiences of inquiry and processes of self-correction that result from inquirers' attempts to identify, define, and resolve social problems. This connects the epistemic normativity of inquiry to the quality of the outcomes that we can expect from it, that is, to their capacity to effectively resolve problems. Thus, in contrast to what Peter believes I believe that there are good reasons to argue that Dewey's problem-solving model is actually able to accommodate value pluralism. One of the reasons has to do with the fact that the expression "problem-solving" fails to fully capture the role of inquiry in Dewey's philosophy and the role problems play within it. Hence, inquiry represents a process of determination of an indeterminate situation where problems are identified but also defined or articulated and only in last instance solved (even if this last "solution" always remains open for discussion, so that actually it can hardly be called "definitive"). Hence, contrary to the idea of a procedure-independent standard of correctness, Dewey does not assume that problems are given as such and that the right solution is somehow waiting for them to be unveiled. Rather, problems are articulated as certain problems in a process that remain open, and which partially depend on the process of collective discussion itself. This view seems able to accommodate value pluralism, since it already acknowledges that there may be a reasonable disagreement about how to frame the problems citizens have to face (Rogers 2009, Festenstein 2018).

What is important at this point is that Peter argues that an epistemic justification of democracy based on her nonconsequentialist notion of scientific normativity can be integrated into a mixed mode of democratic justification in a way that seems to me particularly productive. Hence, more than being in a relation of convergence, Peter proposes a view that identifies a productive tension between intrinsic and epistemic normativities. In contrast to incompatibilism, this tension has the potential of changing and advancing our understanding of (the basic norms regulating) democratic practice. According to Peter, this epistemically motivated reinterpretation can give a more "extensive" meaning (Peter 2009: 126) to intrinsic political values such as political equality and inclusion:

> In Chapter 3, I had characterized deliberative democracy on the basis of two main features: public reasoning and political equality. The epistemic account of deliberative democracy based on a proceduralist epistemology changes the interpretation of these two features in the following way. First, it incorporates the epistemic dimension into a concern with fair procedures by stressing the epistemic value of fair deliberative processes. As such, it interprets political equality more extensively, as including criteria that specify epistemic fairness. That is to say, *it demands that there are criteria that regulate public deliberation at the fact-gathering and analysis stages of processes of policy formulation in addition to the more commonly recognized criteria that refer to equal possibilities to participate in the deliberation over given policy proposals.* The idea is that exclusion from those stages of the policy-evaluation and selection process that are crucial for the shaping of the evidence-basis on which particular policies rest is just as problematic as exclusion from other stages of this process. One way to make sense of this could be by extending the interpretation of political

equality based on primary goods by adding goods that are defined in relation to access to the consultational stages of the policy-making process. For example, beyond rights and liberties, freedom of movement and choice of occupation, powers and prerogatives of offices and positions of responsibility, income and wealth, and the social bases of self-respect, *the list could include goods that lobbying groups need to have influence on the deliberative process, such as access to information, to funding of research projects, and to official and unofficial hearings.* (Peter 2009: 123, my emphasis)

This long passage points to what constitutes in my view the originality of Peter's approach, namely, the idea that by introducing the epistemic dimension as essential to democracy's value it is possible to account for a particular sort of political learning processes. In this characterization of the role played by democracy's epistemic justification in advancing democracy, Peter points to its capacity to expand the range of practices that fall under the category of democratic. By doing this, practices of fact-gathering, for example, come to be seen as falling under the same normative constraints as any other form of democratic practice. If we accept that democracy has an epistemic value and thereby consider democratic practices to consist, among other things, of processes of public inquiry, then a broad range of activities that are typical for inquiry can be disclosed as constitutive part of the democratic process. I propose to call this sort of democratic advancement the "expansion of the range of democratic practice."

Think, for example, about how fact-checking initiatives which have acquired a major role in public debate in the last years due to the proliferation of fake news, bringing to a public awareness of their essential political role. According to Peter's view, then, advancing democracy through epistemic means means coming to consider certain forms of practice as part of democratic life, which also means reconsidering fact-checking as a practice that should fall under the norms of inclusion and political equality. Hence, democratizing fact-checking becomes an essential feature for democracy that gains particular weight if we consider that democracy represents a form of public inquiry. It represents an advancement for democracy which consists in recognizing as democratic a range of practices whose political relevance was previously veiled.

But Peter also describes a second way of democratic advancement in the following terms:

If political fairness is interpreted so as to include epistemic fairness, this gives participants in the deliberative process additional resources to counteract the effects of overly weak or overly strong criteria of political equality. I have argued that if political equality is too weak, some will be effectively excluded from the deliberative process. If epistemic fairness prevails, however, this will allow those affected to draw attention to this situation. Conversely, if political equality is too strong, some will find that the deliberative process rests on substantive judgments that they do not endorse. Again, if epistemic fairness prevails, this allows them to challenge these presumptions. Pure Epistemic Proceduralism is not immune to the threats to legitimacy that the political egalitarians dilemma poses, of course. But by allowing for collective learning about the effects of different constraints on the deliberative process, it gives support to a dynamic interpretation of how these constraints get established. Including conditions of epistemic fairness in the political fairness constraints provides some (procedural) safeguards against the adverse effects of overly weak and overly strong criteria of political equality. (Peter 2009: 132)

The second form of the normative learning process promoted by democracy's epistemic justification consists, according to Peter's description, in the identification and correction of fundamental flaws in the prevailing interpretation of democratic principles and their further transformation and improvement. Hence, even if the interaction between the norms regulating epistemic practice (norms of epistemic fairness, according to Peter and Longino) and the norms of political equality can be one of tension, this tension is not of the kind incompatibilists assume. Introducing an epistemic justification does not mean restricting accepted interpretations of political equality on virtue of the higher value of epistemic concerns. Nor does not it mean, as overlap compatibilists believe, that both forms of justification converge regarding the participation scope and the shape of the practices at stake. Rather, the interaction Peter describes between the two forms of justification consists of tensions that are resolved when we learn to interpret or instantiate intrinsic democratic principles in a richer or more adequate way. This is what is meant by affirming that the interaction between two kinds of democratic justification involves a normative learning process.

As I aim at showing in the coming chapters, this integrative way of articulating the relation of both kinds of democratic values can be also found in Dewey's mixed model of democratic justification. Hence, also for Dewey the epistemic value for democracy has the capacity to stimulate normative learning processes regarding democracy's intrinsic values. As we will see, next to the capacity to expand the range of democratic practice and to promote better understanding of democracy's intrinsic values and norms, the Deweyan account I propose also includes the idea of an epistemically promoted expansion of democracy to nonpolitical spheres of social life. In chapter 3, I will provide, based on Dewey, a pragmatist understanding of the epistemically motivated learning processes of democracy which draws on the idea of social freedom, understood as social cooperation (Honeth 2014a, 2014b). According to this approach, the specific interpretation of intrinsic political values and the norms deriving from them can be advanced when they are able to realize the ideal of social freedom in a more adequate way. The epistemic justification of democracy has, in this view, the function of promoting the advancement of social freedom, understood as social cooperation, in political life.

POLITICAL LEARNING PROCESSES: NORMATIVE DISCLOSURE AND APPROPRIATION

In her characterization of the second kind of learning process democracy may undergo thanks to its epistemic normativity, Peter provides a relatively static view of the normative learning process involved in these internormative tensions, which consists in finding an equilibrium between an overly weak and an excessively strong understanding of political equality. In my view, this understanding omits the reflection on the dynamic and cumulative dimension of learning processes, that is, of the fact that once a new understanding of democratic practice comes to be considered a more adequate understanding, it can play a double function: it can work as a criterium from which to identify possible normative regressions, and it provides a new ground for further political advancement. In my view, a Deweyan approach can offer a rich account that includes an historical reconstruction of the processes of normative interaction at work as well as a more complex characterization of the political function of democracy's epistemic dimension.

It is possible to understand the kind of learning process I have in mind in this Dewey-inspired integrative model of democratic justification by distinguishing two kinds of problems democratic practices and institutions need to face. On the one hand, democracy has to provide solutions to problems related to the adequate realization of intrinsic values. Problems can take very different forms: Does the actual system of political representation realize the fundamental value of collective self-determination? Does this voting system realize the principles of political fairness? Do actual discussion practices in a social movement embody norms of universal inclusion? Do all workers in a cooperative have the same opportunities to participate in decision-making? Within these kinds of problems related to intrinsic values and its normative derivations we should distinguish between the capacity of a practice or institutions to be adequate to the specific understanding given to intrinsic values, on the one hand, and the capacity of those specific understandings to realize the very general spirit of the fundamental values such as freedom or equality, on the other hand. Hence, instituting a democratic practice (let's say, for example, a general assembly guided by rules of consent) may be the solution to the problem of how to embody of a more radical understanding of democracy, but it might also be the solution to the problem posed by the suspicion the less participatory forms of democracy are unable to fully realize the values of inclusion or equal participation when they are well understood. In any case, both kinds of problems concern the embodiment or realization of intrinsic democratic values.

On the other hand, democracy's problems also concern its capacity to identify, define, and solve social and political problems. This kind of problems represents a second-order sort of problems, since they involve a reflexive relation to democratic institutions as practices in their ability to promote good outcomes, here understood in the general sense of effective problem-solutions. These second-order problems are different from the first-order problems arising from the social processes directly involved in the practical realization of intrinsic values. In the latter case, any change or transformation of democratic practices or institutions must be understood as a—more or less precarious—solution to a previous crisis regarding the possibility of embodying intrinsic values (or realizing better versions of them). Regarding democracy's epistemic problems, any change or transformation is analogous to the introduction of a new method in scientific research. So, for example, after realizing that a certain form of democratic decision-making is responsible for the systematic generation of unfair outcomes, based on inaccurate information or on inadequate consideration of values and principles of the participants, citizens may want to try a different methodological solution—that is, a new procedure—to the problem of generating good outcomes.

The present account aims at making explicit the contribution of the second developmental dynamics, the idea of methodological problems, to the problems related to the embodiment and the expansion of the meaning of democracy's intrinsic values. This corresponds to what I will call along this book the political potential of democracy's epistemic dimension. Very briefly, my thesis is that, the kind of practical changes that are directly stimulated by the epistemic dynamics of transformations have the potential of disclosing new, more adequate understandings of the values and norms intrinsic to democratic practice. In other words, the epistemic dynamics has the potential to stimulate new problems regarding the first dynamics. Hence, it can generate "normative crisis" by showing that there are better ways of realizing intrinsic values.

Surely, the last word about the democratic quality of these new practices remains a question to be answered from the point of view of the possibilities of political appropriation on the side of citizens. To come back to the example I presented in my introduction, citizens should ask themselves if the inclusion of undocumented immigrants in political life should be considered an adequate extension of the principles of political cooperation. Sometimes, however, the very possibility that this question is formulated depends on disruptive experiences such as the actual participation of undocumented immigrants in the PAH in their efforts to solve and find a name to the injustices involved in the eviction crisis. Hence, problem-solving can disrupt our interpretations of political practice in ways that promote political learning processes.

At this point there is a risk of falling into a compartmentalization of the field of practical influence of both kinds of dynamics. I understand "compartmentalization" in the following terms: a compartmentalist certainly accepts that the need to identify, define, and solve social problems generates practical innovations. However, these innovations do not substantially affect the immanent norms of democratic practice that set the scope of freedom. Thus, for example, a new communicative mechanism (a new norm for raising hands in an assembly) may be introduced that does not fundamentally alter the established intrinsic values of general inclusion and participatory equality. As long as both values are adequately embodied, the range of possible activities that can be taken to be democratic is open to the epistemic requirements of democratic practice. As a consequence, the area of practical influence attributed to epistemic transformations is substantially reduced to those falling under a particular understanding of democratic practice. As we will see later, this kind of compartmentalization of the sphere of practical influence of both kinds of dynamics corresponds to Honneth's position. This position is at the background of Honneth's critique of Hannah Arendt's full rejection of democracy's epistemic justification. For Honneth, Arendt's monist approach to democracy, according to which democratic practices and institutions only have an intrinsic value, is problematic because it leaves the exact shape political practices should take undetermined. According to it, the epistemic justification of democracy should play a role in giving to political practices their full determinacy: giving the range of possible practices within the limits of democracy's intrinsic values, an epistemic justification of democracy contributes to democracy by promoting the best possible practices from the point of view of their capacity to promote adequate outcomes.

The idea that practical innovations may improve the problem-solving capacity of political practice without substantially changing the meaning of intrinsic values must certainly be considered as an essential part of the larger project of explicating democracy from its epistemic dimension. In other words, the compartmentalist position has certainly something valuable to say about democracy since it provides criteria by which we can judge the democratic value of certain practices. However, my aim is to make a stronger claim, namely, that an important way in which political freedom and equality come to be better embodied or deepened corresponds to the very dynamics produced by democracy's epistemic second-order problems. As I mentioned, this process of political learning regards at least two dimensions: the extension of the range of political practices and the deepening of the norms that are immanent to democratic practice. Even if we will have the opportunity to talk more about the first kind, my analysis will focus on the second one. Hence, deepening the meaning of democracy's intrinsic values and its derivative norms of universal inclusion and participatory equality seems to be essential for the first one, since the expansion of democracy to other activities as well depends on the standards put by our understanding of democracy. In this context, we need to provide an answer to the following question: How exactly do epistemic second-order problems contribute to advancing the first-order problem-solving dynamics of democracy's intrinsic values? In other words, how can epistemic norms influence the way we interpret the intrinsic values and norms that are immanent to political practice?

As I mentioned, the present approach departs from the idea of a static correction of specific interpretation of democratic principles to a more historical view of democratic advancement. According to this view, the kind of practical transformations that constitute a methodological requirement in order to identify, articulate, and solve problems—as for example, when the PAH identifies the need to include all voices as a requirement for effectively fighting massive evictions as moral wrongs and develops specific "methods" or practices to do so—plays an essential role in disclosing new first-order problems concerning the capacity of realizing democracy's intrinsic value. "Correcting" specific interpretations of political equality and inclusion does not mean substituting intrinsic democratic normativity by criteria of epistemic fairness. Rather, it means stimulating a learning process by which epistemically motivated practical innovations may end up being appropriated as better realizations of intrinsic principles or, in other words, as better solutions to the problem of realizing democracy's intrinsic values. This idea will be developed in the next two chapters.

CONCLUDING REMARKS

In this chapter I have outlined different positions available in the literature concerning the relation between democracy's two main values: intrinsic and epistemic. While incompatibilist authors assume the presence of a (potential) tension between both, compatibilist authors believe that the realization of intrinsic values positively contributes to the other and conversely. Within the latter, I have distinguished those who hold that both values are convergent but keep them independent from each other from an integrative position, according to which democracy's epistemic value positively contributes to advancing the realization of democracy's intrinsic values. In line with Fabienne Peter I have characterized this advancement as a double political learning process involving (1) the expansion of the range of practices that count as political, and (2) improvements in the interpretation of democracy's intrinsic values and immanent norms. Regarding the second aspect, I have briefly pointed to the criteria by which these improvements may be evaluated by pointing to Honneth's ideal of social freedom. More will be said about this in the following chapters. I have also argued that Peter's view is too static and that it may fail to account for the accumulative nature of political learning processes. In part, this is due to a static understanding of epistemic normativity. Hence, her view on epistemic normativity is based on a reconstruction of epistemic norms that does not consider that these may evolve according to the needs to articulate and resolve new social problems. In my view, Dewey's view is better positioned in this regard, since it links the normativity of epistemic practices to their capacity to resolve problems. Finally, I have shown in what sense epistemic norms may contribute to challenging and advancing intrinsic norms by pointing to their function of disclosure. This means that the question if a new interpretation of political norms and values is more deeply democratic does not depend on its capacity to resolve problems but on the capacity of the new intrerpretation to be appropriated by citizens as a better ways of realizing democracy. In other words, the epistemic path to democratic deepening is one of disclosure, challenging, and stimulating changes in our well-established interpretations of democracy's intrinsic values and immanent norms.

Chapter 2

Axel Honneth

Struggle for Recognition and Democratic Advancement

The goal of this chapter is to show that Axel Honneth's mixed model of democratic justification, while providing a plausible understanding of the political learning process of democracy, does to give to democracy's epistemic dimension the proper role it can play in this learning process. Hence, as we will see, Honneth gives motivational priority to the intrinsic value of democracy as a motor of political learning, focusing on people's need to be recognized according to these values. At the same time, he limits himself to pointing to the positive epistemic effects of these developments. According to Honneth, these epistemic effects can certainly represent an important source of legitimation of democratic procedures. However, with few exceptions, they do not seem to play any particular role in realizing the normative potential of intrinsic values and immanent norms. This differs from the integrative account of democratic justification that is able to account for the power of democracy's epistemic dimension to promote the revision of well-established—we might also say: "hegemonic"—understandings of democratic values and norms. A detailed exploration of central aspects of Honneth's work is, however, unavoidable since his model of normative learning as the realization of the potential of norms and values will be at the background of the present approach.

THE METHOD OF A THEORY OF JUSTICE (I)

In recent years, as an essential part of his project of renewing social critique, Axel Honneth has concentrated his theoretical efforts on the outline

19

of a theory of justice that constitutes an alternative to two dominant kinds of accounts in social and political theory: on the one hand, constructivistic approaches to justice, which believe, drawing on Kantian premises, that principles of justice can be generated—or "constructed"—through an exercise of reflective thought that abstracts from the social reality to which those principles are to be applied. Hence, even though in some versions they are concerned about the possibility of identifying these principles in existing social institutions and practices, constructivists integrate this concern into their theoretical strategy retrospectively, that is, only once the principles of justice have been inferentially derived. On the other hand, a series of contemporary authors have reacted against the deficits attached to this constructivistic trend in political and social philosophy by returning to a specific form of Hegelianism. These accounts derive the normative basis of a theory of justice from the principles which are de facto accepted by members of society and understand their critical task mostly as revealing the contrast between these principles and a social reality that does not correspond with them. According to Honneth, both methodological approaches to justice bring us to a false dilemma: either we gain a strong normative basis of critique that renounces to its motivational force due to its lack of anchorage in social life or we stick to the principles that we are always following without asking the question about whether these principles are valid. According to Honneth, a theory of justice does not need to choose between presumably incompatible options but—drawing on a central Hegelian intuition—it sees itself both able and compelled to approach the principles identified in social reality as rational or justified. This is the meaning that he gives to the notion of "immanent critique," which constitutes the central task of a renewed form of Frankfurtian social critique: it is a critique whose normative basis is constituted by normative principles that have been reconstructed from social reality and whose validity or rationality has been demonstrated by the theory itself.

For Honneth showing the rationality or validity of the normative principles that are immanent to our social practices cannot be done independently of the fact that these principles are de facto accepted, hence, the very acceptance of those principles represents for immanent critique a reason for their normative validity. Unlike his mentor Jürgen Habermas, however, Honneth does not localize "moral facticity" in the presuppositions of all discourse aiming at a common understanding. The richness of moral experience—that is, the fact that moral vulnerability cannot be reduced to its communicative dimension— prompts Honneth to follow a different strategy of normative foundation, one that draws—more clearly than for Habermas—on philosophical-historical premises. For Honneth, the theoretical step made by normative reconstructivist philosophers from de facto acceptance to the validity of moral principles presupposes the central assumption that the de facto accepted principles or norms are the product of a normative learning process. Hence, for Honneth, asserting the normative validity of already-accepted moral norms—as well as of their specific interpretations—and adopting them as the basis of a critical-theoretical account is only possible under the condition that the latter can be seen as a result of an improvement from older ones.

It follows from this that providing an historical account of the origin of the normative principles that constitute the basis of social critique certainly does not exhaust the normative-reconstructive work of the social critic. The social critic must see that normative principles that, as a result of a learning process, come to "govern" social reality are of such an abstract and open nature that their specific realizations can be such that they either merely partially realize or even pervert their original meaning (Honneth & Sutterlüty 2011). In fact, for Honneth, the history of an historically instituted normative principle can be traced as the history of challenges to the interpretations of the principle on the side of groups who suffer from the effects of its actual specifications in practice. Hence, the history of the principles that acquire a certain level of institutional reality as a result of historical learning processes does not end at the moment of their historical emergence. On the contrary, starting from that very moment a second kind of learning process concerning those practices takes place under the new normative framework constituted by the newly institutionalized principles. These internal or intranormative developments—as opposed to the historically much more exceptional transnormative evolution from one principle to a different one—are characteristic of the kind of dynamics that Honneth explores in his reconstruction of modern forms of life, which includes political life or what he calls the sphere of democratic will-formation. The normative foundation of social critique resides in a view of modernity as the struggle over the interpretation of the principles of individual freedom, a struggle that has contributed to better interpretations of these principles and from which social theorists can learn in assessing social developments.

SOCIAL FREEDOM AS COOPERATIVE ACTIVITY

A central premise underlying Honneth's account of democratic practices and political learning is the thesis that the sphere of democratic will-formation, like the other two central spheres of social action characterizing modern societies—the sphere of intimate relations and the economic sphere, represents specific forms of realization of a particular form of freedom, namely, what he calls "social freedom." According to Honneth, next to two basic modern senses of freedom, negative and positive, we need to distinguish a third sense, a social sense, which accounts for a central dimension of the normative life of modern societies. Against the other two senses, which are concerned with individual freedom as involving the realization and generation of individual intentions generated in isolation from other individuals, the third account of freedom is meant to account for the fact that "the intentions of an agent can only be formed in reciprocal interaction between multiple subjects and thus can be realized without coercion only by acting together" (Honneth 2017a: 177). It is in this deeper sense, which brings together the generation and the realization of individual intentions, that Honneth talks about a "such a form of cooperatively realized freedom" (2017a: 178).

In one of his Dewey Lectures given at the Law School of the Chicago University (2017), Honneth aims at illustrating the kind of phenomena that can only be accounted for through the introduction of this third form of freedom. As a paradigmatic example of social freedom he provides a detailed analysis of practices of democratic will-formation, a characterization that will be especially useful in our further exploration. Hence, from the point of view of the two elements that have been pointed to, Honneth provides the following description. Regarding the social character of the formation of intentions by individuals:

> The determination of the individual will would then be undertaken purely mono-logically and directed toward a merely private realization of its content. This understanding of political expression fails to capture its true dynamics. When the subject contributes to political discourse, she refers in her expression to a chain of earlier statements, which she attempts to correct or improve, such that she can only appropriately be understood as a member of a previously consti-tuted, self-reflexively given, and already present "We." (Honneth 2017a: 179)

Concerning the social character of the realization of intentions:

> This means that the exercise of the "free" action cannot be regarded as complete with the mere proclamation of her belief. For what the individual proposal aims at, and where it finds completion, is in the reaction of the addressed "We," or of its individual representatives, who once again attempt to correct or improve upon the beliefs of other participants with their own. This description suggests that the participants in democratic will-formation must be able to understand their respective statements of opinion as intertwining with one another in such a way that they cannot avoid assuming a "We" that they together sustain through their contributions. (Honneth 2017a: 179)

According to Honneth, then, democratic will-formation must be seen as a cooperative activity through and through, where intentions, which are under-stood as the expression of one's political position, are formed within a larger context that involves a cooperative "we" and where the exercise of a free action can come to its fulfillment only on the condition that others have been able to take a position toward one's own position.

Although we obviously have the tendency to interpret participation in democratic will-formation as an exercise of individual freedom, such freedom cannot readily be described as an exercise of merely negative freedom. This is because the three distinguishing elements of negative freedom have little plausible application to such cases. The actor cannot be represented as a private subject who formulates the intentions of her actions by herself; nor is she "free" in carrying out her action only when other actors do not "arbitrarily" interfere; and finally her action is not complete as an exercise of freedom with the expression of her own opinion, but rather only temporally concludes if the other participants have reacted to it in a rationally comprehensible fashion. The actions of my fellow citizens therefore do not place an obstacle to my own free political act, nor do they merely constitute the conditions of its possibility. Rather their actions are so intrinsically interwoven with mine that it is difficult to speak of an individual act at all. It therefore seems that we can only realize this democratic freedom through a collaborative process, in which we understand our individual expressions of opinion as complementary contributions to a common project of identifying a common will. (2017a: 179)

Social freedom then means the involvement in a cooperative activity—in the present case, that political activity of building or finding a general will—where both the formation of intentions—here, the generation of one's own political position or opinion—and their realization—here, the free expression of one's opinion in the larger context of construction of a general will—are understood as intrinsically social phenomena, where the formation and realization of others' intentions are essentially involved in the formation and realization of one's own intentions.

Honneth goes so far in his characterization of democratic will-formation as a social process that he points to the social character of voting, a practice that is usually seen as the practical realization of an individualistic form of freedom:

A myopic focus on voting fails to recognize that the casting of the ballot is preceded by public discussion, including open media coverage and thus the process of reciprocal influence. Such deliberative discussions are a constitutive rather than merely an incidental feature of democracy (Anderson 2006). Taken in isolation, the casting of the ballot itself can perhaps be thought of according to the model of negative liberty. But this act is only a snapshot of a much more comprehensive process, which is meant to ensure that through appropriate instruments for the exchange of experience and opinion, individual beliefs are not only aggregated but are as far as possible bound together into a rational "general will." (Honneth 2017a: 180)

In the next chapter we will see how, in contrast to this view, for Dewey, secret voting is seen as the unequivocal expression of "individualistic"—that is, the freedom of the individual understood in abstraction of its social relations— in contrast to social freedom. Dewey's characterization goes hand in hand with a reconstruction of the developments of modern democratic practice as involving changes that go from individualistic to strongly social practices of political freedom. Honneth, on the contrary, seems particularly interested in showing how the activity of voting is intrinsically related to other processes of collective will-formation involving the intersubjective exchange of opinions that cannot but be characterized as realizing a social form of freedom. Honneth's reasoning here is intimately bound up with this overall project, which consists in understanding the basic institutions of modernity—modern forms of family and intimate relations, modern free-market economic practice, and modern democratic forms—as institutional realizations of social freedom. As we will see later, a Deweyan approach provides the theoretical means for thinking political progress as involving two kinds of developments: on the one hand, developments concerning different specifications of a prevalent understanding of freedom (individualistic or social) and, on the other hand, developments concerning the transition from individualistic to social freedom, which respond to the intra- and inter-normative levels of progress we have distinguished above.

Finally, for Honneth, those practices realizing social forms of freedom must go hand in hand with a meta-level of social organization that, according to him, must also have a democratic form. In other words, for Honneth the distribution of roles, tasks, and goals at play in the organization of the cooperative practices where social freedom is realized must also have a democratic character. Hence,

[b]ecause such a claim must be reciprocally acknowledged, so that all participants can understand their contributions as fulfilling the autonomous wishes of others, the exercise of social freedom must be bound to the assumption of the recognition of the claim of every other to codetermine the commonly practiced schema of cooperation. Though social freedom can be exercised only in the pursuit of common aims, the determinate content of these aims always remains open for revision and contestation by the members of the "We." (Honneth 2017a: 190)

In general we can say that social freedom understood as a cooperative activity involving the social entrenchment of the formation and realization of intentions has three different versions, each of them corresponding to one particular modern sphere of social interaction: family and intimate relations, economy, and democratic will-formation. Honneth sees in democratic will-formation the enactment of a cooperative activity involving the formation and expression of one's own political position as well as the formation of a collective will. Finally, we must see the realization of freedom for each of these spheres in what Honneth considers to be the unconstrained interlocking of our aims and intentions as well as in the possibility of a democratic regulation of how the different roles in the cooperative activity are to be distributed.

HONNETH'S NORMATIVE RECONSTRUCTION OF DEMOCRACY: AN OVERVIEW

A normative-reconstructive methodology that identifies in modernity the differentiation of three spheres of social action and thereby the institutionalization of three forms of social freedom or cooperation represents the theoretical background of Honneth's account of democracy and democratic practice. Hence, since for Honneth modernity is characterized by the institutionalization of social forms of individual freedom in different spheres of social action, the work of reconstruction that corresponds to the political dimension of a theory of justice with social-critical import consists in a retrospective exploration that shows the history of the better realizations of the principles of political freedom. It is in the context of this historical exploration that we need to approach the question of the transformative and normative work Honneth attributes to the problem-solving function of democratic will-formation. Thus, from this short introduction to his theory of justice we may find ourselves ready to confirm the thesis I have advanced at the beginning of this section: Honneth gives in his overall theory of justice such a central historical role to political freedom that the capacity of democracy's epistemic function to transform our practices in any sense that could be considered "democratic progress" must remain—at least partly—invisible.

The task of showing this epistemic deficit is not an easy one, since Honneth has gone to great effort in order to integrate the epistemic dimension into his overall argument. Hence, one should not forget that for Honneth the sphere of democratic decision-making is constituted by nothing less than cooperative practices aiming at the identification, definition, and solution of problems arising from both political and nonpolitical forms of social interaction. Furthermore, as Honneth puts it in *The Idea of Socialism* (2017), it is precisely this epistemic function of democracy that gives to this sphere of social action a functional priority within the organic whole that includes all social spheres.

In other words, Honneth shows himself to be fully aware of the importance of the epistemic dimension for a theory of democracy. However, as mentioned at the beginning of this introduction, I believe that Honneth is incapable of overcoming the larger lack of integration between the two values of democracy which is present throughout his work, and which assigns both normative and motivational priority to the dynamics of the transformative struggle over the correct interpretation of the principles of political freedom. Just recall that as, I have shown in the previous chapter, my aim is to present a view on political learning processes that gives, as Honneth does, normative priority to democracy's intrinsic values but which distributes the motivational ground for political learning processes (at least) between democracy's intrinsic and epistemic values. In my view, a particularly interesting way of presenting Honneth's position is by drawing precisely on his own reception of John Dewey's theory of democracy, which, as we will see, differs from our own interpretation in important aspects.

The interest of presenting Honneth's Dewey reception in this context is not only due to the centrality of Dewey's ideas for Honneth's overall philosophical view. Moreover, the evolution of Honneth's reception of Dewey's idea testifies a progressive abandonment of Dewey's view on the political role democracy's epistemic dimension can play. It is precisely in the evolution of Honneth's reading that we can identify the contrast between two different options: in a first step, Dewey's theory of democracy is read as defending a purely epistemic view of democracy, one that would account for the transformations in democratic practice from the point of view of the logic of collective problem-solving, as it is identified by Honneth in an early text. Honneth seems to express an ambiguous endorsement of Dewey's pure epistemic view, an ambiguity that already points to the later inversion of the practical priority of freedom and problem-solving. In a second step, Honneth provides a view that gives priority to the progressive dialectics affecting the normative ideal of social freedom, which is developed through a discussion of Dewey's reflections on the media in a true democratic society. This view is crucial for his own normative reconstruction of the sphere of democratic decision-making, as we find it in *Freedom's Right* (2014). In this context, I will explore in more detail the methodological background that lies behind Honneth's reconstructive strategy, as well as consider an integrative strategy that could be implicit in Honneth's argument. In a third step I will explore Honneth's reception of Dewey in *The Idea of Socialism*, which in my view reproduces the subordination of the epistemic dimension at the level of the motivational structure driving social struggles.

DEMOCRACY AS REFLECTIVE COOPERATION: PURE EPISTEMIC DEMOCRACY IN THE WORK OF JOHN DEWEY

In a famous article (1998), Honneth provides, drawing on John Dewey's theory of democracy, the outline of what he takes to be a third way between the two main accounts of democracy that count as alternatives to current liberal views: Habermasian proceduralism and Arendtian republicanism. This third option is presented as superior to the other two, since it is able to integrate two valuable elements that unilaterally characterize each of them. On the one hand, in line with Habermasian proceduralism, a Deweyan account is oriented toward the idea of democracy as a rational procedure. On the other hand, in line with Arendtian republicanism, a Deweyan approach to radical democracy is able to understand democracy as the self-organizing form of an integrated community.

According to Honneth, the necessary integration of both elements into a single understanding of democracy is only possible through the introduction of a central idea that makes Dewey's account especially compelling: the idea of democracy as a reflexive form of social cooperation. As we previously saw, with the expression "social cooperation" Honneth points to the Deweyan intuition according to which individual freedom is not only realized in intersubjective relations of communication, as is the case for Habermas and Arendtian versions of communicative freedom, but also in forms of cooperative activity in which the "communal employment of individual forces to cope with a problem" (Honneth 1998: 767) takes place.

By drawing on the idea of social cooperation, a Deweyan account is able to integrate the Republican intuition according to which democracy is a form of self-government of an integrated community. The specifically Deweyan form of appropriation of this republican intuition—which sees in democracy the self-expression of a community—consists in showing that the political sphere of democratic will-formation represents a sphere of cooperation in which individual freedom can be procedurally exercised. As such, this form of cooperative activity depends on two kinds of prepolitical conditions: on the one hand, the effective presence of cooperative relations in nonpolitical spheres, which are supposed to guarantee the material and symbolic resources individuals need in order to participate and, more importantly, to understand themselves as realizing their individual capacities in political processes and, on the other hand, the democratic organization of these prepolitical spheres, which represents a central factor in the learning and promotion of democratic habits among the individuals concerned.

But Honneth sees also a second, complementary theoretical advantage in the introduction of the idea of social cooperation as the core intuition of a theory of democracy with critical purpose: similarly to the Habermasian approach, and largely in opposition to the Arendtian, a Deweyan account is able to provide criteria of rationality for democratic procedures of collective will-formation. What are these criteria and where do they come from? Here it is especially interesting to follow Honneth in his reconstruction of Dewey's answer to this question, which he characterizes as a purely epistemic account. Let's explore this idea in more detail: according to Honneth, by conceiving of the experimentalist method put into practice by the natural sciences as a general model for the resolution of social problems, John Dewey paved the way to understanding maximal inclusion and political equality as conditions for the enhancement of the rationality of democratic will-formation, thus providing an epistemic justification of democracy:

> In this sense, Dewey could ultimately claim in *The Public and its Problems* that democracy represents the political form of organization in which human intelligence achieves complete development; for it is only where methods of publicly debating individual convictions have assumed institutional form that, in social life, the communicative character of rational problem solving can be set free in the same manner as this is done in the natural sciences by experimental research in laboratories. (Honneth 1998: 773)

This passage points to the positive epistemic features of democratic method, brought together under the idea of an "enhancement of social rationality" effectuated by the procedural features that characterize democratic will-formation. However, pointing to the positive epistemic effect of political freedom is not the only theoretical operation that is attributed to Dewey in this text. On the contrary, according to Honneth, Dewey considers it to be the exclusive mechanism responsible for the configuration of the specific forms taken by democratic practice. Hence, for Dewey

> [t]he political sphere is not—as Hannah Arendt and, to a lesser degree, Habermas believe—the place for a communicative exercise of freedom but the cognitive medium with whose help society attempts, experimentally, to explore, process, and solve its own problems with the coordination of social action. (Honneth 1998: 775)

This pure epistemic approach to democratic practice is clearly reflected in the way Dewey is compelled to conceive of the transformations in democratic institutions and practices:

> [b]ecause the democratic public constitutes the medium through which society attempts to process and solve its problems, *its establishment and composition depend completely upon criteria of rational problem solving.* (Honneth 1998: 778, emphasis added)

The later represents a central passage in Honneth's text, since it shows first the extent to which the historical effectiveness of the idea of communicative freedom is left out of this first reading of the Deweyan model: the "institution and configuration" of the democratic public "depends fully on criteria of problem-solving." For Honneth, Dewey's pure epistemic—or, in the terminology I have used in the previous chapter: epistemic monist—account certainly represents a progression in relation to Arendt's view. Hence, Arendt represents the opposite position insofar as the democratic construction of opinion is exclusively seen as the manifestation of communicative freedom understood in terms of the self-expression of a community. According to Honneth, by making the activity of will-formation "an end for itself" Arendt becomes unable to provide any concrete standard for the institutional configuration of intersubjective construction of opinion in concrete cases. As an alternative to this deficit, the epistemic function of democracy is able to account for the specification of institutionalized forms of democratic practice, and furthermore, for the specific organizations of state agencies as well as their common relation:

Indeed, Dewey goes so far as to conceive of the process of public will formation as a large-scale experimental process in which, according to the criteria of rationality of past decisions, we continually decide anew how state institutions are to be specifically organized and how they are to relate to one another in terms of their jurisdiction. (Honneth 1998: 778)

Certainly, this pure epistemic view that captures the grounds underlying the specific configurations of democratic practice is not incompatible with the view that these practices contribute to the realization of freedom of the individual, understood as the realization of the individual's own capacities in the more general context of the activity of cooperation in the resolution of social problems. However, by reducing Dewey's position to a pure epistemic view, the role of freedom as a principle for determining the specific forms of democratic practice and institutions remains relegated to a secondary role. So we find at this stage of Honneth's work already the elements of what I have called a lack of integration between two practical-developmental dynamics: that corresponding to the practical or methodological requirements that derive from the activity of identification, definition, and solving of social problems and that corresponding to the principles of freedom that are to guarantee the realization of the individual's political capacities. Even if Honneth does see in Dewey the elements of convergence between both logics, at this stage this operation of reconciliation takes the form of a strategy that considers the realization of the political requirements of political freedom as the positive effect of the functional requirements of problem-solving.

It is however not clear in the text to what extent Honneth endorses this pure epistemic view, since he limits himself to pointing to the fact that "Dewey undoubtedly draws near to the model of democracy that Habermas has developed in the form of a discourse theory in recent years" (Honneth 1998: 778). And, as we have mentioned before, Habermas's position is seen as a debilitated version of the Arendtian's freedom-oriented view. As we will see in the coming sections, further theoretical developments seem to reinforce the presumption that, while Honneth did see the theoretical advantages of integrating the epistemic dimension into a theory of democracy, he still would remain Habermasian to the extent that a particular combination of both developmental dynamics will be endorsed. In fact, Honneth's actual strategy will consist in inverting the relation of priority between both elements he has originally attributed to Dewey. From now on, it will be the dynamics of the political form of social freedom that is the determining element—also in his reconstruction of Dewey's arguments—while at the same time the epistemic benefits of this dynamics will be merely made evident.

PUBLIC RATIONALITY AS A BY-PRODUCT OF POLITICAL FREEDOM: DEMOCRACY IN *FREEDOM'S RIGHT*

Against the liberal tendency to think of democratic institutions and practices as the political expression of the freedom of atomized individuals, Honneth proposes in *Freedom's Right* that we understand the normative ideals of cooperation as a characteristic feature of the sphere of democratic will-formation from its very historical origin. Hence, Honneth's self-given task becomes clear throughout his reconstruction: the historical evolution of democratic public life must be read as a—highly ambivalent—process of realization of principles of social freedom that were already immanent to its preliminary institutional forms. The ambivalence of this process becomes evident once we observe how the abolition of obvious barriers to the realization of social freedom has come together with more subtle forms of political exclusion and coercion as the cultural mechanisms of exclusion that Bourdieu describes in *La distinction* (1979). Despite these ambivalences, the history of public will-formation can still be read as one in which the relevant form of normative progress has been achieved.

For Honneth, identifying these achievements and integrating them into a larger process of normative evolution results in two theoretical gains for a critical theory of democracy: on the one hand, such an approach allows for a grounded knowledge about the necessary conditions (social, cultural, material, legal, etc.) for democratic progress. On the other hand, this kind of reconstruction allows the social critic to identify the concrete specification of principles that constitute the normative basis of critique as well as to identify the direction in which new interpretations of given principles will be able to be anticipated. It is now time to see how Honneth describes the dynamics leading to this progress.

THE DYNAMICS OF PROGRESS
IN THE PUBLIC SPHERE

Honneth introduces his reconstruction of the historical evolution of the public sphere by pointing to central Habermasian intuitions formulated in *The Structural Transformation of the Public Sphere*:

> Without being able to go into detail here, the central insight of Habermas' historical study is that the eighteen century bourgeois identification of public opinion with the rationality of political life can only be maintained in a convincing and consistent manner if all people affected by these decisions can be viewed as participants in a non-coercive process of will-formation. From the very beginning, therefore, there was an intrinsic connection between his intention to make politics more rational through a shared process of reasoning and the idea of communicative freedom, because political decisions can only claim to be relational and right if all citizens are equally entitled without coercion, to participate in the process of decision making. (Honneth 2014a: 284)

According to this passage the Habermasian articulation of the two normative functions of democracy consisted in pointing to the necessary connection between the requirement of correction of the decisions resulting from public deliberation and the abolition of barriers of inclusion and equal treatment in deliberation. It would seem, based on Honneth's description of the Habermasian model of democracy—which Honneth himself endorses—that, at least to some extent, democratic transformations concerning the institutionalization and configuration of particular political forms that have meant the expansion of democratic inclusion and the abolition of internal forms of domination have been due to the requirement of rationality of political decision-making. Thus, we would expect from his normative reconstruction that the "democratizing" effects of the epistemic requirement are fleshed out. However, what we find throughout his normative reconstruction of the historical development of democratic public life up to our present time is a quite different strategy: one that sees in these developments the direct effect of principles of social freedom. Hence, early on in his own historical reconstruction we observe that the democratizing potential of this implicit principle is obliterated in the process of constructing an argument for the historical effectiveness of idea of social freedom: in his next steps, Honneth will limit himself to showing that further inclusion and abolition of formal and nonformal forms of domination within public life were converged with the epistemic requirement of a guarantee and enhancement of the rationality of democratic will-formation.

With these considerations in mind we can better appreciate that, in *Freedom's Right*, Honneth provides a normative reconstruction of democratic institutions and practices that sees the historical conclusion and abolition of internal relations of domination as the product of a learning process by which excluded individuals struggle about better interpretations of the norms that govern communicative-political interactions. In the context of this history, the mobilization of epistemic reasons is not effective in a normative-progressive sense: epistemic achievements are seen only as a secondary, positive effect of the extension of rights to participation, opinion, and so on, that takes place as a product of the first transformative dynamic.

Thus, this overshadowing of the problem-solving function as historically effective is particularly evident in the way Dewey's reflections on democracy are mobilized in *Freedom's Right*. Hence, we can easily observe an important shift taken in Honneth's reception of Dewey's work: while in his earlier text Dewey's exploration of the criteria of rationality of democratic will-formation is seen as grounded in purely epistemic reasons, in his later work Dewey's theory is mobilized as providing a view on the institutional settings necessary for democracy as directly deriving from the ideals of social freedom expressed in what Dewey called "the idea of democracy."

> Dewey formulates this idea of social freedom much more emphatically [. . .]. If all citizens were enabled, with the help of the media, to contribute with their own proposals to the public debate over the appropriate means for perfecting the community, then in Dewey's view a state of free cooperation would be attained that would truly deserve the name of 'democratic freedom'. [. . .] As soon as the media fulfil their task of providing the general knowledge required for dealing with social problems, the members of society will be capable, under conditions of equal rights to freedom and participation, to commonly explore appropriate solutions and work cooperatively toward the experimental consummation of their community. (Honneth 2014a: 274)

Hence, while Honneth does not deny the presence in Dewey of an epistemic approach to democracy, he believes that his mobilization of the idea of democracy is to provide a more fundamental normative basis to ground the specific configuration of practices in the sphere of democratic will-formation.

Here we see a reverse of the first interpretation of the first reading provided in "Democracy as Reflexive Cooperation."

THE METHOD OF A THEORY OF JUSTICE (II)

As has been already shown, Honneth's historical reconstruction is grounded in the methodological premises of normative reconstruction, which essentially involve the idea of historical learning processes. A detailed analysis of how we are to conceive of these learning processes is provided in "The Normativity of Ethical Life" (2014). In this text Honneth develops the idea that the project of immanent social critique involves the historical reconstruction of the evolution of normative principles, such that these principles can be described as improvements on previously existing forms. As we have already mentioned, two phases in the normative dynamics of societies must be taken into consideration: firstly, the historical emergence of new normative principles out of a "semantic exhaustion" of older ones—what I have called the "transnormative" level—and, secondly, the history of the different interpretations of an institutionalized principle—what I have called the "intranormative" level. The history of the institutional realizations of modern forms of freedom such as it is provided in *Freedom's Right* falls within the second, intranormative level of analysis, while the question of the historical superiority of the modern conception of freedom as the freedom of the individual is left aside in the book.

According to Honneth, the project of an immanent social critique must be able to describe the intranormative history of modernity as a history of progress in the realization of its central normative principle: that of individual freedom. The dynamics of this progressive realization take the shape of a conflict of interpretation that includes the "confrontations that have been carried out in the interest of an extension of the margin of maneuver of subjectivity, towards the ethical presuppositions of the latter" (Hunyadi: 116, my translation). Furthermore, building on the observation that each form of freedom has its own social place or "right," the reconstructive analysis is focused on the concrete evolution within the specific forms of social freedom that correspond to the different social spheres of action that emerged from the differentiation process that characterizes modernity. As one of the main spheres of modern action, the history of democratic will-formation must hence be explained as the history of the struggle over different interpretations given to the principles of social freedom or cooperation in the above-mentioned sense of an extension of the margins of maneuver of subjectivity.

But how are we to account for the roots of this conflict of interpretations, that is, for the emergence of conflicting interpretations of the fundamental normative principles in the political version of social freedom? According to Honneth,

> [i]n general, all norms that are capable of being collectively adopted and thus of being elevated to the status of ethical principles—such as the principle of ancientry, the principle of care, or the principle of equality—are not only open enough to permit very different kinds of application, but also serve a cognitive function that makes them comparable to spotlights capable of illuminating ever new circumstances and states of affairs. (Honneth 2014b: 823)

Norms and principles can be specified in practice such that their specifications can be subjected to critique and contestation by those participating in the practices embodying them:

> Generally speaking it is therefore part of the everyday exercise of an ethical practice that despite the emergence of shared habits, the application of the standards inherent in the practice remains subject to contestation since there is a continual stream of novel objections and reservation. (Honneth 2014b: 823)

Here we do well to ask: in virtue of what do these objections arise on the side of individuals? Honneth's answer to this question is:

> So conceived, the history of an ethical sphere is *an unplanned learning process kept in motion by a struggle for recognition, since the participants contend for specific ways of applying an institutionalized norm according to their own respective situations and sensibilities.* The further this struggle advances—that is to say, the more revisions have already been made to the practice of a given norm—the more restricted is the dialectical space that remains available for novel objections and grievances. In this way the history of an ethical sphere can be thought of as a conflictual process whereby a certain validity surplus initially inherent in every ethical norm is gradually stripped away. (Honneth 2014b: 823–824, emphasis added)

To summarize, Honneth understands progress within modern social spheres of interaction as a learning process through which the specific forms taken by abstract norms and principles in social practice are challenged by the reinterpretation given by individuals in light of "their respective situations and sensibilities." This activity of "reinterpretation" is possible since norms and principles are to be seen as "spotlights" that are capable of illuminating previously hidden aspects of social and our personal reality. Hence, normative progress should be seen as a normative expansion toward newly illuminated regions of social/personal life, a process that Honneth describes as promoting individualization and social inclusion. In short, Honneth's normative reconstruction, which represents a necessary itinerary both for the justification of the normative standards of critique and for the exploration of the conditions for the realization of social freedom, sees in the progresses made in democratic life the effect of a normative-hermeneutical dynamics by which members of excluded groups learn to see themselves/aspects of themselves in light of the principles of social freedom, thereby forcing through normative changes that point toward further individualization and inclusion.

A LAST EFFORT OF INTEGRATION

From this methodological background it may seem justified to expect the omission of the normative-transformative role of democracy's problem-solving function, which confirms our suspicions advanced in the previous sections. However, in my view, we could still think of a possible strategy to integrate the latter into Honneth's normative reconstruction: since the progressive transformations in our specific understandings of freedom depend on a logic by which individuals learn to see themselves "in a new light," and since we can grasp the process of political cooperation for the solution of public problems as a process where individuals learn to see aspects of themselves as valuable for the resolution of social problems, the progression of freedom can be seen as an epistemically generated process. This is so because problem-solving practices can be seen as the space where individuals learn to perceive "new" aspects of themselves that are not recognized by existing forms of democratic practice. In other words, by conceiving of political freedom as an activity of cooperation in the identification, elaboration, and solution of socially relevant problems, Honneth seems to be able to account for problem-solving as the motor of the dynamics of social recognition: in the context of our common efforts to solve the problems that emerge from social interaction we can come to "articulate" personal capacities and experiences that turn out to be valuable for our cooperative activity and come to represent a motivational basis for a struggle for recognition aiming at new practical arrangements that are able to include this newly articulated and appropriated aspect of ourselves.

But in my view, by following this integrative strategy—which is certainly not explicit in his methodological reflections even if it can be inferred from his reconstruction—Honneth still would miss a central point, namely, the possibility of the transformative logic of problem-solving to promote practical transformations that challenge our actual collective understanding of freedom without the mediation of the just described recognitional mechanism. Hence, from the perspective of an epistemic account individuals do not need to learn see their own particular capacities as valuable for political problem-solving in order to claim for changes in political practice that can come to be retrospectively appropriated as extensions of political freedom. Surely, the central role of the dynamics of recognition is not to be excluded, neither as mediator between actual practical change and reinterpretation of freedom nor as a later result of the effective practice of new understandings of freedom. However, I believe that reducing the political contribution of problem-solving to those practical transformations that have been mediated by individual learning process of self-valuation not only misses the existence of alternative mechanisms leading to political emancipation, but also runs the risk of unnecessarily restricting the scope of the practical innovations we can expect to contribute to a progress of democratic practice. Hence, epistemic requirements may be more radical than the possibilities open by the very recognitional order in which they are inscribed.

"A SOCIAL TENDENCY WITH EVOLUTIONARY POWER": RECONSIDERING PROBLEM-SOLVING

In *The Idea of Socialism* Honneth reinforces his particular way of under-standing the articulation of democracy's intrinsic and epistemic dimensions by identifying in social struggles an "historical tendency" anchored in the motivational basis of the agents of sociohistorical change. Here—in my view—the problematic subordination of problem-solving as a motivational source for social change is indeed subtle, since Honneth's reflections are pervaded by the idea—held both in his older and newer texts—that demo-cratic practice consists in the cooperative research for solutions to social problems. As a consequence, our critical task must consist, as in the previ-ous sections, in exploring the limits of Honneth's efforts to integrate both normative dimensions of democracy. Here, this task will be pursued by placing special attention on Honneth's analysis of the motivational basis of the practical change he identifies as the main motor of historical transfor-mations, to which the broader pursuit of a renewal of the socialist project is linked.

The theoretical task of a renewal of socialism as an alternative to existing forms of socioeconomic organization pursued in *The Idea of Socialism* directs its attention to the ways in which economic organization has come to be seen as the practical realization of social freedom. Briefly, Honneth understands the project of a renewal of socialism as involving the establishment of an experimental culture of inquiry in the economic sphere, which is in its turn seen as the condition for finding out those specific forms of practice and organization that seem to best realize the practical requirements involved in the emancipatory idea of social freedom. According to Honneth, the socialist project—which most centrally consists in realizing social freedom in the economic sphere, even if it sees in the institutionalization of a wider democratic ethical life a condition for the former—cannot exclude any of the three classical forms in which this question has been raised—the Smithian idea of a morally embedded free-market economy; civil societal, cooperativistic control of the economy; and the state-socialistic regulation of economic practice—since they all seem to offer plausible ways to promote cooperative market relations. Moreover, since the question of the emancipatory power of any of these projects cannot be answered a priori, the adoption of an experimentalist culture that explores the consequences of the institutional designs accompanying the realization of each of these possible versions of the socialist project seems to be the only normatively and epistemically valid manner in which to proceed.

When seeking to recover and further explicate an experimentalist approach to economic practice, a relevant question emerges concerning the criteria by which actual experiments should be evaluated. Drawing on Dewey's and Hegel's intuitions, Honneth points to the idea of the normative criterion of the abolition of "barriers to communication" (Honneth 2017b: 65) as a candidate for playing such a role. But, as is characteristic for his reconstructive approach, Honneth aims at seeing in the idea of an "abolition of barriers of communication" not only a fundamental normative basis for the assessment of experimental results whose validity can be theoretically justified but also, and most centrally, he wants to present it as the expression of an historical tendency or dynamics. As Honneth puts it, this principle should not be seen as a "kind of evolutionary force upon which a revised socialism could rely if it wishes to be an expression not of a moral imperative but of an historical tendency" (Honneth 2017b: 60). This idea is important for the socialist project, since

> Early socialists thus ascribed to the proletariat an objective interest in these same changes. Yet after both of these background certainties—the necessity of historical progress and a revolutionary proletariat—had collapsed and become obvious intelectual fictions on the age of the Industrial Revolution, socialism was in danger of losing all anchoring in a progressive historical tendency that lent social grounding to its demands. Therefore, it was and is in danger of degenerating into merely one theory of justice among others, turning its demands into mere normative demands rather than the expressoin of already existing demands. (Honneth 2017b: 63)

Given the fact that the criterion of the "abolition of barriers of communication" is introduced within the context of clear epistemic reflections concerning the quality of political-economic experiments, one could at this stage of the argumentation expect that Honneth takes the historical role of problem-solving more seriously than he has done until now. However, here again, the abolition of barriers to communication is seen as a secondary epistemically positive effect, even if it is again only grounded in people's struggles for political freedom. This becomes particularly clear if we consider the idea according to which the criterion of an abolition of the existing barriers of communication represents an historical tendency. Drawing (again) on his reading of John Dewey's *Lectures in China*, Honneth concludes that:

> From Dewey's perspective, therefore, the periodic revolts of social groups against their exclusion from social interaction ensure that the free and unlimited communication underlying the social gradually becomes reality in the social life-world. Dewey therefore gives a methodological response to the question as to the criterion of the experimental exploration of appropriate solutions to problematic situations. The more those who are affected by a problem are involved in the search for solutions to that problem, the more such historical-social experiments will lead to better and more stable solutions. (Honneth 2017b: 61–62)

In other words, the historical realization of communicative freedom in the political sphere is objectively anchored in the fundamental interest of inclusion in social communication processes, since the exclusion from them cannot be internally experienced but as a loss of freedom in terms of growth. According to this idea, the analysis of the transformative role of social struggles, that is, of their role of motor in the historically ambivalent process of further realization of social freedom, situates the latter at the core of the motivational structure of those struggles. Here again another option is left out of consideration, namely, the possibility that the transformative process functions analogously to a scientific practice of inquiry: in such a practice, available methods and means are put at work and revised and transformed according to their capacity to solve problems. According to this other option, claims for a transformation and deepening of democratic practices would not necessarily arise from an essential interest of the groups to be recognized as participants of democratic will-formation but rather follow immediately from their interest in overcoming injustices related to unrealized forms of freedom, be these political or not.

CONCLUDING REMARKS

Honneth's account of democratic practice has been explored along these lines as involving a problematic subordination of the epistemic dimension of democracy to the normative ideal of social freedom. This subordination becomes evident through the multiple forms in which the motivational and transformative power of problem-solving as an historical force is rejected or, at best, mediated by a dynamics of the struggle for social recognition. Hence, even if we accept that both forms of democratic justification may be at the same time at play as democratizing forces, it seems that democracy's epistemic dimension has an autonomous political potential that goes beyond the hermeneutical possibilities of intrinsic democratic values. Again, this is not to deny that Honneth fails to assign any political relevance to problem-solving, that is, to an epistemic justification of democracy and its historical role. My critique is rather that its power is not integrated into a normative reconstructivistic account that is able to see problem-solving as an independent trigger of democratic advancement. This has become clear in the analysis of (a) Honneth's reconstruction of the progress made within the sphere of democratic will-formation, (b) Honneth's methodological reflections and finally, (c) Honneth's analysis of the motivationally anchored historical tendency toward the abolition of barriers to communication.

Chapter 3

John Dewey

The Political Potential of Democracy's Epistemic Dimension

It is time now to turn to John Dewey's work in order to explore the possibility of providing a mixed model of democratic justification that, while retaining Honneth's view on political learning, it is able to fully account for the role democracy's epistemic dimension can play within it. In my view, the best way to access Dewey's mixed model is to examine his account on the history of modern democracy that we can find in *The Public and Its Problems* (1927). Hence, for him modern democracy represents the result of two dynamics of political transformation, that of the struggle for political freedom, on the one hand, and that of the democratizing requirements of problem-solving, on the other hand. These two dynamics do not only converge but also influence each other. Drawing on his historical reconstruction, we can gain a systematic understanding of the historical relation between democracy's intrinsic and epistemic dimensions. This systematic understanding should not be confused with an epistemic justification of democracy tout court. Rather, the aim of the present exploration is to gain a picture of the interactions between democracy's two kinds of justification that, according to Dewey, are at the source of the institutional developments experienced by modern democracies. Drawing on this picture, my aim is to spell out, in a more systematic form, the ways in which democracy's epistemic dimension can promote political learning processes.

Dewey's reconstruction of the history of modern Western democracy, as we find it in *The Public and Its Problems*, is rather complex, since it involves different phases of development which in turn sometimes contain further subdivisions that need to be spelled out. In general, we can distinguish three phases in Dewey's historical account of the developments

41

affecting democratic institutions and practices since the beginning of the modern era. The first phase corresponds to those transformations in political practice that took place by the end of feudal times and that resulted in the emergence of what Dewey takes to be democratic forms of government in the modern era. Here it should be advanced that the progressive emergence of democratic forms from a context of feudal domination meant, according to Dewey, the progressive institutionalization of one specific form of democracy, one that corresponded to the idea of freedom as realization of individualistic freedom. The second phase refers to the evolution and decadence of those individualistic political institutions and practices. Here Dewey orients his analysis mainly to the institutions of US-American democracy. Finally, a third phase refers to a radical transformation of democratic institutions and practices that, according to Dewey, still needed to take place if democracy is to be saved from its current challenges. Hence, for Dewey, the institutions of his time were marked by the institutional predominance of an individualistic notion of freedom, a notion that was responsible for decreasing the power of institutional and practical renewal that was necessary for the very survival of democracy. Hence, the survival of democracy was seen as dependent on the possibility of deepening democratic practice, even if this collective enterprise involved a clear discontinuity from existing democratic forms. Indeed, what was needed according to Dewey was not more of the same (individualistic) democracy but democracy of a different kind, one that is built on the basis of what Axel Honneth calls "social freedom."

THE EPISTEMIC PATH TO DEMOCRACY: FROM FEUDALISM TO INDIVIDUALISTIC LIBERALISM

In *The Public and Its Problems* Dewey defends the idea that the emergence in modern times of democracy as a political system—also named by Dewey as "popular self-government"—was the result of a series of social tendencies primarily directed to the restriction of the power of government officials "to a minimum so as to limit the evil they could do" (LW 2: 86). Dewey asks, how are we to explain the fact that precisely in a certain moment—and not before—the problem of the "arbitrariness of power" and its capacity to produce "evils" could acquire such a relevance in people's motivational background so that a new form of government would be preferred? His answer is straightforward:

> The transition from family and dynastic government supported by the loyalties of tradition to popular government was the outcome of primarily technological

discoveries and inventions working a change in the customs by which men had been bound together. (LW 2: 144)

In other words, extraordinary changes in technology, science, and economic life took place. These changes generated such a release of human powers and desires that existing feudal domination structures came to be seen as a hindrance to the realization of valuable human possibilities:

The use of machinery in production and commerce was followed by the creation of new powerful social conditions, personal opportunities and wants. Their adequate manifestation was limited by established political and legal practices. (LW 2: 89)

Hence, democracy—in its initial forms—emerges for Dewey as a valuable instrument that should fulfill a new epistemic need in the history of the Western world: that of securing the conditions by which newly discovered human powers would not be hindered by the arbitrary power of governors. This epistemic description of the emergence of political democracy is backed up in Dewey's text by the negative thesis that we are not to find the origin of democracy in the idea of democracy, understood as a general plan that would guide simultaneously different localized processes of institutional and practical transformation:

Much less is democracy the product of democracy, of some inherent nisus, or immanent idea. The temperate generalization to the effect that the unity of the democratic movement is found in effort to remedy evils experienced in consequence of prior political institutions realizes that it proceeded step by step, and that each step was taken without foreknowledge of any ultimate result, and, for the most part, under the immediate influence of a number of differing impulses and slogans. (LW 2: 85)

By denying the existence of an idea of democracy guiding the democratizing reaction against feudal domination, Dewey does not specify at these first stages of his historical reconstruction what is its exact content. Only in later stages will we have the opportunity to deepen into this central aspect of Dewey's theory since, according to him, the idea of democracy must be mobilized in a context of profound political crisis as a way to guide collective action and social reform. For the moment, it is important to consider that the initial stages of democratic government represent the result of local adaptations to new circumstances, circumstances that were initially generated by nonpolitical processes. However, denying the historical effectiveness of a guiding idea of democracy does not mean that ideas or purposes such as the already mentioned one of securing conditions for the release of powers could be guiding these processes. It only states that the unity and commonality of those processes was not the product of the same ideological influence, but that they represented highly contextualized learning processes that finally converged in the institution of democratic forms of government. The fact that these processes led to democracy somehow independently from one another makes sense only if we accept that for Dewey democracy, in its initial forms, represented at that historical time the best response to the nature of the new problems that arose in the larger processes of social transformation: "Looking back, with the aid of ex posto facto experience can give, it would be hard for the wisest to devise schemes which, under circumstances, would have met the needs better" (LW 2: 145). Put in other words:

> "Invent the press and some form of democratic government must emerge." Add
> to this: Invent the railway, the telegraph, mass manufacture and concentration
> of population in urban centres, and some form of democratic government is,
> humanly speaking, inevitable. (LW 2: 110)

To summarize, since the series of highly localized democratization processes reacting against feudal relations were not the direct product of an ideal governing people's political efforts, democracy cannot be seen as the result of a preexisting ideal of political freedom. As it seems, for Dewey, denying the effectiveness of an ideal leaves only open the possibility of spontaneous reactions toward securing values already established. Democracy is, in its initial steps, the result of the efforts for securing something prepolitically valued.

However, this is surely not the end of the story Dewey has to explain about democracy. Dewey's only focus on the instrumental motivations lying behind the emergence of democracy is in fact only apparent. The complexity of Dewey's depiction of the emergence of democratic government from feudal conditions only becomes clear once we see he in fact does not deny the influence of ideas in the processes following this very initial stage and that led to the establishment of institutionally stable forms of democracy. Even if, as we saw, we should not localize these guiding ideas at the very beginning of the story, we should see them as reflective elaborations arising from within the very same process of political transformation that took place during those early years and that ended up having an influence on the latter:

> Theories of the nature of the individual and his rights, of freedom and authority,
> progress and order, liberty and law, of the common good and a general will, of
> democracy itself, did not produce the movement [towards democratic govern-
> ment, JSZ]. They reflected it in thought; after they emerged, they entered into
> subsequent strivings and had practical effect. (LW2: 85)

In short, Dewey's historical reconstruction distinguishes three different moments within initial developments of democracy: first, a very initial stage of nonideally mediated reaction to newly perceived nonpolitical needs; second, the emergence of ideas that represent the normative and theoretical reflection of this immediate reaction and third, the mediation of these reflective elaborations in the further actualization of practical efforts for political transformation. Hence, once a first immediate reaction has taken place, we need to explore if the epistemically motivated transformation of political practice (avoidance of "evils") comes to be mediated by the ideas that emerged as reflective elaborations of the deep transformations affecting modern society. What is important for our analysis is that at this stage of his historical reconstruction, Dewey opens the opportunity to see for the first time historically "at work" the ideal of political freedom and equality expressed in the idea of democracy, hence promoting changes that respond to the practical demands involved in this political ideal. In order to explore these new forms of political transformation in which both epistemic demands and the practical demands of political freedom are at play, we need to make a short detour to analyze the specific nature of the ideas that emerged as reflective elaborations of existing democratic movements, ideas that Dewey enumerates in the passage just quoted.

Hence, from Dewey's short enumeration we are able to divide those theories, views, or ideas that represented theoretical elaborations of the new experiences fostered by ongoing social and political transformations in two different kinds: on the one side, we can identify those who refer to aspects that are protected and promoted by political institutions and political practice—"rights of the individual," "progress and order"—and which clearly concern the epistemic function of democracy, since protection and promotion of rights, social processes, and organization constitutes the task on behalf of which control of officials through popular government represented the best historically available method. On the other side, Dewey's list of normative ideals or values also includes elements that directly concern democracy as institutionalization of political freedom such as the "common good" and "general will." Surely, this distinction is blurry since some of the mentioned normative ideals such as "progress" and "liberty" can be applied to both groups: they can be both ideals to be realized by democracy or through democracy.

Hence, despite their diverging way to relate to democracy—the first, as task to be accomplished by democratic self-determination, the second as normative ideals realized through the exercise of democratic practice, it is a central idea that the elements of both groups of ideals are to be seen, according to Dewey, as particular specifications of a more general notion of freedom that arouse at the time of liberation from feudal power structures. This general

notion became a governing principle of the initial stages of modernity determining both the epistemic tasks for democracy and the realization of political freedom in democratic practice: that of freedom of the individual seen
in abstraction from its social relations. According to Dewey, the theoretical
elaborations that emerged with the release of human powers conceived of this
release in terms of liberation of the individual against society at large, and
saw the individual and society as realities that opposed each other.

Dewey puts the question about the causes of the emergence of the individualistic understanding of the experience of liberation from those social
relations that governed in feudal times. And his own answer is straightforward: Coming from a time in which political power was directly entrenched
with the major part of existing social institutions such as those of economy
and religion, the conclusion was easily inferred that the historical experience
of liberation from feudal oppression must have meant the liberation of the
individual from its social ties in toto. By identifying "society" or "the social"
to those oppressing institutions of feudal society, those who tried to make
sense of their new experience of liberation were conducted to barren the way
to a social understanding of freedom, something the negative consequences
of which would become generally apparent only in later stages of democratic
institutionalization and practice.

This individualistic understanding of the experience of liberation from
feudal structures coined both groups of normative ideas we have analyzed: on
the one side, democracy, insofar it has an epistemic function, has the task to
protect and guarantee the conditions that promote principles of individualistic
freedom. According to Dewey, this very specific form of understanding the
task of democracy influenced the specific configurations taken by democratic
institutions and practices since, in analogy to the application of a new method
in science, they were perceived as the best method historically available for
the realization of a predemocratically given epistemic task. Hence, as Dewey
shows by quoting the work of authors such as James Mill, the specific shape
"democratic forms" were sensed to take was theoretically developed in the
light of the task they had to accomplish:

> What arrangements will prevent rulers from advancing their own interests at
> the expense of the ruled? Or in positive terms, by what political means shall the
> interests of the governors be identified with those of the governed? The answer
> was given, notably by James Mill [. . .]. Its significant features were popular
> election of officials, short terms of office and frequent elections. (LW 2: 93)

On the other hand, democracy itself—including not only what Dewey calls
the "state machinery" but also the communicative practices of emerging public spheres—came to represent a practical realization of the political version

of this modern understanding of freedom, that of the individual in abstraction of its constitutive social ties.

Let's summarize before carrying out further our exploration. For Dewey the institutionalization of specific forms of popular government out of feudal conditions was the result of a process whose beginning was non-political in nature: it concerned scientific, technical, and religious transformations resulting in the unexpected release of human powers. Political changes are to be seen as a response to the sensed need to get rid of the obstacles as well as to protect and foster the conditions of this release. At the same time, due to the existing entrenchment between political power and other social institutions, the normative elaborations of the experience of liberation of powers took an individualistic overtone. So that we can say with Dewey that an individualistic understanding of freedom became the normative vanishing point of institutionalization processes in the beginning of the modern era. For democracy this meant firstly that the task of political action was limited to the protection of individual rights and of natural economic law. This task determined the specific institution and configuration of political action, so that particular democratic forms crystallized as methods that would set limits to the arbitrariness of power, thereby protecting those rights and natural economic laws. Secondly, it means that democracy itself came to be seen as the social institutionalization of the autonomy of the individual, in a sense that would oppose it against "the Social."

We have now gained an overview on the main factors lying behind Dewey's view on what he considers to be the initial forms of the political transformation that led to democracy: on the one side, those developments leading to the formation of initial forms of popular self-government acquired their specific form, representative democracy, insofar as they worked as methods for protecting and promoting individualistic freedom. On the other side, at some later moment, the ideal of political freedom as realized through democratic institutions and practices had a role to play in these transformations. The question about how both developmental dynamics historically converged in actual political transformation is answered in different passages of *The Public and Its Problems*. Hence, Dewey affirms that "the identification of democratic forms of government with this individualism was easy. The right of suffrage represented for the mass a release of hitherto dormant capacity and also, in appearance at least, *a power to shape social relations on the basis of individual volition*" (LW 2: 101, emphasis added) and: "Popular franchise and majority rule afforded the imagination a picture of individuals in their untrammelled individual sovereignty making the state" (LW 2: 101). In both passages the same idea is at play: the specific configuration taken by political forms, initially developed purely out of epistemic needs or interests, was retrospectively conceived of as expressions of political freedom. This identification was possible because both the task of democratic practice and institutions and the ideal of freedom they were meant to realize were the result of the very same historical experience: that of a liberation of the individual against society as a whole. Since both elements were derived from the same normative source, namely, individualistic freedom, the particular institutional forms taken by at those initial stages were such that they fitted the communicative premises underlying an individualistic ideal of freedom: coming together in political action meant managing to aggregate and impose one's individual will, that was conceived of as existing before political communication, something that perfectly fitted the political arrangements that were supposed to guarantee individual liberty and the free play of natural economic laws.

While in the first stages of political transformation toward popular self-government we find an actual relation of convergence and mutual reinforcement between the methodological needs derived from the protection of individualistic freedom and the "individualistic" understanding of self-determination, we seem able at the present stage to identify a possible source of future tension among these practical and institutional developments. Hence, the normative principles that are to be realized by and through democracy may diverge to such extent that societies can come to enter into a crisis of its political practices and institutions. Thus, it is conceivable that the epistemic tasks of democracy—that is, the kind of problems democratic institutions and practices are to deal with—may experience changes to such a degree that the methods that should fulfill those tasks overflow the limits of what can be practically institutionalized under the point of view of individualistic political freedom. In other words, epistemic or methodological requirements may be at the source of practical and institutional transformations that exceed the practical requirements of the historically specific form of understanding the intrinsic value of democracy. In this first sense, the epistemic dimension of democracy would be responsible for a crisis that can only be solved if the limits of our collective understanding of political freedom are expanded such that the new institutional and practical requirements could be fitted within it.

THE EPISTEMIC PATH WITHIN DEMOCRACY: FROM INDIVIDUALISTIC TO SOCIAL LIBERALISM

Dewey's *The Public and Its Problems* does not only reconstruct the history of the emergence of democracy in modern Europe coming from feudal mode of social and political organization, but it also provides an account of the further developments of democracy up to his time. In fact, for Dewey, the history of democracy in the last two centuries should be read from the point of view of its crisis in the late 20s. One that affects the principles of freedom that, in different forms, have governed social and political life from the times of liberation from feudal organization. As we have already seen, these principles are characterized by strong individualistic premises: freedom and liberation are those of an individual detached from its social relations. According to Dewey's diagnostic, the crisis of democracy that has taken the form of political apathy and the retreat of political action represents a proof of the deficient nature of this conception. Hence, he characterizes the last two centuries of popular government as the history of individualistic freedom's self-nullification. For Dewey the only way out of the actual crisis involves bringing an alternative notion of freedom into play that recognizes from the outset the social nature of the autonomous individual. Simply put, what is needed are reforms aiming at a transformation of the ways in which citizens communicate and inquire into social problems, reforms that correspond to a notion of social freedom which at the same time contribute to the further institutionalization of freedom in political practice.

In the context of these more general projects of social and political reform, the problem of the transformative role played by problem-solving function of democracy is apparently reversed: if reform is supposed to derive from an ideal of social freedom that challenges actual communicative practices, is there any sense in which the problem-solving function of democracy influences these changes? In other words, does the transition from individualistic to social freedom depend to some extent on the very dynamics of political problem-solving? Or do we have to limit ourselves, at this stage, to see in problem-solving a normative function merely subordinated to the new form of freedom (social) that jumps on stage independently of it?

In order to answer these questions, I will shortly reconstruct Dewey's narration of the history of US-American democracy, a history that has gone through two different phases and which, according to him, must be followed by a third one if democratic institutions and practices are to have any continuity at all. These phases correspond to (1) the emergence of democratic forms under "pioneer conditions"; (2) the progressive retreat of political forms or "crisis of democracy"; and finally (3) the necessary arrival of social liberalism, that is, the needed consolidation of social freedom as the governing normative notion of the time to come.

Dewey describes the origins of American political institutions and practice as directly emerging from what he calls "pioneer conditions." These conditions were those characterizing the life of the immigrants who constituted the first British colonies in the North American continent. In his description, Dewey mentions four of them: First of all, pioneers brought to the new continent old political habits and ideas they had acquired in Great Britain, these political habits reproduced the practical demands of what we have called "individualistic freedom"; secondly, communities emerging in North America were isolated from each other, a situation that promoted some kind of regulative idiosyncrasy and the lack of standards for the production and assessments of institutional forms such as those related to the education of the children. Thirdly, for Dewey pioneer times were characterized by the prominence of the conflict between the individual and nature; and finally, the existence of basic needs that could not be met but by the local community such as basic education, construction of common buildings, and so on. These conditions promoted what came to be called Jeffersonian democracy: local communities, face-to-face communication, election of well-known representatives based on their experience, prestige, and knowledge.

According to Dewey, the notion of freedom immigrants brought from England and other European regions and which was sedimented in their political habits corresponded to the kind of individualism we have already studied in the previous section. Furthermore, the conditions under which what came to be identified with the Jeffersonian ideal of democracy arouse contributed to a consolidation of this imported European political habits:

> The pioneer, [. . .] had no great need for any ideas beyond those that sprang up in the immediate tasks in which he was engaged. His intellectual problems grew out of struggle with the forces of physical nature. [. . .] The type of character that evolved was strong and hardy, often picturesque, and sometimes heroic. Individuality was a reality because it corresponded to conditions. (LW 5: 85)

However, very quickly technical developments changed the social conditions under which pioneers had developed their practices and institutions so enormously that locally developed political institutions and practices would soon prove to be insufficient. In Dewey's text, we can identify three ways in which technological innovations such as the invention of the telegraph, improvements in transportation and industry challenged and contributed to the further development of existing political practice and institutions: First, technological transformations concerning transport and communication were responsible for a high level of homogenization of views and perspectives that made possible the political integration of very different communities arriving from overseas: "Our modern state-unity is due to the consequences of technology employed so as to facilitate the rapid and easy circulation of opinions and information, and so as to generate constant and intricate interaction far beyond the limits of face-to-face communities" (LW 2: 114). There was a second sense in which technological transformations, such as the use of machines for electoral calculation or the emergence of the technical means and economic conditions for the emergence of mass media, contributed to challenge and transform existing political institutions and practices.

Third, and most centrally to our argument, technological revolutions generated new problems of significantly different nature than those the Jeffersonian community had to deal with. The following passage sums up pretty much all the changes affecting the nature of the new problems democratic forms had there on to deal with:

> But it is no longer physical wilderness that has to be wrestled with. Our problems grow out of social conditions: they concern human relations rather than man's direct relationship to physical nature. [. . .] The problems to be solved are general, not local. They concern complex forces that are at work throughout the whole country, not those limited to an immediate and almost face-to-face environment. (LW 5: 85–86)

In my view, this description captures three central senses in which problems changed: first, the new problems arising from the scientific, industrial, and technological revolutions were eminently social, that is, they had to deal with the organization and harmonization of social relationships. At the same time, the new problems were also more general in scope: they affected both geographically and numerically larger parts of the population. Finally, scientific, technological, and industrial developments contributed to the enhancement of the complexity of the problems affecting citizens so that both the causes and the effects of social interactions became especially difficult to trace.

Dewey notes at this stage that the transformation of political practice and institutions that followed these changes in social conditions was a highly ambivalent process. In fact, for Dewey the former are not to be seen so much as transformation of practices in the sense of the methodological adaptation to the new problems under new means of communication and inquiry than as a retreat of democratic forms tout court. This retreat of democracy had two major expressions: First, an expanded sense that political action in its current, limited form is not of much value. As Dewey points out, in this context of political apathy "the still more inclined to generalization assert that the whole apparatus of political activities is a kind of protective colouration to conceal the fact that big business rules the governmental roost in any case" (LW 2: 118). The second expression of the retreat of democracy was the emergence of an alternative understanding of politics as administration of public issues that legitimized the action of technocrats at the expense of that of democratic publics. At this stage of our exploration, we still need to explore in more detail the causes that, according to Dewey, have led to such a critical situation for democracy instead of to further methodological transformation by which political forms would be able to come to the new problems already described. Note here that the problem here concerns the very reproduction of democracy as a political form. Certainly, the crisis of democracy had to do with the very emergence of new problems old institutional and practical arrangements could not deal with: the main question for Dewey is why the necessary transformations in political practice and institutions did not take place following social developments.

In *The Public and Its Problems* Dewey labels the situation just described of political apathy and rise of expertocratic forms of government as well as the resulting crisis of democratic institutions and practices as the "eclipse of the public," which gives name to one central chapter of his book. Hence, the problem of democracy is not only that the rise of complexity has made the resolution of public problems more difficult for existing political institutions, but also that those affected by the public consequences of association have become unable to perceive these consequences both as affecting them and in need to be taken care of. In other words, the rise of social complexity constitutes a political challenge both at the level of institutional problem-solving and at the level of collective self-perception necessary for the emergence of a democratic public. The public cannot perceive itself and, hence, undertake the kind of political activities that would make democracy flourish again from its actual critical situation. Here it should be noted that for Dewey, these developments represent a normative challenge for all those who believe in democracy understood as popular government, independently of their particular understanding of it. Most centrally, Dewey points to the fact that the actual situation represents a challenge for the very public philosophy (Ansell 2011) that is responsible for the actually existing institutional forms of democracy. This public philosophy is, as we have seen, that one who considers democracy as the realization of individualistic freedom. Hence, in the actual situation,

> Instead of individuals who in the privacy of their consciousness make choices which are carried into effect by personal volition, there are citizens who have the blessed opportunity to vote for a ticket of men mostly unknown to them, and which is made up for them by an under-cover machine in a caucus whose operations constitute a kind of 'political predestination.' There are those who speak as if the ability to choose between two tickets were a high exercise of individual freedom. But it is hardly the kind of liberty contemplated by the authors of the individualistic doctrine. (LW 2: 120)

Let's get things together and bring Dewey's argument one step further: In the chapter "The Eclipse of the Public" Dewey tells us the story of a deep transformation in political practice. From local, face-to-face interaction-based political practice, based on knowledge and prestige of officials which is seen as a specific form of realization of political freedom in its individualistic sense, US-American politics has evolved into a situation in which less and less people participate in elections and democratic politics is seen more and more as mere façade, or else it is reduced to the administration of technical matters. For those who consider democracy and politics in general as a façade (radical socialists and implicitly, business people), popular government is seen more and more as superfluous since the effective power appears to be beyond the reach of any form of popular control. For those who are willing to reduce politics to administration of technical matters, popular government is not only considered as involving superfluous institutional setting but also as an obstacle to effective problem-solving. This state of affairs marked by political apathy, democratic inaction, and rise of technocratic forms of government is normatively problematic in an immanent sense: the promises of liberation implicit in the political culture of modern liberal democratic states are blocked by the very institutional realization of the ideals that constitute the normative core of that public philosophy: those of individualistic freedom. This self-nullifying effect of hegemonic public philosophy however becomes only evident once technological developments have generated social changes involving an enormous rise of social complexity.

In this context, existing political practices and institutions prove themselves unable to fulfill one basic epistemic function: that of sustaining the cognitive conditions of collective self-perception. These conditions concern the possibility of citizens to perceive themselves as affected by the consequences of social transactions. This is so because in their actual, individualistic form, these institutions and practices prove themselves unable to sustain and promote the necessary communicative infrastructure as well as the logical requirements—that is, requirements related to the methods of social inquiry put at work in the social sciences as well as in mass media and public debate—that are needed for collective self-perception.

Hence, according to Dewey, the communicative infrastructure and the logical quality of public inquiry in times of individualistic freedom took their specific shape from wrong premises, which can be brought together under the idea of the "omnicompetent individual":

> Two essential constituents in that older theory, as will be recalled, were the notions that each individual is of himself equipped with the intelligence needed, under the operation of self-interest, to in engage in political affairs; and that general suffrage, frequent elections of officials and majority rule are sufficient to ensure the responsibility of elected rulers to the desires and interests of the public. (LW 2: 157)

For Dewey, the theory of the omnicompetent individual is wrong in two senses: it has historically proved to be wrong, since it has served to shape and justify institutional and practical forms of democracy that are not able to maintain themselves in time and space. In a second sense, the theory is wrong because it lays on a wrong conception of human intelligence and communication. Hence, according to Dewey, intelligence is an eminently social achievement.

A philosophical reconsideration of the social-epistemic premises underlying the individualistic conception of freedom makes clear that conditions of higher complexity just make more evident the insufficiency of this notion: the intelligence and communication needed for tracing publicly relevant consequences cannot be achieved if existing institutions remain within the framework of an individualistic conception. Hence, according to Dewey the survival of democracy depends on the emergence of a new public capable of generating new forms of democratic practice. However, this emergence should not be seen as the reemergence of an old public. Since the "pioneer conditions" that brought about Jeffersonian democracy are hardly given, a new public seems unable to rest on the communicative infrastructure of only rarely existing forms of face-to-face communication. Furthermore, the general notion of freedom governing the normative life of this new public must be of a different sort: In its realization, it must indeed be able to sustain the complex communicative infrastructure that is needed in times of high complexity as well as to promote the rationality of public inquiries. Hence, the kinds of social interaction that prove themselves to be necessary to sustain this infrastructure at the political level are much more demanding than those which can be inferred from a notion of individual freedom. Thus, what democracy needs is the generation of practices that practically exceed the normative requirements linked to the governing principles corresponding to individual freedom. Under current circumstances, for democracy to survive, the new public must have the realization of a social understanding as its normative vanishing point:

> The crisis of democracy demands the substitution of the intelligence that is now accepted. The need for this change is not exhausted in the demands for greater honesty and impartiality [. . .] The social use of intelligence would remain deficient even if these moral traits were exalted, and yet intelligence continued to be identified simply with discussion and persuasion [. . . .]. Approximation to use of scientific method in investigation and of engineering mind in the invention and projection of far-reaching plans is demanded. (LW 11: 51–52)

Up to this point, the problem-solving function of democracy seems to be at the basis of the needed deep transformation in democratic institutions and practices. Given the fact that problems have become social, complex, and large, only new forms of political practice that realize freedom of an essentially different sort of that of individualism seems able to guarantee the communicative infrastructure and inquiry practice necessary for the collective self-perception of the public as well as for the identification, formulation, and solution of new problems. Here we see at work the tension that we pointed to in the previous section: the problem-solving function of democracy involves the demand for new practices and institutional arrangements that exceed the limited and limiting content of a governing notion of freedom. Hence, with this idea we would seem to come to a final version on Dewey's view: on the one side, the epistemic function of democracy may be mobilized by social actors in a way that reduces the reach of an institutionalized meaning of freedom, on the other side, this very same function may force established institutions and practice to transformation in a sense that practically exceeds the governing meaning of freedom, thereby forcing its further expansion.

THE EPISTEMIC PATH TO A MORE SOCIAL DEMOCRACY: THE IDEAL OF DEMOCRACY

However, it is not difficult to see at this stage that an important aspect is lacking in my reconstruction of Dewey's view. Unlike in the case of the liberation from feudal times, in the critical analysis of his time, Dewey does not see this new, challenging understanding of democracy as having directly emerged from the epistemic needs agents experienced resulting from the different nature of new problems they had to deal with. Dewey's idea is a much complex one: surely, once the communicative conditions for the identification of public problems are set, epistemic needs will contribute to stabilizing the newly reached meaning of social freedom. Epistemic needs arising in the new era of technological developments made the institution of social freedom in democratic practice normatively necessary; however, in times of the eclipse of the public, the necessity and the sense of the "social" meaning of freedom cannot be primary derived from the particular political experience of dealing with new problems. For political actors, the practical necessity and the general sense of social freedom can only emerge only once the necessary communicative infrastructure for the emergence of a public has been put at work. As it is announced in the following passage, the only way out of such a vicious circle is constituted by the introduction of the idea of democracy:

> The old saying that the cure for the ills of democracy is more democracy is not apt if it means that the evils may be remedied by introducing more machinery of the same kind as that which already exists [. . .]. But the phrase may also indicate the need to returning to the idea itself, of clarifying and deepening our apprehension of it, and of employing our sense of its meaning to criticize and re-make its political manifestations. (LW 2: 144)

Note the difference with Dewey's description of the emergence of popular forms of government: At those initial stages, no idea or project of democracy was needed to direct the actions of the individuals toward institutional reform that resulted in democratic forms. Ideas appeared as reflective elaborations of these first experiences and were marked by the idea that the freedom realized through democracy was that of the individual against the society that oppressed it. At the present moment, the situation is such that communicative conditions are needed for. And according to Dewey, these conditions can only be promoted through the mobilization of a clearer and deeper understanding of democracy. It is important to note the sort of operations Dewey sees involved in the mobilization of the idea of democracy: we have to "[return] to the idea itself," and "[clarify] and [deepen] our apprehension of it" and "[employ] our sense of its meaning to criticize and re-make its political manifestations."

According to Dewey's words, then, the idea of democracy represents a normative ideal that can be reinterpreted in a more adequate way such that we gain practical standards that allow for critique and reform. But what is the origin of this normative ideal? What is its content and how can it be reinterpreted in a deeper way? In trying to answer the last question, one would be tempted to identify the idea of democracy with that of social freedom tout court. Hence, one would say in the very same moment where the epistemic dynamics of democracy seems unable to promote by itself the necessary institutional forms and practices for its own survival, only by mobilizing a normative ideal that derives sociality from other sources. In my view, however, Dewey's position is more complex: The idea of democracy is surely linked to the idea of social freedom but, as it is also the case for Jürgen Habermas, it also involves the epistemically grounded idea that democratic practices must be socially "thick" if they are to fulfill their task of protecting/promoting the conditions of social freedom.

Let's take a short look at Habermas's view. In *Between Facts and Norms* (1998b), Habermas proposes to understand his deliberative theory of democracy as an alternative to two traditional approaches: liberalism and republicanism. Each of them sees the paradigmatic form of democratic practice—for which Habermas also uses the expression "democratic process" (Habermas 1998b: 296)—as lying on different normative grounds. On the one hand, for liberals

> Rules of compromise formation are supposed to secure the fairness of results through universal and equal suffrage, the representative composition of parliamentary bodies, the mode of decision making, rules of order, and so on. Such rules are ultimately justified in terms of liberal basic rights. (Habermas 1998b: 296)

Habermas makes here a direct reference to basic liberal rights as grounding the rules of democratic practice, understood, in contrast to a richer account of deliberation, as the mere generation of compromises. However, liberalism's grounding strategy is not an intrinsic one. Rather, the talk of liberal rights refers to the quality of the results of any democratic process. They set the limits to what kinds of results we should expect from democratic practices. Hence, Habermas stresses the idea that liberalism "is oriented not toward the input of a rational political will-formation but toward the output of government activities that are successful on balance" (Habermas 1998b: 298). The rules guiding the practice of generation of compromises are those that guarantee that the results of the democratic process will be fair and will fulfill the task of "the constitutional framework for an economic society that is supposed to guarantee an essentially nonpolitical common good by satisfying personal life plans and private expectations of happiness" (Habermas 1998b: 298).

Habermas characterizes the normative expectations of the liberal conception of democratic practice as "weak." Hence, as we can infer from the enumeration of democratic practices above (building compromises, elections, representation, and decision-making) liberalism does not demand a normatively substantial understanding of the practices involved in democratic self-determination in the same sense deliberative democrats do. On the contrary, it limits its practical requirements to the institutionalization of the minimal political rules of fairness that, in the last instance, serve the goal of promoting well-functioning economic relations as well as to guaranteeing that political decisions will respect basic liberal rights. Here we can track an ambivalence in Habermas's characterization of the normative sources lying in the liberal position. Hence, it is not clear if the "normative weakness" of liberal democratic procedures is due to the centrality given to their epistemic role—coming close to a monist epistemic position—or to the nature of the outputs expected from democratic practice—in this case, the protection of classical liberal rights and the efficient regulation of a capitalist free-market economy. Otherwise formulated, does the increasing weight of democracy's epistemic dimension involve a decrease in the normative substance of democratic practice, or is the very nature of the expected outcomes, that is, the specific epistemic tasks given to democratic practice, at the heart of a limited understanding of democratic practice?

His further reflections on the issue suggest that not the strategy of a purely epistemic justification, but the specific nature of the results expected from the democratic process is at the heart of the theoretical "choice" among different, weaker or stronger understandings of the normative substance of democratic practice. In other words, it is because it attributes to democracy a limited epistemic task that of protecting preformulated liberal rights and regulating the economic sphere that liberalism does not require, from an epistemic point of view, stronger forms of communication for the formation of a collective will. In my view, both authors, Habermas and Dewey, share in their critique of liberalism—understood in its individualistic sense, as opposed to a more social understanding of liberal politics—the view that the practical requirements involved in realizing democracy's instrumental value depend, at least to a certain degree, on the nature of outcomes expected from the democratic process: if these outcomes are merely meant to protect the negative rights of the individual as well as the well-functioning of economic relations, then the normative requirements for the epistemic processes generating results in line with this limited view of human freedom need also to be necessary limited.

To come back to Dewey, we get a sense of this complex view in the following passage:

> For democracy signifies, on one side, that every individual is to share in the duties and rights belonging to control of social affairs, and, on the other side, that social arrangements are to eliminate those external arrangements of status, birth, wealth, sex, etc., which restrict the opportunity of each individual for full development of himself. (LW 14: 349)

Dewey's characterization is based on a difference that is central for our analysis. Hence, we see in it two different forms of freedom at work, whose complex relation needs to be spelled out here. On the one hand, Dewey talks in terms of a "[share] in the duties and rights belonging to control of social affairs," thereby pointing to the ideal of autonomy or self-government as an integral part of the idea of democracy. On the other side, democracy also involves the freedom involved in the self-realization of the individual: "the opportunity of each individual for full development of himself." Iris Marion Young (2001) reserves the names of "self-determination" and "self-development" for both normative ideals, which according to her must be part of a theory of democracy that values the latter for its capacity to realize justice.

In the context of the present reconstruction, the most interesting for us is the fact that both forms of freedom (self-determination and self-development) are related to each other in two different senses, whose reconstruction will bring the epistemic function of democracy to the normative core of its immanent idea. In a first sense of the relation between both normative ideals, for Dewey, the conditions for individual self-development can only be protected or promoted if individuals have an actual share in the control of the social affairs that concern them. In other words, self-development is, at least to some extent, only possible if citizens fully participate in practices of self-determination, thereby taking control upon the results of the political process. On the other hand, the participation in collective practices of self-determination must be seen as contributing to the self-development of the individuals in a second sense: in political practice, individuals realize themselves as political beings, thereby contributing to the normative ideal of self-development to the extent that participating in political life represents a value in itself.

As it seems, for Dewey the idea of democracy represents a standard for political critique and reform that involves both, the ideals of autonomy and of self-realization. At the same time it states that participation in practices of autonomy is a necessary condition for the protection and promotion of individual self-realization, which points to the idea of democracy as a method for the resolution of social problems. Furthermore, it implies that participation in practices of autonomy represents a particular kind of self-realization: the realization of our capacities as autonomous or political beings. According to Dewey, a deep understanding of this particular combination of both ideals involves becoming aware of the social "thickness" of democracy. Regarding political or democratic practice, the previous ideas suggest two ways of conceiving them as social in the strong or thick sense implicit in the notion of social freedom: first of all, as with any other form of self-realization (at work, in the family), democratic or political self-realization is a social enterprise. Second, as an instrument for the protection or promotion of self-realization, democratic institutions and practices must also be social if they are to work as methods for the promotion of conditions for individual self-realization, elements implicit in the notion of the identification, definition, and resolution of the problems that arise in modern social life.

In conclusion, by mobilizing the idea of democracy for the goal of promoting social reform such that the communicative infrastructure necessary for the cognitively dependent emergence of a public, Dewey mobilizes both kinds of arguments at the same time, those related to democratic practice as the realization of the ideal of autonomy and self-realization, and those related to democratic practice as an instrument for identifying, defining, and resolving social problems. To this extent, and contrary to Honneth's interpretation, Dewey remains faithful to his particular epistemic account of democracy and democratic transformation all the way through.

DEWEY'S SYSTEMATIC ARGUMENT

It has come now the time to recapitulate and formulate Dewey's systematic view underlying the different steps of his historical reconstruction. For carrying out this task it seems especially useful to bring into discussion the distinction between what I will call the intranormative and the transnormative levels of practical transformation. The intranormative level of practical transformation refers to changes in specific interpretations given to general normative principles realized in our practices. Even though they may clearly differ from each other, specific interpretations and their particular realization in practices remain within the limits of what can be derived from a certain normative principle. At this level, normative progress concerns the capacity of the given interpretations of a norm to be experienced as better or more adequate than the previous ones. Hence, Dewey's critique of the self-nullification of individualistic forms of democracy is to be seen as based on this kind of intranormative transformation: according to him, actual democratic practices cannot be seen as an authentic realization of the principles of individualistic freedom. But the intranormative sense of progress does not need to apply only to individualistic freedom: social freedom may be also subjected to the very same dynamics involving better or worse interpretations of the social nature of freedom. At the transnormative level, normative changes are more radical: they concern the more abstract principles of freedom (individualistic or social) at stake. So, as we saw, for Dewey, individual freedom's self-nullification compels those who believe in democracy to change the basic principle the latter is meant to realize: given the impossibility we need to mobilize a clearer and deeper—and this means: a social—idea of democracy that newly generates the institutional and practical conditions for its own reproduction.

Within this general framework, Dewey makes an essential contribution to the project of reclaiming the historical effectiveness of the epistemic dimension of democracy to the extent that he provides an historical reconstruction of democracy that identifies the dynamics involved in methodological innovations at work at both levels of practical transformation: intra- and transnormative. Let's analyze both levels separately:

The epistemic dimension's role on the specification of general normative principles: For Dewey, principles of freedom—individualistic or social—are too abstract to provide by themselves sufficiently concrete standards for action. Hence, these abstract principles need to be interpreted such that their meaning can be specified. Dewey's reconstruction points to a concretizing effect of methodologically motivated practical change. So, for example, the practice of secret voting cannot be directly derived from the principle of the autonomous individual, even though it can be reflectively identified as realizing this principle. The task of democratic forms being the identification, definition, and solution of problems defined by a specific notion of (individual or social) freedom, political forms also take a specific form that corresponds to these epistemic needs. So far the general notion of freedom can harmonize with newly generated practices, the latter can be seen by political actors as realization of political freedom. To this extent, we can speak in terms of the

epistemic function of democracy working as a motor of the practical realization freedom: next to a Honnethian dynamics by which the principles of freedom produce their specifications by their own in struggles for recognition, the
meaning of those principles can also be transformed by the dynamics arising
from epistemic needs. Surely, once it has been epistemically transformed,
the new meaning of freedom can be mobilized by agents in their critique of
political practice. To this extent, we cannot exclude the possibility that both
epistemic and freedom-related reasons will be mobilized at the same time
in social critique and practical transformation. Furthermore, the epistemic
transformation of the meaning of freedom has also its own limits: once progress in the meaning of freedom is made, factually held epistemic reasons that
demand exclusion from the practices of collective will-formation or which
promote restrictive understandings of ideals of equal participation cannot be
seen but as normative regressions.

The epistemic dimension's role in the socialization of democratic practice:
At the second, transnormative level of analysis, we have to do with the transformation of institutions and practice corresponding to two different general
notions of freedom, individualistic and social. Here there is a first sense in
which the epistemic dynamics of democracy may contribute to this change:
by becoming aware of the social nature, measure, and complexity of public
problems, citizens may prefer new methods, methods that exceed the practical meaning of individualistic conceptions of democracy. However, since this
"realization" is dependent on conditions that individualistic social freedom
cannot give to itself—which concern the communicative infrastructure necessary for the self-identification of a public—we enter into a vicious circle
from which the dynamics of problem-solving cannot take us out. In such a
situation, Dewey proposes to mobilize the idea of democracy as an ideal of
social freedom in the design of institutional transformation: only by mobilizing this idea will we be able to construct the communicative infrastructure
which is necessary for the self-maintaining of democracy in times of high
social complexity. However, by mobilizing the idea of democracy we cannot
still say that the transition from an individualistic to a social understanding
is based merely on a self-promoted expansion of the institutionalized meaning of autonomy and self-realization. Hence, the idea of democracy involves
more than freedom as autonomy: it also involves self-realization of the
individual within the community and the double mentioned epistemic connection between self-realization and autonomy. At the same time, the ideal
of democracy does not emerge as the idea of an actualization of the potential
of actual political practice, but furthermore, as the idea of the actualization
of a potential which is inscribed within society at large. Therefore, the mobilization of the idea of democracy has to be thought as the mobilization of a
double ideal of freedom which is epistemically and/or socially mediated. The

idea of democracy can be seen as the realization of a principle of social life: it brings with itself the experience of the epistemically necessary expansion of an individualistic understanding of freedom. Hence, the deep institutional and practical transformation that is involved in the evolution from individualistic to social freedom as principles of institutionalized forms of political practice represents a project that draws its normative value from the social experience of the epistemic need involved in self-determination. The problem-solving function of democracy can not only be made responsible for the better realizations of a principle of freedom but also for deeper changes in it.

EXCURSUS: HABERMAS' GENEALOGY OF A POSTMETAPHYSICAL NEED FOR JUSTIFICATION

In *Truth and Justification* Habermas provides what he calls a "genealogy of the postmetaphysical need for justification" (Habermas 2003: 266) that comes close to some of the fundamental insights we can find in Dewey's *The Public and Its Problems*. Even if it is not clear if Habermas gives to this social need a strong casual role in the institutionalization of deliberative procedures, one cannot but be astonished to observe the parallelisms between both historical accounts of modern life. Hence, both see in the institutionalization of democratic procedures a functional response to the requirements of the new epistemic needs generated by the normative transformations that accompany modern life. However, there lie important differences between both authors. One of them is that Habermas and Dewey identify different aspects of modernity as relevant causes at the origin of this epistemic need. While Dewey points to the release of potentialities made possible by new scientific and technological developments of the modern era, Habermas focuses on the process of functional differentiation and the consequent pluralization of forms of life and anonymization of social interactions that characterizes the historical development of modern life forms. As we need to show in more detail, these processes are at the source of new understandings of justice that cannot be responded to but through the institutionalization of deliberative practice.

Habermas begins his genealogical analysis by outlining the normative and cognitive features of an imagined premodern society. He proposes we imagine a strongly hierarchical and repressive society (according to our own standards) where a shared worldview is able to explain all inequalities as responding to the necessary reproduction of the common good, which is perceived by the members of that premodern society as what is "equally good for everyone" (Habermas 2003: 265). In other words, social inequalities and relations of domination appear as justified in the eyes of those concerned in virtue of the capacity of the shared worldview to characterize them as the natural articulations of the more abstract principle of equality that is involved in all notions of justice. With the processes of functional differentiation that characterize modern societies, the basic relations among their members also change: interactions become anonymous and take place among individuals who cannot see each other as similar any more. In this context, the old mechanisms of normative integration must be substituted by new ones that respond to this modern condition: "As the intersubjectively shared worldview is shattered and the traditional form of life disintegrates, the collective good that is intertwined with both of them becomes problematic" (Habermas 2003: 263). At this stage two different aspects need to be taken into account: on the one hand, the perceived plurality of forms of life has as a consequence of the ontological foundations of the old normative order no longer being obvious; the contrary, the moral universe of members of modern societies starts to appear as "constructed." On the other hand, integration under new conditions of plurality only becomes possible under "an agreement about more abstract, general norms that are not tailored to specific cases in advance" (Habermas 2003: 263). It is at this moment that the "egalitarian implications of justice" (Habermas 2003: 263) become apparent to individuals: justice in the sense of "equally good for all" cannot any more justify highly hierarchical orders. On the contrary, since it is meant to cope with a rich spectrum of social roles and experiences, the principle of "equally good for all" must go hand in hand with (a more) equal consideration of different forms of life. At this stage, Habermas points to the fact that, historically, the progressive realization of the "egalitarian implications of justice" was limited by the strong ethical integration of national states. However, Habermas points to the fact that the progressive multiculturalization of national communities has once more brought to the fore the "the universalist implications of justice" (Habermas 2003: 264).

Both processes, the newly experienced need for legitimization of the moral order and the progressive making explicit of the egalitarian implications of the justice principle involved in the formulation "equally good for all," make of the institutionalization of discursive rationality as a mechanism of social integration that is typical of modern societies a functional requirement, hence:

The expectation of legitimacy—that only norms that are "equally good for everyone" merit recognition—can be fulfilled only by means of a procedure that ensures the inclusion of everyone who is potentially affected as well as impartiality in the sense of equal consideration of all interests involved.

It is not all that surprising that the communicative presuppositions of rational discourse should meet the requirements of such a procedure. For moral knowledge, unlike empirical knowledge, is inherently used for purposes of critique and justification. Moral knowledge consists of a stockpile of convincing reasons for consensually settling conflicts of interaction that arise within the lifeworld. Hence the communicative model for deliberation about and justification of disputed propositions fits with a posttraditional, purged idea of justice. After the collapse of comprehensive worldviews and ethoi, this idea can be articulated only in terms of the impartiality of belief and will-formation within an inclusive justificatory community. In practical discourses, "impartiality" as discursive vindication of criticizable validity claims coincides with "impartiality" as a posttraditional idea of justice. (Habermas 2003: 265–266)

According to Habermas, then, only a procedure that is able to include individuals that are strange to each other and that is able to equally consider the interests of each is able to generate "concrete" notions of justice in the context of "equalitarian universalism," which are required for social integration in a context of high levels of pluralism. To this extent, Habermas seems to imply that the institutionalization of deliberative procedures that is typical of modern democratic societies has one of its historical motors in the instrumental need for generating even stronger egalitarian notions of justice, a need that arises in the wider context of social differentiation and intercultural integration. While, as we saw before, the last word about valid outcomes is to be found in the actually existing processes of democratic will-formation, this constructive element finds its counterweight in the preprocedural task that is set by the very developments of modern forms of life: that of the deployment of the egalitarian potential that is inherent to notion of justice.

As we will see however, even if Dewey and Habermas share the idea that epistemic needs have had democratizing effects, the differences between both views do not only concern the nature of those epistemic needs. Furthermore, Dewey's experimentalism involves a kind of practical pluralism—according to which, experimentalism can be realized in many different ways, and not only through deliberation, understood as argumentative exchange—that is not compatible with Habermas's understanding of deliberation. This affects the way both authors understand democratic progress: while for Habermas it means the progressive institutionalization of deliberative procedures, for Dewey it involves the generation of innovative practices that realize experimentalism in an open-ended list of political practices.

WHEN PROBLEM-SOLVING DOES NOT ADVANCE DEMOCRACY

As I indicated in chapter 1, that democracy's epistemic function as an autonomous dynamic has played and can play a progressive role in the advancement of existing democratic forms is for many authors not an obvious fact. In the literature we do not only find systematic positions that cast doubt into the capacity of problem-solving to promote democracy. Furthermore, we also find historical accounts that, contrary to that of Dewey, identify problem-solving as the source of the perversion, regress, or blocking of democratic advancement. Hannah Arendt and Peter Wagner have provided historical accounts of political transformation that focus on some of the dangers of subordinating political freedom to the resolution of social problems. As I aim to show, however, this subordination does not concern democracy's problem-solving function per se, but has rather to do with their view on the specific problems that at some historical moment have come to the foreground of political life. In the case of Arendt, these problems refer to what she calls the "social question," which she identifies as nothing less than the origin of the state of terror that followed the French Revolution. On the other hand, according to Wanger, the European political and economic elites were able to effectively mobilize epistemic reasons that blocked the possibility of developing the democratic promises of the modern revolutions. While by themselves they do not stand in direct contradiction with my Deweyan account, by shortly discussing their positions I hope to provide a clearer view on the Deweyan position I am defending here.

HANNAH ARENDT AND THE EPISTEMIC PATH TO POLITICAL PERVERSION

As we mentioned in chapter 1, Hannah Arendt explicitly denies the compatibility between the search for truth—understood as "factual truth" (Arendt 1967: 122) and politics. In her own words, truth "precludes debate, and debate constitutes the very essence of political life" (Arendt 1967: 115, quoted from Estlund 2008: 21). Beyond her systematic view, however, Arendt has also formulated an historical argument against any attempt to subordinate political freedom to the needs of the epistemic dimension of democracy. In fact, in her historical-philosophical characterization of the American and French Revolutions (2006), Arendt attributes to the instrumental function of democracy exactly the opposite effect to the one I have presented along these lines. According to Arendt, it is precisely the emergence of the idea that democratic government has as its task the resolution of social problems—and more particularly, those concerning what she calls the "social question"—what is at the origin of the turn of revolutionary movements from the pursuit of political freedom to the worst forms of human despotism. This historical tendency is explained by the different nature of the activities involved: on the one side, democratic forms are seen as an achievement drawn from the political and economic elite's striving for freedom. On the other side, the "social question,"

which refers to the states of misery of great parts of the population is introduced artificially in this struggle for freedom. Its introduction is artificial
since the "social question" is directly linked to realm of necessity, that of us
as natural beings with basic needs, while politics belongs to the ontologically
delimitable field of free action. Hence, putting democracy at the service of the
resolution of "social" problems must be seen as submission of freedom under
the reign of necessity, thereby subverting the original intention of the struggle
for a republican–democratic political order. According to Arendt, the terror
of the French Revolution constitutes the major expression of this regrettable
historical development, which cannot be but described as the perversion of
democracy by its subordination to its problem-solving function:

> The direction of the American Revolution remained committed to the foundation
> of freedom and the establishment of lasting institutions, and to those who acted
> in this direction nothing was permitted that would have been outside the range of
> civil law. The direction of the French Revolution was deflected almost from its
> beginning from this course of foundation through the immediacy of suffering; it
> was determined by the exigencies of liberation not from tyranny but from neces-
> sity, and it was actuated by the limitless immensity of both the people's misery
> and the pity this misery inspired. The lawlessness of the 'all is permitted' sprang
> here still from the sentiments of the heart whose very boundlessness helped in the
> unleashing of a stream of boundless violence. (Arendt 2006: 82)
>
> Since there were no sufferings around them that would have aroused their
> passions, no overwhelming urgent needs that would have tempted them to
> submit to necessity, no pity to lead them astray from reason, the men of the
> American Revolution remained men of action from the beginning to the end,
> from the Declaration of Independence to the framing of the Constitution.
> (Arendt 2006: 85)

This characterization of the perversion of the original movement toward
freedom can be interpreted as involving two different arguments, an antiepistemic and an ethical argument. According to the latter, political perversion
is due to the kind of moral reaction the presence of social misery generates
on the actors involved in the revolution: one of pity and compassion. As it is
illustrated by the actions of Robespierre, compassion is responsible for the
abolition of any moral limits to the exercise of political practice. Hence, the
moral feeling of compassion is able to subordinate all further moral considerations that would limit the action of revolutionaries. On the other hand,
regarding her antiepistemic argument, the intrusion of the real of necessity
into the realm of politics—which takes the form of a subordination of the
liberating goal of revolutionary practice—radically cuts the process of realization of freedom:

It was under the rule of this necessity that the multitude rushed to the assistance of the French Revolution, inspired it, drove it onward, and eventually sent it to its doom, for it was the multitude of the poor. When they appeared on the scene of politics, necessity appeared with them, and the result was that the power of the old regime became impotent and the new republic was stillborn; freedom had to be surrendered to necessity, to the urgency of the life process. (Arendt 2006: 50)

By talking in terms of "surrender to necessity, to the urgency of the life process" Arendt points to what I have called an epistemic subordination of political practice—in this case in the form of revolutionary action. Hence, the urgency and necessity make politics—a communicative activity of collective self-articulation—a mere means to the ends nothing else can be said about but that they are necessary. Let's turn now to Wagner's view before discussing both positions in more detail.

PETER WAGNER AND THE EPISTEMIC PATH TO POLITICAL BLOCKADE AND REGRESSION

Peter Wagner has pointed to a widely shared naive tendency to view the political revolutions around the eighteenth century as representing real "democratic revolutions." On the contrary, according to Wagner, European societies in fact did not develop a democratic self-understanding during the democratic revolutions. Rather, it is easy to recognize a rejection of the idea of collective self-determination. This fact becomes especially clear if one looks at the way classical Greece and Rome were conceived as political experiences in the political imaginary of the moderns. According to Wagner, references to Greece are not to be seen as involving a direct reference to democratic ideals, rather, "in line with Aristotle's usage of politeia, the term refers to the form of a political order, to a 'polity,' as we can now felicitously say, not to the extent of popular participation in political decision-making, in contrast to dēmokratia" (Stråh and Wagner 2017: 75). According to his view, the "polities that emerged from the 'democratic revolution' were elaborated in conscious rejection of Greek democracy by the elites of European societies" (Stråh and Wagner 2017: 75). In contrast to the historical reconstructions we have presented in part I, Wagner rejects in these lines the idea that the political revolutions of the eighteenth century have generated first, limited institutionalizations and imaginaries of democratic self-government which have been subsequently ref and transformed through different processes involving to a large extent social struggles for democratization. On the contrary, Wagner points to a clear rejection of popular self-government on the side of European elites. Especially interesting in our context is Wagner's consideration of the reasons for the active rejection on the side of European elites of the ideals of democratic self-determination. Hence, according to Wagner, we have to explain this rejection as resulting, among others, from the kind of worries that affected European elites. These worries involved the articulation of different understandings of freedom that emerged late-Enlightenment revolutions: "as personal freedom from arbitrary and unjustified rule and for self-expression and self-realization (Taylor 1989), as commercial freedom that was expected to both to promote peace and wealth (Hirschman 1977), and as collective self-determination" (Stråh & Wagner 2017: 76). For Wagner, the historical problem of articulation of different modern forms of freedom was responded to with the liberal concept of freedom, a notion that combined the safeguard of the rights of individuals against arbitrary intervention. Interestingly, according to Wagner, this concrete articulation left the kind of political freedom involved in democratic self-determination excluded from consideration: "The idea of enlightened rule was widely accepted in nineteenth-century political liberalism, a rule that accepts limits to state interference with private lives, even protects private liberties, but is entirely devoid of any democratic self-understanding" (Stråh & Wagner 2017: 76).

As readers may note, Wagner's own version of the history of modern political institutions differs to a large extent from the one sketched by Dewey in *The Public and Its Problems*, contradicting a basic thought that Dewey seems to share with Habermas's characterization of the liberal model of democracy. Hence, for both authors, liberalism takes a thin form of democratic will-formation as a methodological requirement meant to guarantee that political decisions do not contradict the negative rights of the individual. Surely, as we have already mentioned, this thin methodological requirement goes for Dewey hand in hand with a notion of collective self-determination that simultaneously arises in Modernity. However, as we saw, the struggle for self-determination takes place in a time where the social as a whole is seen as repressive. Equality relevant in the present context is Wagner's presentation of the reasons underlying the active rejection of popular self-government in those early political revolutions: what one could see as a severe restriction of an emerging institutionalization of democratic ideals—or what Wagner considers to be purely a rejection of democracy in favor of the institutionalization of a republican order—should be seen as the result of the "epistemic worries" of the European elite. Hence, one may conclude that there seems to be historical evidence of the regressive role the epistemic value of democracy has had for democratic practice.

This is, however, not the only form in which epistemic considerations have been mobilized in the history of modern democracy. Hence, Wagner points to the "limitation of the substantive reach of democratic decision-making" (Stråh & Wagner 2017: 81) by the stabilization of basic laws through constitutional means:

On the one hand, the modern political self-understanding can be seen as [. . .] built on the unanimous and unalterable commitment to some 'universal' principles and 'inalienable' rights [. . .]. On the other hand, constitutional limitations also addressed a different concern, namely the possibility of a 'tyranny of the majority' (Tocqueville) that used its democratically acquired power to further its own interest rather than the common good. (Strah & Wagner 2017: 81)

Here we see how the democracy's epistemic justification—here understood as democracy's capacity to promote the common good against the interest of specific groups—was effectively mobilized in the restriction of constitutional rights to political participation. In conclusion, as Wagner shows, epistemic arguments have been historically mobilized against the possibility of expanding democratic participation.

The two positions just sketched not only illustrate a way in which the epistemic dimension of democracy may be said to have antidemocratic consequences. The thesis I have defended up to this point, namely, that we need to see democracy's epistemic dimension as a motor of democratic progress, however, stands only in partial contradiction to the two accounts I have just sketched. We do not need to deny the historical claim that epistemic reasons have been mobilized de facto in order to justify political exclusion, to reduce the reach of democratic participation, or to limit the scope of issues about which democratic decisions should be made. In this regard, our mixed model of democratic justification provides an interesting solution to the problem of any democratic regression that is epistemically motivated. Hence, once a progress in political freedom and equality has been reached (either in a struggle for political recognition or by the normative appropriation of changes that were in their origin epistemically motivated), any attempt to reduce the scope and reach of democratic progresses must be subject to strong justificatory pressure. This is so because such a reduction cannot be seen but as a problematic perversion or regression of the new meaning of democracy we have gained as the result of a learning process. Put in other words, any attempt to limit or reduce democratic achievements that comes from the need to solve a problem must be experienced as reduction in freedom and equality.

Apart from this, Arendt's and Wagner's concerns help us to better understand the scope of what we understand by democracy's epistemic dimension. Hence, we can attribute to it a democratizing power only to the extent that the problems that constitute the tasks to resolve by democratic practice are not of the kind Arendt and Wagner describes in her account. Let's recall that the former understands the "social question" as a set of needs of the miserable, about which no discussion is needed while Wagner shows how elites have historically had a strong weight in the definition of problems. Both, indisputable problems and problems that have been unilaterally defined by elites have had antidemocratic consequences.

But, as we will see in part II, our Deweyan account assumes that problems that have to do with justice including "social" justice have an articulatory dimension which makes them in principle always open for discussion. In other words, there is nothing like indisputable problems and solutions. In talking about the needs of naked life of the masses, Arendt denies the possibility of rearticulating the social question, of understating it from different moral perspectives, of rearranging evidence so that the question takes a new light, of finding new evidences and imagining different solutions, of including the voices of those living under conditions of misery, and so on. In our view, however, even in the case of the most basic human needs, hermeneutical possibilities must remain open since there is certainly not only one way of satisfying such needs. In his turn, Wagner shows how those epistemic considerations mobilized in order to block the progression of political freedom were actually formulated by political and economic elites. To this extent, the kinds of tasks to be solved by political practices and institutions were limited to those promoting the interests of powerful groups at the expense of others. However, the fact that common problems are defined by elites does not mean that they cannot be defined otherwise or that their definition is able to grasp the real nature of the problem. On the contrary, we should assume that by excluding important segments of population affected by common problems, unilateral definition of problems is prima facie unable to promote real solutions to existing problems. Wagner's argument against the political potential of democracy's epistemic dimension can be then nuanced by the assumption that democratic restrictions responded to the elite's concerns to ensure that social problems were defined and solved in a way convenient for them.

In sum, defending that democracy's epistemic dimension can play an important role in advancing democracy must assume an understanding of social problems that avoids two possibilities: that they are irrefutable and that they can be unilaterally defined. Both elements will be discussed in more detail in chapter 5, where we show that Dewey's experimentalism provides a convincing connection between people's needs to fight injustice and their democratic claims.

CONCLUDING REMARKS

To recall, in chapter 2, I had argued that Honneth does not fully account for the motivational and innovative potential of democracy's epistemic justification. Certainly, he does not deny the epistemic value of democracy, that is, their capacity to enhance the quality of the outcomes of the political process when they are realized in practice. However, by putting all weight in the struggle for political recognition, he dismisses the capacity of our attempts to solve problems to challenge established understandings of democratic values and to promote new, better ones. In this chapter I have shown that Dewey's account does not suffer from this shortcoming. On the contrary, by exploring the complex interaction between intrinsic and epistemic dynamics of political change, I have identified the strong transformative power that Dewey attributes to people's need to solve their collective problems. This role consists in promoting both intra- and inter-normative political progress: to promote better realizations of political freedom, taken as the fundamental democratic value, and to promote, given the institutional preponderance the individualistic variant of political freedom, a social version of the latter. We will see in chapter 5 that Dewey also provides systematic arguments that are able to underpin such an historical view. Finally, I have also considered two historical accounts that set doubt on democracy's epistemic dimension's capacity to advance democracy. These accounts show how historically, epistemic reasons and dynamics have been at the ground of political perversion and regression, or have directly blocked any attempts at advancing democracy. Indeed, Wagner's view seems to be also valid for describing the present situation of many democratic societies. Arguments drawing on democracy's supposed inability to solve problems and guarantee economic welfare are mobilized in the media as well as in certain academic departments in order to defend restrictions in citizens' participation or the substitution of experts for democratic representatives. Here, again, this observation is far from justifying the rejection of the political potential of democracy's epistemic dimension. Hence, as in the case of the European elites of the nineteenth century, the standards for which democracy's problem-solving capacity is measured by those critical perspectives are set by strong interest groups who see in democratic self-determination as threatening for their own interests. From this perspective, the thesis that the struggle against injustice and the search for just social relations has a potentially democratizing force remains untouched. Hence, as we will see, the fact that problems are defined by a powerful minority is, from the point of view of the epistemic quality of the process, problematic. Hence, problems can only be effectively solved if they are fully articulated in an inclusive and egalitarian process of political participation.

Part II

EXPERIMENTALISM AND SOCIAL MOVEMENTS' DOUBLE COUNTER-HEGEMONIC POWER

Chapter 4

From Contents to Practices

Points of Departure

From the background of the mixed model of democratic justification I have previously developed, the aim of part II is to fledge-out the idea that social movements can represent central epistemic motors of democratic deepening. In other words, my aim is to substantiate the thesis that, due to their epistemic motivations, that is, the fight against injustice and the pursue of more just social relations, social movements are able to deepen the ways in which citizens realize democracy's intrinsic values. To put it in terms that will recurrently appear throughout the coming chapters, in the collective enterprise to identify, define, and struggle against injustices, mobilized groups have the potential to generate counter-hegemonic forms of political inquiry, and hence, counter-hegemonic forms of political practice that challenge hegemonic understandings of democracy and promote political learning processes. My thesis is that the epistemic practices of social movements have a double, deeply interconnected counter-hegemonic potential: they can contribute to the emergence of an oppositional consciousness, that is, of an awareness of injustice and they can promote counter-hegemonic forms of public inquiry, and therefore, of democratic practice.

Let me explain all this in more detail. Hegemonic forms of public inquiry, as they are put at work in parliaments, in the media and other spaces of public debate, contribute to the reproduction of some perspectives on social problems, tending to favor those views that perpetuate social groups in their power positions. So, let me just take an example that will appear in later chapters, namely, the specific status often attributed to public problems as something "fixed," that is, something that is fully given previously to the inquiry process. Taking public problems as fixed entities by certain forms of public inquiry often contributes to the reproduction of problems that have been already defined by economic, political, or epistemic elite. Due both to this unilateral process of articulation as well as to the fixed status given to public problems, most citizens are unable to (re-)formulate new public problems in light of their own particular experiences—problems that are often very different from the ones powerful individuals articulate. Conversely, by taking problems as "unfixed" entities whose exact definition very much depends on the process of collective inquiry, social movements open cognitive opportunities for including new perspectives, for using citizen's imagination, for reactualizing old concepts, and so on, which can lead to the articulation of new problems. In other words, by taking problems as unfixed entities, citizens are able to redefine important aspects of social reality in ways that scape the symbolic power of social elites. Danny Trom and Bénédice Zimmerman also point to this phenomenon, namely, to the necessary changes citizens make in their inquiries, in their account of social mobilization:

> It seems that the work on categories [and problem-definitions, JSZ] carried on in moments of mobilization makes participants embark upon kinds of inquiry of different scope, depending on the available categories. This activity is not exclusively objectified in rhetoric [. . .]. It also requires the pursue of operations such as unveiling and demonstration. These operation are strongly instrumentalized, oriented towards the transformation of the conceptual tools through which public experiences are structured. (Trom & Zimmerman 2001: 308, my translation)

New problems and categories are counter-hegemonic to the extent that they challenge established power structures and hierarchies. That existing cultures of public inquiry very often play in favor of dominant groups is certainly not alien to John Dewey. Likewise, that collective struggles usually involve epistemic struggles aiming at the overcoming of these kinds of "public pathologies" did not escape him either.

In the next chapters my aim is to explore the counter-hegemonic innovations of social movements from a specific point of view, namely, that concerning the most fundamental operations of experimental inquiry. Dewey called the set of those operations as well as their mutual relations the "logic" of inquiry. In these pages I will avoid the term "logic" as much as possible in order to avoid misunderstandings and talk in terms of "fundamental" or "most general" operations of inquiry. Hence, what Dewey meant by "logic" did not have the implications we usually give to this term. The logic of inquiry could not be separated from the presence of rhetorical, aesthetic, moral, or emotional elements that are an essential part of any inquiry. In any case, my aim is to develop the thesis that social movements are able to challenge existing hegemonic cultures of public inquiry from the point of view of the most fundamental operations of experimental inquiry.

In fact, seeing social movements as counter-hegemonic epistemic innovators opens different paths of theoretical and empirical exploration. And certainly, the exploration I propose to pursue, based on the idea of fundamental operations of inquiry, represents only one possible epistemic approach to the political potential of social struggles. In my view, however, introducing the perspective of the fundamental operations of inquiry can contribute to an unveiling of subtle forms of exclusion and a plurality of forms of political learning. And here is where the work of Dewey can again play a central role, since he developed a full-fledged theory of those fundamental operations. Particularly I will focus on Dewey's theory of inquiry as it is most exhaustively developed in his *Logic: The Theory of Inquiry* (1938), a work that I will read as a theory of experimentalist epistemic practice that offers an open and normatively substantial model of collective intelligence. Based on a reconstruction of Dewey's intuitions, I propose to understand the particular innovations observable in social movements as involving the adoption of major traits of experimentalism. As we will see, these traits can take very different forms, even if they can be seen as embodying certain fundamental operations of inquiry—and their mutual relations, as I will show.

One can reformulate the task that will be pursued along these lines in the following terms: to show that social movements can contribute to the emergence of experimental cultures of public inquiry, cultures which have a double counter-hegemonic potential: that of generating counter-hegemonic views on social reality and that of generating counter-hegemonic forms of democratic practice. Even if I believe that this task can be pursued with the help of Dewey's own theoretical tools, it also entails going beyond Dewey's own work. Hence, despite he believed in the necessity to regenerate the public culture of inquiry as a remedy to the democracy of the United States, he never seemed to express a particular hope that social movements would contribute to doing so. In his search for how to promote experimental methods of inquiry into the broader public life of his time, Dewey did not seem to take into consideration the potential of situated publics to challenge and influence existing pathological cultures of public inquiry. Rather, what we find in his work are more general considerations about the need for institutional reforms and the essential social role education should play. This does not mean, however, that he never considered the idea that in social mobilization, what he called dominated groups would be able to develop experimental forms of public inquiry against the background of existing pathological forms. How exactly Dewey articulated this particularly interesting idea will be the object of study in part III, where I will focus in the factors involved in such collective learning processes. Hence, by conceiving of social movements as counter-hegemonic methodological innovators in a fundamental sense I hope to fill a gap in Dewey's work that, however, needs to be seen as continuous with his own way of understanding social and political life.

Before beginning my exploration, however, some previous clarifications should be made about its exact reach and its goal. Firstly, one of the risks of approaching social movements from the point of view of the proposed epistemic perspective is to reduce the range of relevant practices we can observe in everyday politics to what I have called "epistemic practices." While we will have the opportunity to define and investigate in more detail the notion of "experimental epistemic practice" proposed here, reducing the plurality of practices put at work by social movements to a set of epistemic operations is far from the aim of the present reflections. Furthermore, the practices involved in the identification, definition, and search for solutions to social injustices are not qualitatively, emotionally, or aesthetically neutral since they are inscribed in a larger context of what some authors have called a "public experience." Moreover, epistemic practices such as organizing a workshop or starting a discussion group cannot be isolated in most cases from other nonepistemic practices. So, for example, organizing a protest is certainly not only an epistemic practice since it involves aesthetic and moral or what Dewey called "qualitative experiences" that cannot be reduced to cognitive operations. However, to the extent that a protest is taken as an experience from which a movement can draw conclusions regarding, for example, further strategies of resistance or the exploration of aesthetic possibilities, it can be certainly part of a larger epistemic set of practices. Far from promoting reductionism, taking an epistemic point of view should be rather seen as an analytical strategy oriented toward the exploration of a dimension of social movements that, only with few exceptions, has been not sufficiently examined. The thesis that, in virtue of the adoption of experimental inquiry, social movements are both able to articulate injustice and advance democracy should be seen as complementary to other essential considerations regarding the role of art, morals, religion, and so on, can play.

Secondly, giving oneself the task of exploring, through an epistemic path, the democratizing potential of social mobilizations does not mean denying the presence of regressive or antidemocratic practices observable in many social movements. Thus, in many cases social mobilizations reproduce existing authoritarian hierarchies. In the words of Tilly and Wood:

> [S]ocial movements do not necessarily espouse or promote democracy. Movements form far more frequently around particular interests and grievances than around demands for democratization as such. Form early on, relatively democratic movements regularly provoked undemocratic countermovements, such as the United Kingdom's early-nineteenth-century opponents of Catholic rights. In more or less functioning democracies, furthermore, social movements

recurrently pursue antidemocratic programs such as exclusion of immigrants, or racial, ethnic, and religious minorities. Sometimes they pursue the abolition of democracy itself in the name of a totalitarian creed such as Mussolini's Fascism and Hitler's Nazism. (Tilly & Wood 2016: 126)

Hence, the present account does not assume an idealized view of the practices of the oppressed even if an important number of empirical studies have pointed to the democratizing role of social movements. Two main concerns arise in the present context, which relate to the very historical articulation of the advancement of democracy with the struggle against injustice. On the one hand, one may question the positive correlation I aim at establishing between the pursuit of justice and democratization, in the sense that we may be able to identify how the defense of just causes goes hand in hand with a limitation or inversion of democratic practice. On the other hand, one may want to ask if the pursuit of collective goals involving the exclusion of rights—like, for example, the French case of the manif pour tous or Germany's PEGIDA and their critique of the "Lügenpresse"—is compatible with a deepening or even a defense of democratic practice. Hence, as the example of the manif pour tous shows, at least from a superficial perspective, we can observe the compatibility of goals involving the limitation of rights of a part of the population with the defense of democracy. To formulate both objections briefly, neither does the pursuit of just outcomes seem to be necessary related to the extension and deepening of democracy, nor does the pursuit of unjust outcomes seem to have necessarily antidemocratic consequences.

In my view, a first answer to these very important objections would consist in biting the bullet and reformulating the purpose of the present project in a conditional form. Accordingly, we could say that if social movements have positively contributed to democratic life or can do so at all, then we would miss a relevant dimension of their democratic contribution if we did not consider their capacity to produce practical innovations that deepen the meaning of democracy. As Charles Tilly and many others have shown, it is not especially difficult to find historical support for this idea (Tilly and Wood 2016, Della Porta 2013). In the present context, the analysis I aim at developing would represent a contribution to a better understanding of this practical contribution social movements make to democratic life. A second answer would consist in addressing these objections in a way that casts doubt on their basic premises. Basically, we would have to state that neither the nondemocratic pursuit of justice nor a democratizing pursuit of injustice can take place in the long run. Both are very strong theses that would require long consideration, since they involve complex normative and empirical reflections that cannot be pursued in the present context. However, it still may be useful to indicate the sense in which a strong correlation between democratization and the pursuit of justice may be thinkable in light of both critiques.

On the one hand, one may have good reasons to doubt that any pursuit of just causes can go hand in hand with antidemocratic organization. More concretely, one may doubt that, in the long term, the exclusion of perspectives that goes hand in hand with antidemocratic movements may not negatively affect the capacity of the group for making sense of people's experiences in a way that injustices can be collectively articulated. This idea would be in line with Habermas's view on the strong correlation between public and private autonomy. In an essay published in 1998 Habermas provides an example of the capacity of deliberative procedures to generate norms that are in accordance with basic human rights, stressing thereby the epistemic, outcome-based value of democratic practice. Habermas stresses the idea that public autonomy realized by deliberative procedures, on the one hand, and private autonomy as it is expressed in human rights, on the other hand, cannot stand in a hierarchical relation to each other. On the contrary, both public and private autonomy presuppose each other. On the one hand, no exercise of public autonomy is possible without the institutionalization of those private rights that make the exercise of political rights possible. On the other hand, citizens "can arrive at a consensual regulation of their private autonomy only if they make adequate use of their political autonomy as enfranchised citizens" (Habermas 1998a: 261). An "adequate" use of the political autonomy of citizens represents for Habermas the condition for a consensual regulation of private autonomy.

This idea already points to the epistemic value of the exercise of political autonomy, that is, of democratic organization. In what sense should we understand it? According to Habermas, the idea of an interdependence between public and private autonomy provides an answer to the question regarding how exactly the exercise of private autonomy should be conceived of. In his essay, he points to the fact that this question—that is, what it practically means to realize our private autonomy—has been differently answered by liberals and by proponents of a social state. In the first case, a reductionist view of individual rights is defended which has shown itself to be unable to satisfy the conditions of social justice, while in the second case a social-democratic pursuit of individual autonomy has showed tendencies to paternalism. In both cases the exact determination of what it means to be an autonomous subject is left to preconceived notions of the individual and the social. In contrast to both positions, Habermas calls upon the essential connection between an "adequate" use of political autonomy and the learning processes that bring individuals to clear notions of their private autonomy. This is especially clear in the case of feminist struggles for political inclusion. According to Habermas, feminists have taught us that the individual rights that are meant to guarantee to women the autonomy to pursue their lives in the private sphere cannot even be adequately formulated unless the affected persons themselves first articulate and justify in public debate those aspects that are relevant to equal or unequal treatment in typical cases. The private autonomy of equally entitled citizens can be secured only insofar as citizens actively exercise their civic autonomy. (Habermas 1998a: 264)

From this fact, we should conclude that "the private autonomy of equally entitled citizens can be secured only insofar as citizens actively exercise their civic autonomy" (Habermas 1998a: 264). This is so because only through participation in procedurally regulated public practice are women able to consider the relative relevance of experiences and life situations for a determination of individual rights.

Habermas's characterization is especially interesting in the context of debates about epistemic conceptions of democracy, since, according to David Estlund and others, democracy has an epistemic function to the extent that, by following its procedures, we can arrive at "right" conclusions or outcomes in response to the question about what is to be done. Many epistemic democrats draw on Joshua Cohen's characterization of epistemic democracy, according to which "right" conclusions are independent of actual democratic process leading to this conclusion (1986). According to Estlund, Habermas is a special sort of epistemic democrat—that is, one that assumes the presence of a procedure-independent standard for correctness—even if he himself would consider his account to be purely proceduralistic (Estlund 2008: 88–89). He grounds his thesis on the basic distinction Habermas makes between ideal and real democratic practice since drawing on this distinction he admits that in really existing democratic practices we may not always reach what would otherwise constitute the outcomes of ideal rational deliberation:

Deep deliberative democracy judges actual political processes by independent standards, too. The reason is that the use of a hypothetical deliberative procedure as the standard for evaluating actual democratic decisions is one way of holding outcomes to a standard that is logically independent of their actual procedural source. (Estlund 2008: 89)

In my view, Estlund's characterization of what he calls Habermas's "deep epistemic" democracy is adequate only to a certain extent. Hence, as we have seen in the example of feminist struggles, even if Habermas acknowledges that the difference between ideal and real procedures makes his view epistemic, we cannot conceive of the ideal outcomes of the democratic process as preexisting the very process in the way they do for authors like Estlund. Hence, the specific forms of exercise of private autonomy cannot be set prior to the very actual political process where specific norms are generated. Only through actual participation in procedurally regulated political practice can we reach an understanding of private autonomy that can be accepted as just for all, since only in such a case can actual concrete life situations and needs be properly articulated and balances among them produced. The political task of promoting the exercise of private autonomy implies a certain degree of normative indeterminacy that is to be gradually reduced by a procedurally regulated process of political participation.

Coming back to our question, Habermas points to the fact that only the inclusion of women in deliberative procedures of the feminist movement has shown to be the most adequate method to generate adequate outcomes. This has to do with the fact that the very indeterminacy of private autonomy can only be adequately determined by the concrete and irreplaceable experiences of those who are to exercise that autonomy. In more general terms, we could say that a nondemocratic organization, to the extent that it potentially blocks the voicing of those experiences, must be systematically unable to generate adequate outcomes, that is, adequate ways of realizing principles of autonomy. In a nonstrictly epistemic but still relevant sense, one may see the experiences of alienation of the main figure of Ralph Ellison's novel *The Invisible Man* as paradigmatic examples of the kind of incompatibility we are dealing with in this context. Here the main figure finds among in the authoritarian, hierarchical and opaque organization of the struggles of people of color the ground for an alienating self-relation that undermines any possibility of generating a proper perspective on the experience of the black American.

On the other hand, one may also have good reasons to doubt the democratizing potential of those groups struggling for the limitation of the rights of historically oppressed minorities. Hence, one may assume that their particular definition of justice is incompatible with the inclusion of the perspective of those negatively affected by such a view. One may thereby come to see behind a superficial commitment to democracy and enactment of democratic forms of operation a set of more invisible, micrological power relations and authoritarian forms of organization that can only be disclosed in empirical observation, and that may also become evident in subsequent political developments following the higher stages of the movement. Again, even if these very brief considerations need to be supported by further normative and empirical explorations, they both point to the possibility of a stronger—even if not necessary—connection between democracy and justice.

In the rest of this chapter I explore three central approaches to the epistemic and political contribution social movements can make to democracy—those provided by Iris Marion Young, Elizabeth Anderson, and James Bohman. This exploration will allow us, first of all, to distinguish in more detail what I call a "content-based" approach to the political contribution of social mobilizations from a "practice-based" account, one drawing on the theoretical developments of our previous political-epistemic considerations. Second, by examining Iris Marion Young's theory of democratic inclusion and, more concretely, her notion of internal exclusion, we will have the opportunity to introduce the idea of an epistemic level of social exclusion: one that is generated by dysfunctions concerning the fundamental operations underlying (public) inquiry. Even if these "dysfunctions" or "pathologies" will be explored in the next chapters, my aim is to show that they represent an important source of exclusion of the voices of oppressed groups from democratic debate. Finally, I propose to gain a more precise understanding of the epistemic goals that are to be seen as the basis of practical innovation. More concretely, I will argue, against Bohman, that Dewey's idea of effective "problem-solving" represents a more adequate understanding of the epistemic goal of social movements than the idea of "world-disclosure." My goal is not only to point to differences of my account with those of the three mentioned authors, but also show how much the present view can learn from them. Hence, to this extent, they represent unavoidable points of departure for an epistemic exploration of the contribution social movements can make to democratic life. The purpose of the coming exploration consists in gaining precious theoretical tools for the study of the political potential of social movements, but also in pointing to what still needs to be done if we want to theoretically substantiate the idea of a connection between their struggle against injustice and their democratizing potential.

TOWARD AN EPISTEMIC, PRACTICE-BASED APPROACH TO SOCIAL MOVEMENTS

In her critique to deliberative approaches, Iris Marion Young has criticized tendencies to overemphasize the role of neutrality as a value for political deliberation. According to many deliberative democrats, as a condition for the legitimacy of the results of political decision-making processes, those participating in these processes must be ready to leave aside their individual interests, needs, and perspectives, and only defend those positions that can be accepted from a universal point of view. This should be possible by a specific form of democratic deliberation, that of the exchange of reasons. From the perspective of an epistemic justification of democracy, Young argues that excluding from democratic decision-making the perspective of groups occupying lower social positions must go together with an impoverishment of the epistemic quality of the former. Excluding the situated perspective of those entitled to participate in collective will-formation reduces the amount of points of view that may prove useful for reducing existing injustices and further promoting just relations in democratic societies. Since, according to Young, we should not value democracy only for its intrinsic value—that is, for its capacity to embody collective self-determination—but also for its epistemic capacity to abolish existing injustices and promote just conditions for all, democratic practice must be open to this plurality of perspectives. This plurality is meant to guarantee that those suffering a social injustice can make visible and reflect both on their own experiences and their normative evaluation of unjust social conditions. Deliberative neutrality, which is the main feature of argumentative exchange, is hence seen as indirectly contributing to the reproduction of existing injustice. It must be substituted by a broader view of democratic communication that promotes both the conservation and the inclusion of the voices of the structurally oppressed. As it is well known, Young proposes in her broad view to include, next to deliberation, narration, greeting, and rhetoric as legitimate forms of political practice.

One important question that arises in this context concerns how we are to understand the idea that individuals (and groups) have a "situated perspective" or possess a "situated knowledge" in virtue of their "social position." More particularly, in line with authors such as Charles Mills (1998), Young is interested in the situated perspective of "oppressed" groups. Who are the oppressed and what is their "position" in the social world, according to Young? The expressions "situated perspective" and "social positions" already point to a spatial understanding of social reality. Indeed, according to Young, the social world cannot be reduced to the sum of experiences and actions of the members of society understood as individuals: on the contrary, these experiences and actions need to be contextualized at a supra-individual level comprising social structures that determine people's life opportunities to a large extent: "appeal to structure invokes the institutionalized background which conditions much individual action and expression, but over which individuals by themselves have little control" (Young 2001: 92). Hence,

> an account of someone's life circumstances contains many strands of difficulty or difference form others that, taken one by one, can appear to be the result of decisions, preferences or accidents. When considered together, however, and when compared with the life story of others, they reveal a net of restricting and reinforcing relationships. (Young 2001: 93)

To this net of restricting and reinforcing relationships that determines people's opportunities and life chances and over which individuals have little control, Young gives the name "structures of inequality":

a person's social location in structures differentiated by class, gender, age, ability, race, or caste often implies predictable status in law, educational possibility, occupation, access to resources, political power and prestige. (Young 2001: 95)

Finally, the detection of such structures of inequality determining the life opportunities of individuals allows the identification of social-structural groups, which Young defines as "a collection of persons who are similarly positioned in interactive and institutional relations that conditions their opportunities and life processes" (Young 2001: 97). From social positions defined in social-structural terms, different groups come to have situated perspectives and forms of knowledge which makes their point of view different from other groups:

[a]mong the sorts of situated knowledge that people in differentiated social positions have are: (1) an understanding of their positions, and how it stands in relation to other positions, (2) a social map of other salient positions, how they are defined, and the relation in which they stand to this position; (3) a point of view on the history of the society; (4) an interpretation of how the relations and processes of the whole society operate, especially as they affect one's own position; (5) a position-specific experience and point of view on the natural and physical environment. (Young 2001: 117)

In short, according to Young, individuals live under social structures that determine their life chances and which are very often unequal, thereby creating groups of individuals that share similar experiences and views concerning the structures governing the social world and the relation to the natural environment that is marked by their social position. However, Young's interest is not only to account for the diversity of social perspectives. Her focus is rather on the situated perspective of social-structural groups that suffer under unequal social chances:

People differently positioned in social structures have differing experiences and understandings of social relationships and the operations of the society because of their structural situation. Often such differences derive from the structural inequalities that privilege some people in certain respects and relatively disadvantage others. (Young 2001: 98)

For Young the perspective of the oppressed is of special value for a critical theory of democracy since it is a perspective that tends to be excluded from the loci of democratic decision-making and it represents a particularly valuable source of information for democratic processes aiming at abolishing existing injustice and promoting just life conditions. The idea of the "epistemic privilege" of the oppressed that goes hand in hand with this theory must, according to Young, be understood in a weak sense: even if their perspective as victims of unequal distribution of power and opportunities is of special relevance for any attempt to promote more just conditions, and their voices must therefore be effectively included in any democratic process, "[t]hey too are liable to bias and self-regard in overstating the nature of situations, misunderstanding their causes, or laying blame in the wrong place" (Young 2001: 117).

The idea of the particular value of the situated perspective of the oppressed plays an important role in Young's theory of democratic practice. It is part of her mixed model of democratic justification, which combines both democracy-intrinsic and epistemic reasons for the inclusion of the oppressed. On the one hand, the situated perspective of the oppressed must be included to the extent that it contributes to the promotion of justice and hence has an indisputable epistemic value. On the other hand, by promoting a wider understanding of legitimate political communication, the inclusion of the voices of the oppressed contributes to the realization of a democracy-intrinsic value, namely, that of their opportunities for collective self-determination.

Before coming to a more detailed exploration of Young's mixed model of justification, I would like to point that Young's epistemic argument for inclusion, as it has been presented here, takes into consideration only one possible understanding of the epistemic contribution social movements can make to democratic decision-making. Hence, as I have already mentioned, social movements do not seem to only be carriers of situated perspectives, but they generate their own ways (or methods) to generate, elaborate, and communicate those situated perspectives. To understand this difference, it may be helpful to shortly turn Helen Longino's distinction between "knowledge as content" in contrast to what she calls "knowledge-productive practices." For Longino, who has worked on a social account of scientific practice, these two senses often get confused in their analysis. In a first sense, according to Longino,

> 'knowledge' refers to content, whether an accumulation of representations or of skilled ways of doing things. [. . .]. Representational content can be stored—in documents, in memory, linguistically or imagistically—and is transmissible. The content of practical knowledge may sometimes, when codifiable, be stored and transmitted through documents, but it is also stored and demonstrated bodily. (Longino 2002: 108–109)

In the second sense, knowledge refers to knowledge production or "knowledge-productive practices," which include all practices—intellectual or material—occurring within a context of inquiry that have a bearing on the outcome of inquiry. [. . .] Scientists don't just reason; they interpret observations and experiments, they support or critique conjectures or hypotheses, they derive consequences, they extend models to new domains. (Longino 2002)

Longino underlines that these activities of knowledge production constitute essentially social activities:

They [i.e. scientists] have multiple reasons for the particular choices and decisions they make in the course of all these activities, reasons that include feasibility, potential for application, aesthetic values, interest from other colleagues, interest from potential consumers, intelligibility of colleagues, resonance with metaphysical or ideological commitments. These are the kinds of factors included under the umbrella of "the social." (Longino 2002: 98)

In analogy to scientific practice, we need to differentiate in any epistemic approach to social movements their role as providers of knowledge as content from their role as generators of knowledge. This is something that seems to be failing in Young's epistemic justification of inclusion of the perspective of oppressed groups. In my view, we fail to grasp the whole political potential of social struggles when we only focus on their capacity to provide situated perspectives understood as "contents" to democratic decision-making processes, thereby not taking into account the practical dimension of their epistemic contribution to democratic life. We need to change from a vision of social movements as information-providers to one as valuable coinquirers. Thus, this is not only justified from the point of view of the study of political potential of those movements but has also important consequences for the epistemological status of social analysis. As Casas-Cortés et al. have pointed:

when we recognize movements as spaces and processes in which knowledges are generated, modified, and mobilized by diverse actors, important political insights are gained—both into the politics of those contemporary movements, as well as into those of society more broadly. This recognition bears important implications for social movement researchers. It requires that we shift the mode of engagement in our research, blurring well-established boundaries in social science between the "subjects" and "objects" of knowledge production—a shift that has certainly been called for in anthropology for at least 20 years and by the critique of positivist and Cartesian epistemologies, more broadly. (Casas-Cortes et al. 2018: 20)

Apart from the methodological concerns of social analysis, this change of perspective is also needed in the context of the actual debates on modern moral progress. Hence, in my view, the study of the moral progress of modern societies presupposes changes in the ways in which societies think about moral problems. Here it is important to consider to what extent, those groups struggling for changes in our moral perceptions have had to innovate in ways of thinking and to what extent these innovative ways have influenced societies at large. In recent years, Anderson has focused her theoretical efforts on showing the extent to which the mobilization of oppressed groups plays a role in the moral progress of societies. Anderson understands moral progress as the transformation of the moral view of the dominant groups of society in a way that they are able to integrate the moral view of the dominated. Historically, this transformation has very often taken the form of struggles between dominant and dominated such that dominant groups have been compelled to go through a kind of moral learning process involving the final integration of the perspective of the dominated.

Let's briefly analyze Anderson's view on the historical role played by mobilized groups. Firstly, mobilized groups, by virtue of what Anderson calls, along with Charles Tilly, their actions of contention, play a central role in challenging the views of those who occupy positions of power within society. More specifically, Anderson attributes to members of these groups the ability to correct the biases of the powerful regarding what is morally right by producing disrupting experiences that challenge the preexisting beliefs of those in power. To the extent that they disrupt people's ordinary moral beliefs, the experiences generated by mobilized groups can be said to foster a self-reflective attitude on the side of the dominant—an attitude that unleashes the potential integration of the perspective of dominated groups. Let's call this role ascribed to politically mobilized groups the role of "challengers" of hegemonic norms and worldviews. As challengers, mobilized groups stimulate what moral reflection in such a way that the powerful become able to overcome the one-sidedness of their own moral views (which is for Anderson a first step toward moral progress as it has been defined above).

According to Anderson, however, appealing to the challenging role of contentious politics put at work by the mobilized is not enough to explain how societies may morally progress, since the mere reflexive integration of the view of the oppressed is not a guarantee of the validity of the norms and principles that arise from this integration. In line with Dewey's experimentalism, a further element in the realization of morally progressive social reform that is responsible for the validity of the normative changes that take place is the test in which dominated groups have an actual say in determining the moral quality of the consequences generated by these changes. Moral and social transformations effected through social struggle must be tested in a process in which oppressed groups have a say in determining the quality of the consequences generated by them. Here again, Anderson understands the contribution of oppressed groups in terms of an information-providing function, only that in this case, the information provided tells us something about the consequences of the implementation of normative changes and is thereby made relevant for testing the general validity of normative innovations.

In conclusion, Anderson's account of moral progress overlooks the possibility of conceiving of the contribution of the oppressed to moral progress in terms of practice. In my view, one of the reasons why this is has to do with the fact that she sees the emergence of the experimentalistic attitude that is a necessary requirement for the integration of the perspective of the oppressed as a mere result of the clash between dominant and dominated groups that takes place in social struggle. Hence, it is the experience of a moral challenge generated by group's repertoires of contention to the dominant that brings the latter to adopt an experimentalist attitude regarding their own views. While this double, moral and epistemic, learning process takes place on the side of the dominant groups, Anderson does not consider that the very condition for the struggle of oppressed groups in situations of extreme symbolic domination consists in the development of a local experimentalistic culture of inquiry by those groups that makes the generation of new frames (McAdam & McCarthy 1996) of injustice possible at all. While moral progress presupposes the transformation of the methods of moral reflection on the side of the dominant, its very condition must be found in those stages of struggle where the oppressed learn to see themselves as such.

Coming back to Young's view, it would be unfair to situate her approach to democracy within the limits of a content-based account of the democratic role of social movements. Hence, even if she offers a content-based justification for democratic inclusion, Young is certainly aware that social movements can be generators of valuable forms of political practice. Here I propose to identify those elements in her account that can be seen as a point of departure toward a practice-oriented epistemic consideration of the political potential of mobilized collectives. They only represent, however, initial steps, since, as I aim to show, Young is not able to fully integrate them in her normative account of democratic practice in the full sense that has been developed in part I.

Social movements as schools of democracy: the first element that constitutes a substantial step toward a practice-based account of the political-epistemic role of social movements is Young's awareness of the fact that civil-societal organizations—which include social movements—can come to constitute places where democratic practice is learned:

> The image of civic associations as free self-organization without the disciplinary regimes of coercion and bureaucracy is at best an exaggeration that feeds disenchantment with state institutions. A great number of voluntary associations,

however, are directly democratic. People form and run them according to rules
they collectively adopt. To this extent even private associations can be schools
of self-government. (Young 2001: 165)

According to Young, it would be a mistake to idealize civic associations as
immediately putting in practice democratic forms of organization. However,
Young notes the existence of many associations organized by democratic
principles that can work places where we exercise and promote democratic
habits.

Social movements as places of practical innovation: For Young, civil-
societal organizations can not only play such an important educative role but
they represent also loci for actual practical innovation:

> Beyond such general virtues of participation, the self-organizing activities of
> civil society contribute to self-determination, and, to a lesser degree, self-devel-
> opment, by supporting identity and voice, facilitating innovative or minority
> practices, and providing some goods and services. (Young 2001: 165)

Young argues that civic associations contribute to the relation of a fundamental democratic value, that of self-determination, by "supporting identity and
voice" and "facilitating innovative and minority practices." In other words,
social movements are able to put into practice innovative forms of politically
relevant communication that are able to realize the values of self-determination in more inclusive ways. Such "innovative and minority" practices are
able to include the voice of those whose views usually remain unconsidered.

Testimonio and consciousness-raising meetings: Young provides illustra-
tions of some of those innovative practices in her pluralist account of democratic communication. So, for example, communicative practices that fall
under the label of "testimonio" are characterized as an example of the inclusive effects of narration or story-telling. "Testimonio" refers to how "[s]ome
resistance movement leaders in Central and South America narrate their life
stories as a means of exposing to the wider literate world to the oppression of
their people and the repression they suffer from their governments" (Young
2001: 71). These inclusive effects are not only valued for their direct enactment of the value of self-determination, but also for their epistemic benefits:

> Especially in mass society, where knowledge of others may be largely mediated
> by statistical generalities, there may be little understanding of lived need or
> interest across groups. A norm of political communication under these condi-
> tions is that everyone should aim to enlarge their social understanding by learn-
> ing about the specific experience and meanings attending other social locations.
> Narrative makes this easier and sometimes an adventure. (Young 2001: 77)

In general, the three central intuitions represent basic elements of the kind of practice-based account of the political contribution of social movements I aim at providing here: (a) that social movements are social spaces where democracy is exercised and learned; (b) that social movements are practical innovators with the ability to realize the value of "self-determination" in different, and sometimes, better ways; and finally (c) that some of these highly localized practical innovations should be integrated into a pluralistic understanding of democratic practice. There are, however, two main senses in which the account I aim at developing goes beyond Young's ideas.

First of all, Young includes in her pluralist account of democratic communication examples of epistemic practice such as testimonio and consciousness-raising by virtue of the fact that they are able to include situated perspectives that would otherwise remain unspoken—something that has, according to her, both democracy-intrinsic and epistemic benefits. However, a subtle but important difference separates Young's view from the one I aim at developing here. Hence, such practices are in her account merely taken as instantiations of a model that she develops from an external point of view and which remains closed to further innovation. By this I mean that Young provides a mixed justification of her pluralist model of democratic practice that remains in principle closed to any possible further democratic learning, including those promoted by the epistemic dynamics of the oppressed in their efforts to frame injustice/pursue just social relations. To this extent, her account can hardly be open to an even more pluralistic understanding of democratic practice, one that is necessarily dependent on the very practical transformations that have taken place and will take place in actual social struggle.

Second, Young's reflections also remain, in my view, insufficient to the extent that they seem unable to account for a deep level of practical transformation involved in local epistemic innovations, one regarding the fundamental operations of the collective inquiries carried on by social movements. This affects, due to the connection between epistemic innovations and democratic deepening, the capacity of her view to grasp the variety of ways in which intrinsic values of democracy can be better realized. What this mean can be understood if we turn to Young's theory of exclusion as the critical-theoretical counterpart of a theory of democratic development. Hence, as we can infer from the previous passages, the power of social movements to realize the intrinsic value of democratic value of self-determination has to do with their capacity of inclusion. For Young, realizing self-determination in better, deeper, or more adequate forms means including in equal terms the voices of the previously excluded. In this context, we should clarify the way we should understand "exclusion" and "inclusion" as measures for the better or worse realization of intrinsic democratic values.

EPISTEMIC EXCLUSION AS A FORM
OF INTERNAL EXCLUSION

In this respect Young herself has offered an important conceptual tool to political theorists by introducing a basic distinction between two forms of political exclusion: external and internal. My thesis is that Young could still have gone a step further in her analysis of internal forms of exclusion and thereby grasped a further sense in which people's voices and perspectives are excluded from the democratic process. By "epistemic exclusion" I refer to excluding mechanisms involved in the basic operations of democratic inquiry, mechanisms that leave individual experiences and voices out of the range of relevance for the process of collective inquiry. These mechanisms can persist even when pervasive forms of external and internal inclusion have been abolished. Let's turn to Young's famous distinction in order to clarify this idea.

According to Young, there is not only one way of excluding the perspective of individuals from democratic decision-making processes. In a first sense, exclusion refers to the fact that "individuals and groups that ought to be included are purposely or inadvertently left out of fora for discussion and decision-making" (Young 2001: 54). As paradigmatic examples of external exclusion Young mentions the material inability to participate in democratic fora:

> Perhaps the most pervasive and insidious form of external exclusion in modern democracies is what I referred to in the previous chapters as the ability for economically or socially powerful actors to exercise political domination. [. . .] Inequalities of power and resources frequently lead to outcomes such as these, where some citizens with formally equal rights to participate nevertheless have little or no real access to the fora and procedures through which they might influence decisions. (Young 2001: 54)

Next to this first, particularly obvious sense of exclusion, Young points to cases where members of socially oppressed groups are politically excluded even if their presence in decision-making processes is formally and materially warranted. For Young, the fact of participating or being present in decision-making processes cannot warrant that members of minority groups may have an effective influence in the process. Accordingly, we need a further notion, that of "internal inclusion," that is able to account for those cases:

> Having obtained a presence in the public, citizens sometimes find that those still more powerful in the process exercise, often unconsciously, a new form of exclusion: others ignore or dismiss or patronize their statements and

expressions. Though formally included in a forum or process, people may find that their claims are not taken seriously and may believe that they are not treated with equal respect. The dominant mood may find their ideas or modes of expression silly or simple, and not worthy of consideration. They may find that their experiences as relevant to the issues under discussion are so different from others' in the public that their views are discounted. I call these familiar experiences internal exclusion, because they concern ways that people lack effective opportunity to influence the thinking of others even when they have access to fora and procedures of decision-making. (Young 2001: 55)

According to this characterization, internal inclusion of a group involves the reaction of dominant groups in regard to the social-structural position of the oppressed groups or to some identity features that can be derived from that very position, as for example, certain modes of expression. In other words, when the members of an oppressed group try to make their voices heard within democratic processes, they are rejected on account of the dominant groups' own prejudice. For Young these "familiar experiences" represent the range of possible internal exclusions that a critical theory of democracy should address. In fact, their existence and possibility represent the core argumentative basis for a broader view of legitimate democratic practice that goes beyond current deliberative views:

A theory of democratic inclusion requires an expanded conception of political communication, both in order to identify modes of internal inclusion and to provide an account of more inclusive possibilities of attending to one another in order to reach an understanding. (Young 2001: 56)

In my view, however, we are able to identify a second kind of internal mechanism limiting people's capacity to influence the democratic process, one that does not have the prejudices of dominant groups as its immediate basis. Hence, we can actually find many cases where, even if prejudice—be it based on social structures or on cultural elements—is not present in communicative interaction, oppressed groups may still fail in having their situated views play an effective role in the decision-making process. This is the case for the kind of mechanisms involved in what I have called "epistemic exclusion," a form of internal exclusion which, while certainly having negative effects for groups situated in positions of social disadvantage, does not necessarily have identity prejudice as the basis of exclusion.

By "epistemic exclusion" I understand then those mechanisms limiting the effective possibility of influencing the processes of democratic decision-making based on a different ground, namely, on the epistemic status of the constitutive elements of the inquiry process, namely, its fundamental operations. Up to this point, we still have not examined what I have previously called the fundamental operations of experimental inquiry. However, we can recall here the idea that social problems are sometimes considered to be something fixed, something that preexists the processes of collective inquiry and which merely needs to be discovered, and then solved. It is easy to see that the prevalence of such an understanding of social problems in public life plays can have exclusionary effects. Hence, the idea that social problems are fixed entities makes any attempt to reformulate commonly accepted problems, normally formulated by symbolic, political, or political elites, from the light of the situated perspectives of oppressed groups, futile.

To sum up, by examining Young's theory of social movements I have first distinguished between two forms of epistemic justification for including them as legitimate political actors in public life. The first way is based on the idea that social movements often provide unique information and points of view, due to their specific social position of their members. This point of view represents necessary inputs for realizing democracy's epistemic task consisting in the promotion of just social relations. The second way is based on the idea that social movements develop valuable forms of epistemic practice that differ from those we can commonly find in larger contexts of democratic decision-making and will-formation. These methods are valuable not only because they have a positive effect in our capacity to identify and solve problems, but also because they contribute to advancing intrinsic democratic values. As I have shown, Young only develops a systematic content-based justification of inclusion of the voices of those groups. Something similar happens to Anderson's approach to the contribution of struggling groups to moral progress. Hence, instead of seeing in those movements the space for the generation of experimentalist cultures of inquiry that make moral progress possible at all, it focuses on their role as "challengers" and "testers." Certainly, neither Young nor Anderson's accounts exclude the possibility of a practice-based account to political and moral progress. In the case of Young, she provides also essential insights for the practice-based epistemic account: (1) the idea that movements are schools of democracy, (2) the thesis they are practical innovators able to promote inclusion, and finally (3) the identification of nonargumentative, inclusive, forms of democratic practice as forms of democratic deepening in social movements. However, these insights need to be further complemented since they are unable to account for two main aspects linked to grasping the full political potential of social movements: the open nature of the range of possible forms of democratic practice and communication, and the idea that internal exclusion can have its origin in the most fundamental operations of the collective inquiries carried out in public discussion.

JAMES BOHMAN: SOCIAL MOVEMENTS
AND WORLD-DISCLOSURE

Apart from Iris Marion Young and Elizabeth Anderson, James Bohman's work represents a major contribution to this series of theoretical attempts at grasping the epistemic contribution of social movements to democratic and moral progress. In what follows I will briefly reconstruct Bohman's pluralist view of democratic practice, as providing an alternative to Habermas's understanding of the relation between democratic practice and inclusion. Bohman's work stands very close to the project pursued throughout this study. Unlike Bohman, my aim is, however, to understand the epistemic work of social movements as problem-solving in contradistinction to Bohman's focus on their world-disclosive function. Hence, understanding world-disclosure as the only normatively relevant "epistemic achievement" of mobilizations runs, among other, the risk of disconnecting the analysis of their epistemic work from the experiences (of injustice) that are at the heart of social mobilization.

In *Public Deliberation: Pluralism, Complexity and Democracy* (1998), Bohman aims at providing a model of democratic communication that is able to overcome the deficits he identifies in deliberative views such as that of Jürgen Habermas. Bohman believes that proceduralist accounts that reduce democratic communication to rational discourse or argumentation, together with "precommitment" models, "presuppose sameness of belief and desires in ways that make them inappropriate for ongoing political debate" (Bohman 1998: 47). According to Bohman, the ideal of rational deliberation is problematic to the extent that it sets overly demanding criteria for its realization—which he considers to be specialized argumentation, unanimity, and impartiality—in actual political practice. In his view, we can only gain a pluralistic and dynamic understanding of public communication if we abandon proceduralism and draw on the model of politics as joint action. Under this model, we must see political communication forms as "mechanism[s] for restoring ongoing joint activity" (Bohman 1998: 59). Bohman provides an open-ended list of such mechanisms, which include argumentation, "explicitation," and experimentation, among others. For Bohman, plurality and dynamism of communicative mechanisms represent a requirement from the point of view of the different strategies by which people may come to "agree" on conflicting matters.

In order to avoid the problems attached to Habermas's approach, Bohman distinguishes between a proceduralistic or discourse-theoretical and a dialogical account of democratic communication:

> The joint activity through which deliberation takes place within the public sphere is dialogical and not merely discursive. Discourses employ specific

regulative standards of justification, and they are typically structured toward one sort of claim or another. For example, scientific discourses are oriented towards claims of truth, whereas legal discourses are constrained by the arguments and claims that are consistent with the body of law. By contrast, dialogue is the mere give and take of reasons. It does not necessarily aim to produce well-justified claims, rather, it aims to produce claims that are wide enough in scope and sufficiently justified to be accountable to an indefinite public of fellow citizens. (Bohman 1998: 57)

In this context, Bohman provides a nonexhaustive list of dialogical mechanisms which have as a common thread "that they produce 'deliberative' uptake among all participants in deliberation—that is, they promote deliberation on reasons addressed to others, who are expected to respond to them in dialogue" (Bohman 1998: 59). These mechanisms are (1) making "explicit what is latent in [speakers'] common understandings, shared intuitions and ongoing activities" (Bohman 1998: 59); (2) the "back-and-forth exchanges around differences in biographical and collective historical experiences" (Bohman 1998: 60); (3) communication concerning "how to apply a given norm or a principle to a particular case" (Bohman 1998: 61) or what Klaus Günter calls "discourses of application"; (4) articulation, which consists not "in the specification of a norm that is at issue, but making its content richer and more complex" (Bohman 1998: 62); and finally (5) the mechanism of "shifting and exchanging perspectives in the course of the dialogue—shifting between speaking and listening" (Bohman 1998: 63).

Apart from this "open-ended" list of communicative mechanisms Bohman also introduces a second central element of his alternative to Habermas, namely, the question about the innovative power of social movements in the context of the necessary renewal of democratic institutions and deliberative practices of democratic publics. According to Bohman,

> even with well-ordered democratic institutions, a public can still fail to deliberate well; its citizens may not be able to produce publicly acceptable solutions to the problematic situations that initiate their deliberation. If such cognitive failures cannot be traced back to institutional flaws, the public can only examine itself for failures of public reason. (Bohman 1998: 199)

Hence, "when deliberation fails, citizens may need to change their public reasons; but they also may need to change the situation itself, the framework in which they deliberate" (Bohman 1998: 200). According to Bohman, democratic publics usually have in their capacity for self-reflection and self-scrutiny their own resources for renewal. However, "[w]hen community-wide biases restrict the scope of such self-scrutiny, usually leaving relevant problems off the agenda, deliberative institutions can lose their problem-solving capacity and public communication breaks down in unnoticed ways" (Bohman 1998: 200). In such cases of communicative obstruction "a new public must emerge to create new institutions and new opportunities for deliberation" or "as Dewey puts it in *The Public and Its Problems*, the public changes institutions indirectly by forming a new public with which institutions must interact" (Bohman 1998: 201).

In continuity with Dewey's thesis about the dynamic power of "new publics," Bohman introduces the idea that social movements react to the communicative obstructions, as well as the power relations they help to sanction, affecting democratic publics and institutions. More particularly, Bohman draws on frame analysis to describe how mobilized groups come to present new public problems or offer different understandings of accepted ones, a process that does not proceed without difficulties:

> As William Gamson notes, cultural codes entrench taken-for-granted meanings, making them given "facts" rather than social constructions [. . .] Such transparent descriptions and accepted meanings guide definitions of problematic situations [. . .]. Collective actors in social movements have to challenge this taken-for-granted character and show these meanings to be only some of many possibilities, as the women's movement has done with gender identity. (Bohman 1998: 209)

What is especially interesting in the present context is Bohman's understanding of the "innovative" function of mobilized groups: according to him, the best way to grasp this function is by drawing on the Heideggerian notion of world-disclosure, a notion that he uses in order to describe the very cognitive activity put at work by mobilized groups. Bohman defines world-disclosure as the activity of social innovators (intellectuals and social movements) consisting in "breaking down old patterns and illuminating new possibilities of seeing, thinking, or speaking, as when the new greeting 'citizen!' articulated the Jacobin ideal of equality and disclosed a social world without deference" (Bohman 1998: 215). Critical world-disclosure also involves changes affecting the very practices by which citizens collectively inquire about the world: "what [the process of disclosing new possibilities] means can be best analyzed not in terms of a contrast between innovative and everyday discourses but in terms of the contrast between a disclosive relation to the world and a rigid one" (Bohman 1998: 217). Hence, "[i]f the linguistically constituted public world can become rigid, it can also become fluid in deliberative dialogues when speakers try to correct failures in interaction" (Bohman 1998: 221).

In the present context, Bohman's analogy between scientific and public reason seems especially relevant, since it shows his interest in the innovative epistemic features of collective practices:

> People see the relevance of confirming evidence more readily rather than they see that of falsifying evidence. Especially when they are "degenerating", past theories and beliefs can become rigid gestalten to which evidence must conform [. . .]. In such cases, normal science's productive problem solving deteriorates into theoretical blindness and ad hoc gerrymandering. [. . . .] The dialogical and open-ended interaction of theory and experience becomes frozen in a rigid framework. (Bohman 1998: 220–221)

And further:

> Whereas rigid beliefs and expressions are caught in a circle of self-confirmation, disclosure opens up the possibility of perceiving falsifying evidence as relevant to one's theoretical beliefs and assumptions. (Bohman 1998: 221)

In calling our attention not only to the capacity of social movements to challenge our patterns of relevance in the world but also on what he calls the "fluid" quality of the communicative practices involved in world-disclosure, Bohman comes close to the Deweyan practice-based view that will be developed in the coming chapters. Hence, Bohman includes, like Young, many of the "fluidifying" practices generated in social mobilization such as consciousness-raising in his open-ended account of the mechanisms of public deliberation (Bohman 1998: 61).

However, a central difference between our and Bohman's account should be mentioned here. Hence, according to the previous passages, Bohman considers practical innovation to be a methodological requirement derived from the epistemic goal of world-disclosure, while up to this point we have considered problem-solving or truth-seeking to be this epistemic goal. While world-disclosure in the sense employed by Bohman represents an indispensable goal of the counter-hegemonic practices of those suffering from the effects of existing power relations, it would be wrong, however, to reduce epistemic innovation to the requirements of world-disclosure. Certainly, Bohman does not detach the latter from people's endeavors to arrive at more adequate interpretations of the world. On the contrary, there is a sense in which new interpretations can be said to be more adequate; namely, when these interpretations can be reflectively appropriated by citizens:

> It is not enough to open up possibilities, although that may be a first reflective step; these new possibilities must be reflectively appropriated, as is the case

in the aesthetic sphere as well. Thus, to be critical, the expression must have a reproducible effect on the audience, as well as open up possibilities and relevances. (Bohman 1998: 226)

Bohman is particularly interested in separating truth from world-disclosure, even if he does not aim at rejecting the search for truth as part of the political process. Different features separate "truth" from "world-disclosure": (1) "disclosure is audience-relative, whereas truth in the strong, normative sense is not" (Bohman 1998: 226); (2) "disclosure is not truth itself, but it enables truth to emerge in public reflection," such that disclosures "concern what makes truth possible" (Bohman 1998: 226–227). Bohman reserves the notion of truth for the larger process of democratic communication: "The democratic requirement of public verification is part of the test of whether the new understanding can elicit and promote continued cooperation" (Bohman 1998: 227), while world-disclosure— together with the innovative practices that make it possible—represents the only epistemic contribution of mobilized groups can make to this larger context.

In my view, limiting the epistemic achievement of social movements to world-disclosure, that is, to providing the conditions that enable truth to emerge in public reflection may not only be at odds with the goals pursued by those participating in the mobilization, but also set too strict limits on the kinds of practical innovations one can expect from social movements. Hence, if we want to see certain practical-epistemic innovations, such as the practices of experimental testing that are part of an experimentalist culture of inquiry, as emerging from the epistemic needs of social struggles, we must take into account their own efforts at trying to come to true outcomes, no matter how weak the sense of the adjective "true" might be. While for Bohman the fluidification of democratic communication is bound up with the exercise of opening up possibilities of world-interpretation, the present account will see fluidification as an effect of the collective need for generating correct or true views about the world, that is, to effectively identify, define, and resolve problems. Movements are not only practical innovators in their efforts to make people see the world in a different light, but also, and most centrally, in their attempts to articulate injustice in the way that best accounts for their own experience, which surely includes world-disclosure as a necessary operation of inquiry but which is definitely not exhausted by it.

HEGEMONIC AND COUNTER-HEGEMONIC EPISTEMIC PRACTICES

In our critical engagement with some central normative and democracy-theoretical reflections in Young's, Anderson's, and Bohman's work, we have been able to point to the strong link between the more or less established public practices through which public problems are framed and the power structures they contribute to stabilizing. Along these lines I have been using the adjectives "hegemonic" and "counter-hegemonic" to describe those epistemic practices in a sense that should already be clear at this point: while hegemonic epistemic practices tend to stabilize or reproduce meanings, perspectives, and worldviews that in their turn contribute to a stabilization or reproduction of existing unjust power relations, counter-hegemonic epistemic practices introduce new methods and operations that contribute to generating alternative meanings, perspectives, and worldviews. By doing that, they contribute to the transformation of the status quo. We can find a classical example of the counter-hegemonic power of such epistemic innovations in the literature on testimonio, which, as practice aiming at truth, has been attributed an indisputable political function in the visibilization of the crimes of Latin American dictatorial regimes. Before turning, however, to a more detailed exploration of what I mean by "epistemic practice," it is worth examining to what extent the notion of epistemic practice can be part of a larger context of a critical theory of the public sphere. Hence, the shift of emphasis from knowledge as content to epistemic practice I propose must be responsive to the larger context in which democratic practices are embedded.

In her famous text *Rethinking the Public Sphere* (1992) Fraser has developed an alternative view to Habermas's account of the public sphere which is able to integrate those feminist critiques pointing to important flaws of the Habermasian account. For Habermas, deliberation, which represents paradigmatic form of public discussion, is seen as guided most fundamentally by the norms of universal inclusion, equality of status, and the norms of argumentative discourse, publicity, and veracity. In *The Transformation of the Public Sphere* (1991) these basic norms are considered to be immanent to what Habermas called "public reasoning," which he saw as the form of political practice resulting from the "change of function" of the sphere of literary discussions and cafes that bourgeois class organized in the eighteenth century. According to many feminist authors, Habermas's reconstruction of the bourgeois public sphere should be rejected as part of an emancipatory project since, from its very beginning, the bourgeois public sphere is so essentially linked to mechanisms of exclusion that any projected rehabilitation of the notion would contribute to reproducing these very mechanisms. Fraser certainly does not go as far as many of these authors, who prefer to reject the notion of public sphere in toto; however, she believes that feminist critiques represent important challenges that need to be integrated into a notion of the public sphere that, rather than idealizing it, sees public life as a social process pervaded by struggles among different public spheres. More concretely, and in accordance with some reconstructive-historical observations regarding the coexistence of alternative public spheres like feminist and proletarian publics, Fraser proposes to see public life as involving the existence of hegemonic and counter-hegemonic publics: while the former are able to remain within positions of domination thanks to exclusionary mechanisms that are constitutive of their practices, and which have as their main feature imposing a certain view of social reality—that which best fits the interests of dominant groups—counter-hegemonic publics are able to generate "parallel discursive arenas where members of subordinated social groups invent and circulate counterdiscourses, which in turn permit them to formulate oppositional interpretations of their identities, interests, and needs" (Fraser 1992: 67).

In the context of an epistemic and practice-based account of the political contribution of social movements we need to explore the extent to which the idea of epistemic practice can be integrated into Fraser's own view of public life, a perspective that is certainly not far from her own analysis. Hence, according to Fraser, feminists identify at the heart of the bourgeois public sphere, since they seem to point to some relevant features characterizing communicative practices and, more concretely, what has been described in previous chapters as the immanent normativity of democratic practice:

> Briefly, scholars like Joan Landes, Mary Ryan, and Geoff Eley [. . .] argue that, despite the rhetoric of publicity and accessibility, that official public sphere rested on, indeed was importantly constituted by, a number of significant exclusions. For Landes, the key axis of exclusion is gender; she argues that the ethos of the new republican public sphere in France was constructed in deliberate opposition to that of a more woman-friendly salon culture that the republicans stigmatized as "artificial," "effeminate," and "aristocratic." Consequently, a new, austere style of public speech and behavior was promoted, a style deemed "rational," "virtuous," and "manly." (Fraser 1992: 59)

While the notion of "democratic practice" does not appear in Fraser's text, it is obvious that the description provided in terms of "behavior" and "ethos" as well as of "woman-friendly salon culture" as "artificial," "effeminate" as opposed to "rational" and "manly" corresponds to the kind of perspective we aim at developing here. What authors like Landes, Ryan, and Eley identify, according to this passage, are precisely exclusionary mechanisms that touch on the very immanent normativity of the communicative practices of political will-formation. According to feminist critics, we must understand the dynamics affecting the immanent normativity of the communicative practices of literary publics as the result of power mechanisms aiming at reproducing male domination without having recourse to direct repression, something that Fraser subsumes under the Gramscian notion of "hegemony."

As mentioned, even if Fraser rejects the radical conclusions of such a critical-historical approach to the emergence of the bourgeois public sphere, she believes that we can only provide a critical account of the public sphere if we abandon some central Habermasian premises, such as the idea of the possibility of "bracketing differences" in public communication, a unifying view of the public sphere, a clear-cut difference between the public and the private and, finally, the assumption of the sharp distinction between state and public sphere as a requirement for the well-functioning of the latter. Regarding the first idea, that of "bracketing differences" of status, Fraser points to the assumption that the bourgeois public sphere can be a kind of "zero degree culture [. . .] so utterly bereft of any specific ethos as to accommodate with perfect neutrality and equal ease interventions expressive of any and every cultural ethos" (Fraser 1992: 64). This is, according to Fraser, the result of a dangerous abstraction, since in fact what we find de facto is a plurality of cultural forms on which exclusionary mechanisms are erected: "The result is the development of powerful informal pressures that marginalize the contributions of members of subordinated groups both in everyday life contexts and in official public spheres" (Fraser 1992: 64). Hence, similarly to Young, for Fraser

[t]his history records that members of subordinated social groups—women, workers, peoples of color, and gays and lesbians—have repeatedly found it advantageous to constitute alternative publics. I propose to call these subaltern counterpublics in order to signal that they are parallel discursive arenas where members of subordinated social groups invent and circulate counterdiscourses, which in turn permit them to formulate oppositional interpretations of their identities, interests, and needs. Perhaps the most striking example is the late-twentieth century U.S. feminist subaltern counterpublic, with its variegated array of journals, bookstores, publishing companies, film and video distribution networks, lecture series, research centers, academic programs, conferences, conventions, festivals, and local meeting places. In this public sphere, feminist women have invented new terms for describing social reality, including "sexism," "the double shift," "sexual harassment," and "marital, date, and acquaintance rape." Armed with such language, we have recast our needs and identities, thereby reducing, although not eliminating, the extent of our disadvantage in official public spheres. (Fraser 1992: 67)

As is the case for many other feminists, Fraser points here to the capacity of social movements to generate a different perspective on the world as well as our identities and needs. However, in contrast to the previous passages, Fraser's analysis does not fully develop the idea that in feminist or proletarian movements those forms of behavior that were reflectively rejected by the bourgeois public sphere as "effeminate" or irrational may have had the chance to develop as legitimate or "acceptable" forms of political practice. Hence, the practical-innovative potential of counter-hegemonic publics cannot be reduced to the reproduction of existing cultural patterns, even if the presence of these patterns represents a condition of possibility for certain forms of internal inclusion in Young's sense. Furthermore, an emancipatory account of the public sphere needs to be able to account for the potential groups possess to produce new practical ethos and new cultures of public inquiry, or even to mobilize existing ones in counter-hegemonic ways.

The notion of public sphere or public life underlying the present account comes close to that of Fraser insofar as it distinguishes between hegemonic and counter-hegemonic public spheres within the context of a pluralistic understanding of the public sphere. As we already know, in contrast to Fraser, however, who seems particularly interested in questions regarding what we have called "content," the present account stresses the practical dimension of counter-hegemonic publics, which becomes particularly clear if we consider publics as communities of inquiry. While hegemonic practices of public inquiry contribute by their exclusionary effects to the reproduction of hegemonic views, struggling communities of inquiry come very often to see themselves compelled to develop not only different perspectives but also, and most basically, the need to generate counter-hegemonic methods of inquiry. These methods, which have come to be rejected as "effeminate" or "vulgar" by dominant social groups, are counter-hegemonic to the extent that they allow for the generation of counter-hegemonic perspectives regarding people's "identities, interests and needs." Hence, counter-hegemonic movements are loci from which groups can challenge the culture(s) of public inquiry dominant in the public sphere by enhancing the standards of what should count as a democratic practice as well as by providing new methods that are de facto able to conform to accepted norms.

A pluralist view of political-epistemic practices sees in the emergence of differently "situated" inquiries the possibility of more general learning processes affecting other local but also hegemonic forms. Ultimately, if we follow this proposal, we should conceive of public life as constituted by a plurality of self-transforming, mutually influencing, power-related methods of inquiry. In my view, such an epistemic, practice-based perspective on social struggles in the public sphere would provide a productive ground for studying the interaction among different communities of public inquiry as well as the conflicts, mutual influences, and learning processes concerning the methods they reproduce and develop. Accepting that methods may be clustered in epistemic cultures or cultures of public inquiry we may be able to characterize social movements, but also parties, media, private organizations, and so on, both at a national and transnational level. In this larger context, the localized epistemic practices social movements develop in their attempts to identify, define, and solve concrete problems can be seen as part of this larger process involving conflict, interaction, and mutual influence among publics as well as between those publics and the state.

THE NOTION OF EPISTEMIC PRACTICES IN SOCIAL MOVEMENTS

But what are epistemic practices in social movements? How do they look like? How easily can we identify and distinguish them? Can we find them isolated from other practices or are they essentially connected to other, nonepistemic dimension of social mobilization? The notion of epistemic or knowledge-practice or cognitive praxis has been studied in sociological approaches of social movements. Hence, as Chesters and Welsh remind us:

> Social movements have long been bearers of knowledge about forms of oppression and injustice, expressing political claims, identifying social and economic grievances and bringing new or neglected issues to public prominence. They have been in the forefront of debates about how social divisions including gender, race, sexuality, age and religion structure society and reproduce power structures including prevailing norms and values. They have also been prominent in highlighting the social and environmental implications of the application of new sciences and technologies from manufacturing processes to nuclear fission, genetically modified organisms to cloning and nanotechnology. Social movements produce knowledge that is often challenging to those in power or which might be difficult for a society to confront—levels of sexual abuse, the treatment of the mentally ill, the stigmatisation of those with HIV/AIDS etc. (Chesters & Welsh 2010: 105–106)

Until recent times, however, we do not find systematic accounts on the side of sociologists or social theorists. Under the label of "knowledge practices," important sociological attempts have been made to describe the cognitive work that takes place in contexts of social mobilization (Arribas Lozano 2018, Cox 2014, Della Porta & Palava 2017). For Casas-Cortés and her colleagues, knowledge-practices

> range from things we are more classically trained to define as knowledge, such as practices that engage and run parallel to the knowledge of scientists or policy experts, to micro-political and cultural interventions that have more to do with "know-how" or the "cognitive praxis that informs all social activity" and which vie with the most basic social institutions that teach us how to be in the world.

As examples of knowledge-practices, they mention

> encounters ranging from heated online and journal debates over the nature and
> meaning of Italy's movimento no global, in which new forms of situated and
> reflexive theoretical production are defined; to hours of direct-action strategiz-
> ing in meetings at Chicago's cooperative bookstores, where theories of embod-
> ied democracy are derived; to campground conferences on Native American
> territories, where native knowledge contributes to the science of environmental
> justice issues; constitute, among other things, important sites of knowledge cre-
> ation, reformulation, and diffusion. We call these diverse practices "knowledge-
> practices." (Casas-Cortés et al. 2008: 19–20)

Even if the present account is certainly sympathetic to such a pluralist and
micrological approach, the preference for the term "epistemic practice" is
justified from the particular task of this book, namely, the attempt to account
for the epistemic dimension of social movements as part of the power of
democracy's epistemic dimension to promote political learning processes.
Nonetheless, in this book expressions such as knowledge-practice, knowledge-producing practice, epistemic practice, or collective inquiry are to be
taken as synonymous.

Even if up to this point I have focused on epistemic practices as generating
the cognitive conditions for articulating and fighting injustice and promoting
just social relations, it is obvious that epistemic practices must also respond
to other epistemic needs like, for example, technical questions about how
to organize online communication. However, even in technical questions
it is difficult not to identify a perspective of justice. This becomes clear by
examining the different kinds of knowledge that are produced in a social
movement. Firstly, to use a Deweyan expression, social movements need
to produce knowledge on the problematic situations that are at the source
of mobilization, such as the ecological crisis, the situation of women, or the
introduction of an "unjust" law. This knowledge regards both the description
and the normative evaluation of the situations of injustice that is at the source
of their collective struggles as well as the search for alternative scenarios. Iris
Marion Young has provided a list of the "objects" social movements need to
inquire into:

> Among the sorts of situated knowledge that people in differenciated social
> positions have are: (1) an understanding of their position, and how it stands in
> relation to other positions; (2) a social map of other salient positions, how they
> are defined, and the relation in which they stand to this position; (3) a point of
> view on the history of the society, (4) an interpretation of how the relations
> and processes of the whole society operate, especially as they affect one's own

position; (5) a position-specific experience and point of view on the natural and physical environment. (Young 2001: 117)

Gaining knowledge about these situations is also a question of assessing the situation from the point of view of its normative quality. A situation—the working conditions in nuclear centrals, the salaries of healthcare workers, the construction of a water dam, the attacks on LGTBI+ community, the invisibilization of the work of women, and so on—must be considered as bearing a certain kind of "injustice." At the same time, alternative situations pointing to more just relations must be often imagined. This kind of normative work is particularly difficult in a context of value pluralism, but it is necessary to build an oppositional consciousness and, in the long run, to change the public perception of the problem in question. It should be added here that, in this collective process of assessment or normative framing of the situation, the norms and values at play ("What kinds of injustices are at stake?") can also be (re-)defined according to new hermeneutical possibilities inherent to the values at hand. In Deweyan terms, the relationship between the "objective" situation and the values and norms used to assess it is transactional: the two poles may come to transform each other in unexpected ways.

Secondly, epistemic practices also respond to the need of generating practical knowledge about how to organize the movement. Movements need to organize communication, develop mobilization techniques, to organize "camps" or "occupations," to draw posters or write leaflets, to protect themselves physically and symbolically from attacks by other political actors, to express themselves in the media, to take care of its members, and so on. In a so-called climate camp I observed and took part in summer 2019, epistemic needs ranged from the need to build a water system to the cooking of pizza for several hundreds of participants, the organization of night-watch turns to the organization of courses, workshops, and theater plays. This sort of practical knowledge also has a normative dimension: Who can legitimately be called upon to participate in certain unpleasant tasks? Who is allowed to participate in activities and to whom? Should certain members or subgroups remain excluded from some kinds of activity?

Thirdly, epistemic practices also produce reflexive knowledge about the methods that are meant to produce the previous kinds of knowledge. It is hence a methodological knowledge and involves questions of the sort: what methods of observation and fact recollection are the best? What is the best way to potentiate the sharing of experiences that is the most adequate to the movement? What are the best methods of discussion, the more interesting forms of organizing a public debate? Who can and who should participate in collective decision-making? And how? What are the possible formats for decision-making activities? Should one prefer consensus or majority rule? How to deal with disagreement and, more concretely, radical disagreement? Here, the question about the democratic potential of movements comes to the fore. Hence, the question if more democratic methods are more appropriate to generate more just and efficient decisions is crucial for democratic advancement. Here again, a normative moment cannot be separated from the production of methodological knowledge: is it, for example, acceptable and appropriate to invite experts external to the movement? Should we provide informal meetings to promote inclusion?

Finally, social movements also have to deal with questions regarding their own identity or identities: "Who are we?", "What unites us as a group?", "What do we struggle for?", and "How do the various subgroups in the movement hold together?" As I aim at showing drawing on Dewey's expressive approach to social movements, the possibility of developing a collective identity must be understood as a process of collective self-articulation that is highly influenced by all other activities of inquiry. Hence, as Dewey shows, the possibility of collective self-reflection is linked to the pursuit of collective inquiries.

In order to characterize what epistemic practices in social movements are and what makes them different from other kinds of practice we can also find, it is helpful to come back to the more general notion of social practice. Hence, epistemic practices can be characterized as those practices regulated by epistemic norms and whose main goal represents the generation of knowledge and solution of problems. As Rahel Jaeggi points out, all social practices are "rule-governed":

> [Social practices] always involve sequences of actions governed by rules and regulations, hence by a division of the possibilities of action into what is and is not appropriate to do. This means that practices involve not just regularity but also rule-governedness. As Titus Stahl puts it, "The central idea is that a practice invariably involves an internal distinction between right and wrong action" (Stahl 2013, 263). The decisive point is that the operative criteria are *internal to practice*. (Jaeggi 2018: 56, author's emphasis)

Next to guidance by rules or norms, goal-orientation is another of the characteristic features of social practices. In fact, the presence of a determinate goal defines, according to Jaeggi, a set of individual actions as corresponding to a certain practice:

> Practices as I understand them here posit and have purposes and, among other things, are determined by these purposes. So they are what they are because of

the purposes that they pursue or are pursued with them. The practice of shopping or of standing in line at the checkout and paying serves the purpose of buying groceries; the practice of attending seminars serves (among other things) the acquisition of knowledge; the purpose of playing (basketball) is recreation, physical training, or social connectedness—or it is practised just for fun, but even then it is good for something. Practices should be individuated in terms of their purposes. This means that a sequence of actions is recognized as a certain practice based on knowledge of their purposes. ("Are you just standing here for a chat, or are you in line to pay?" Depending on my answer, I am engaging either in the practice of shopping or in that of small talk. (Jaeggi 2018: 59)

Jaeggi makes three important clarifications about the goal-orientation of practices: firstly, social practices can have different goals, which can be intentional or not, implicit or explicit. The goals of practices can be intentionally and consciously pursued, while in other cases goals are realized without any explicit awareness of them. For example,

The purpose of the conversation in the grocery store is not just to make a successful purchase but also to flirt with the shop assistant, and the activity as a whole may serve as a distraction from work. Playing basketball may serve all three of the purposes mentioned (training, having fun, and communication) together. Strictly speaking, one would have to say in such cases that a single practice is not determined in several ways but that one and the same sequence of actions simultaneously constitutes several practices—flirting as well as shopping. (Jaeggi 2018: 59)

These considerations have consequences for any attempt to develop an approach to the normative dimension of political practices in social movements. On the one hand, epistemic practices follow epistemic norms or rules, those regarding the realization of epistemic tasks with the goal of solving a problematic situation. At the same time, as social practices they can have different goals at the same time and, in consequence, different normativities in correspondence with these goals. Accordingly, we need to think of what we have called "epistemic normativity" as cohabiting with other practical goals and other forms of normativity. This brings us back to the idea of a tension between democracy's epistemic and intrinsic values (and their derivative norms). So, when we are doing politics, epistemic norms responding to the goal of making the right decision or finding reliable information cohabit with political norms that have in the realization of political freedom their goal. It is precisely at this level of cohabitation—together with the relation among different practices—that a large number of the normative tensions and political learning processes may arise. Hence, these are precisely the tensions where the potential extensions of intrinsic values and norms are disclosed. So, when members of groups traditionally or legally excluded from political participation see themselves motivated for problem-solving reasons (e.g., fighting against massive evictions) in political action, the clash between different normativities, epistemic and political, can be resolved by rethinking the specific sense we give to norms of inclusion.

To sum up, epistemic are those practices in social movements in which participants, consciously or not, contribute to the identification, definition, and resolution of the problems they need to deal with. As such, epistemic practices produce knowledge, both about problems and the best way to cope with them and about the larger context where these problems take place and are resolved. Epistemic practices are not always only epistemic: sometimes the goal of a practice is not only to resolve a problem, but to embody certain values, or to achieve a certain aesthetic goal. And even if some practices may be purely expressive or artistic, epistemic practices should not be separated from art and rhetoric, hence, the latter are also constitutive elements of a process in which knowledge can be generated. Importantly, epistemic practices also deal with knowledge about values, norms, and collective goals.

CONCLUDING REMARKS

This chapter has discussed some fundamental aspects of an epistemic approach to social movements that takes them seriously as inquirers, instead of merely as content-providers. Concretely, I have examined the idea that social movements can play a double counter-hegemonic role: they produce counter-hegemonic views of society and its problems, and they generate counter-hegemonic forms of political practice. Drawing on previous epistemic approaches to social movements I have developed the idea of "epistemic exclusion" as a specific form of internal exclusion and rejected the idea that social movements should be merely taken in their world-disclosive function. Instead, they should be taken as problem-solvers. This said, we should be aware of the risk of taking a reductivistic view on Dewey's understanding of problem-solving. Hence, for Dewey, in order to be solved, problems need to be articulated as such. This process of articulation certainly involves disclosing the hermeneutical and ontological possibilities of the social world. Finally, I have revised the existing literature on knowledge-practices in order to fledge-out a notion of "epistemic practices" that is useful for approaching social movements. The aim of the next chapter is to examine Dewey's notion of experimental inquiry in order to theoretically substantiate the idea of that experimental epistemic practices in social movements have a double counter-hegemonic potential.

Chapter 5

The Double Counter-Hegemonic Potential of Experimentalist Practices

The aim of this chapter is to present Dewey's experimentalist theory of epistemic practice in such a way that it can account for what happens in social movements when they act as double counter-hegemonic innovators. In other words, my aim is to explore the prospects of Dewey's notion of experimental inquiry for accounting for the capacity of social movements to challenge hegemonic ideologies that deny or naturalize relations of oppression and injustice on the one hand, and hegemonic understandings of democratic practice that reduce it, for example, to mere electoral procedures, on the other. Hence, when, for example, in a movement's weekly assembly participants try to figure out where and how they should organize a protest, when in a meeting they consider the pros and cons of collaborating with public institutions, or when in a workshop they try to find the best way to frame a particular unjust situation, what we find, apart from many other elements such as aesthetic and moral experiences, are a series of epistemic practices put at work in order to figure out the best possible answer to their questions. These practices include, for example, collecting evidence that support a certain path of action; introducing new perspectives from participants in smaller workshops; explaining personal stories; making a documentary film; explicitly discussing about values and norms in online forums; inviting artists, experts, journalists to discuss certain topics; or organizing feedback session about action strategies that have been previously tried. In the same manner, when participants organize a workshop on experiences of gender-based exclusion or on care relations in the movement, they behave, among other things, as inquirers that are able to identify and define problems and look for creative solutions. These epistemic practices can be characterized as experimental if they satisfy certain conditions. The aim of this chapter is to explore what these conditions are while at the same time showing that they are responsible for what I have been calling movement's double counter-hegemonic potential.

At first sight, it might seem strange to introduce abstract epistemological reflections into the study of the collective practices of social movements. Moreover, given that Dewey himself bases his epistemic views on the analysis of scientific practice, one might wonder if the chosen strategy is adequate for accounting for the sort of things that take place in a movement's assembly, a workshop, or an online meeting. However, one of the most fascinating Deweyan intuitions is that scientific practice should be seen in continuity with any other kind of practice in which we try to identify problematic situations and try to figure out how they can be best solved. Thus, the introduction of abstract epistemological reflection is, in my view, that it can provide valuable keys for the analysis of what it is actually done in collective inquiries that take place outside the laboratory. Here it should be advanced that the notion of experimental inquiry Dewey develops refers to more than just the implementation of experiments and testing as a form of acquiring reliable knowledge. According to the reading I propose, Dewey's experimentalism refers to a form of inquiry that includes and is able to (re-)connect the fundamental epistemic operations of problem-definition, hypothesis-formation, reasoning, and experimental testing. I will have the opportunity to explain what this all means in the coming sections of this chapter. It is worth noting, however, that by the term "(re-)connect" I refer to the capacity to make each of these basic operations dependent on the other ones. For example, in experimental inquiry, the formation of an hypothesis of how a problem could be best solved cannot be separated from the process by which problems themselves need to be defined. In other words, we should not propose solutions without taking into consideration that we are at the same time contributing to the definition of problem the solution is meant for. In the same guise, according to experimentalism, we cannot define a problem without considering the possible solutions a certain definition of the problem may suggest. As I will show, at a more fundamental level, experimentalism consists in (re-)connecting the operations of inquiry that relate to facts and those dealing with ideas (including values and norms). As we will see, the way operations with facts and operations with ideas are connected with each other in inquiry is to a great extent responsible for its double counter-hegemonic potential of social movements.

Next to the question about the relation of dependency between the different fundamental operations of inquiry that is essential for experimentalist inquiry, I will also present a second feature of experimental inquiry that is particularly relevant in the present context. Hence, this feature is essential for the capacity of experimental inquiry to play a double counter-hegemonic role, providing counter-hegemonic views on social reality and deepening democratic practice. This feature corresponds to the expressivist or articulative nature of experimental inquiry. In this chapter I propose to examine the specific sense(s) in which inquiry practices involve an articulative moment expressed in Dewey's definition of inquiry as the progressive determination of an indeterminate situation. Hence, it is precisely the presence of different articulative moment in inquiry what makes project of the application of Dewey's epistemic views to the study of the experiences of injustice particularly compelling. Inquiry represents a process of articulation of our moral experiences that is open and fluid enough to generate an oppositional consciousness. At the same time, by providing an expressive reading of inquiry I aim at exploring an epistemic justification of democratic inclusion that is able to systematically account for the progressive "deepening" and of democracy as an epistemic requirement of peoples' epistemic goals. In other words, through an expressive understanding of inquiry as articulation we can gain an epistemic defense of democracy, that, in contrast with current accounts, requires democracy to become a continuous and pluralist process of democratization that has the idea of cooperation or social freedom as its major orientation.

In the present chapter I will therefore follow several steps. First of all, my aim is to show how Dewey's logical analysis can be related to an account on the epistemic practices of social movements. Hence, Dewey's logic is about exploring the most fundamental operations that inquirers undergo in their everyday practices of knowledge production. Accordingly, I will develop the Deweyan insight according to which we can approach epistemic practices from the perspective of the degrees of generality of the operations they put at place. Hence, in the analysis of inquiry we identify the most fundamental operations—Dewey calls them "logical forms" (LW 4: 117, LW 12: 11)—that are at the base of the particular methods of inquiry that are put in practice in everyday epistemic practices. I have previously referred to these fundamental operations as problem-definition, hypothesis-formation, reasoning, and experimentation. I have also mentioned that, even more fundamentally, inquiry consists of operations related to facts and to ideas, since facts and ideas are the most fundamental elements of any inquiry. Dewey's point is that these fundamental operations can be embodied in an open-ended variety of particular epistemic practices. To this extent, Dewey's logic is compatible with the idea that experimental practices can be realized in a plurality of ways. After that, I will present the idea that Dewey's theory of inquiry can be understood as a theory of the immanent normativity of epistemic practices in the most general form they can take, thereby stressing the prescriptive function of the fundamental operations I have mentioned.

After having clarified both relation of logical operations to everyday epistemic practices and the prescriptive status of the former, I will reconstruct

Dewey's outline of the general pattern of inquiry as the set of the four basic operations of inquiry. I will proceed in two different steps. First, I will explore what I have called the most fundamental level of logical analysis, one concerning the operations of inquiry dealing with facts and with ideas. In the second step, I will explore in detail each of what Dewey takes to be the four main operations of inquiry: problem-definition, hypothesis-formation, reasoning, and testing of hypotheses. They represent four different fundamental ways in which facts and ideas are put in relation to each other and they need to be approached in detail in order to provide a general view of experimental inquiry. After having exposed the meaning of each of the operations I will show that for Dewey experimentalism denotes the presence of a fluid relation between the four fundamental operations of inquiry, which involves, in the last instance, a fluid relation between the facts and ideas at play in inquiry.

This will be followed by a discussion of on an expressive reading of Dewey's theory of inquiry, which, as I mentioned, refers to the idea that inquiry is not merely about finding given problems and providing solutions to them, but about articulating those problems in a way that provides them with a "specific shape" (Taylor 1985: 374). Furthermore, as I will show, inquiry is not only about articulating problems, but also about articulating what Dewey calls "suggestions" into ideas that play a role in any inquiry as well as the identity of those who participate in the process of inquiry.

In a further step, I will show to what extent experimentalism's two main features (fluidity and articulation) contribute to the generation of counter-hegemonic perspectives that make possible the emergence of collective oppositional consciousness. My aim is to draw on T. W. Adorno's notion of reified thinking in order to show how experimentalism has the potential of challenging existing structures of power which remain hidden by hegemonic methods of inquiry. I will examine also in what sense experimentalism has the potential to deepen the democratic quality of epistemic practices. Here is where the possibility of providing an epistemic justification of democracy comes into play. Hence, providing such a justification involves showing that, in order to effectively solve social problems, experimentalist epistemic practice must realize democratic norms of inclusion and equality in ways that often involve deepening the specific understandings we usually give to these norms. In other words, an epistemic justification of democracy should be able to show that, in order to account for social injustice, search for just social relations, and meet the practical requirements of mobilization, members of social movements need to deepen their relations of political cooperation in an open-ended variety of ways.

Finally, in the two last sections of this chapter, I will consider, drawing on Emmanuel Renault's idea of a "feeling of injustice" and José Medina's notion of "resistant imaginations," how these abstract considerations about Dewey's experimentalism can be brought back to the analysis of the concrete epistemic practices of social movements. On the one hand, the inquiries of those struggling against injustice and for more just social relation can be understood as collective articulative processes that go from a vague "feeling" to more articulate notions of injustice guiding their self-comprehension and their particular actions. On the other hand, the expressive understanding of inquiry is able to accommodate the idea that imagination plays an essential role in the generation of an oppositional consciousness.

THE MOST GENERAL METHODOLOGY

The opening sections of Dewey's *Logic: The Theory of Inquiry* point to the following basic thesis: out of the plurality of particular methods of inquiry available, some fundamental operations can be traced that can be common to all of them. The set of these operations can hence be seen as the most general form of inquiry, what Dewey calls "the pattern of inquiry." Apart from these general traits, epistemic practices also have particular traits, such as, for example, those characterizing the particular methods of biological inquiry in contrast to those of physical inquiry. Again, the plurality of those particular methods of inquiry is multiplied by further specifications. For example, different methods of biological inquiry can be developed depending on specific epistemic goals and research interests. As a matter of fact, we actually should talk in terms of "degrees" of particularity, which go from the most general form of inquiry to the most particular method that is actually applied in inquiry. While on the one end of the spectrum we find the general form or the "pattern" of inquiry, at the other end we find practices of inquiry actually taking place—practices that implement particular methods that in their turn embody more general methodological forms all the way up to the most basic operations of inquiry. Hence, we need to see, as Dewey contends, that fundamental operations are not different from what we could call a methodology.

The distinction between these three levels of methodological generality—general fundamental operations, more or less particular methods, and primary practices embodying fundamental operations—provides the background for a more central thesis underlying Dewey's logical reflections. Hence, according to Dewey, fundamental operations—which represent the actual object of logical reflection—should not be understood as constituting a general method a priori, that is, a method that would be given prior to the actual exercise of epistemic practice. On the contrary, for Dewey "all logical forms [. . .] arise within the operations of inquiry and are concerned with the control of inquiry so that it may yield warranted assertions" (LW 12: 11). Otherwise formulated: "[I]inquiry into inquiry is the causa cognoscendi of logical forms, [while] primary inquiry is itself causa essendi of the forms which inquiry into inquiry discloses" (LW 12: 12). Actual epistemic practice or primary inquiry is, according to this formulation, at the origin both of the particular methods (biological, physical, etc.) and, most importantly, at the very source of the general forms that are to be examined by logicians. This fact is essential for understanding the prescriptive force of logical forms: the epistemic validity of fundamental operations, their prescriptive force, is not derived from some sort of consideration prior to the actual practice of inquiry. On the contrary, it is essentially connected to the latter, hence "the forms originate in operations of inquiry" (LW 12: 11, author's emphasis).

THE PRESCRIPTIVE FORCE OF LOGICAL FORMS

Before exploring the exact nature of this connection we need to clarify what exactly it means for Dewey that logical forms have a prescriptive character, something that is already announced in the first of the two previous quotations. Hence, "[s]ince inquiries and methods are better or worse, logic involves a standard for criticizing and evaluating them" (LW 12: 13). The logic is a prescriptive discipline to the extent that, by examining the most general structure of inquiry, it sets the general conditions that must be met by all particular methods that are to be followed in actual practice:

> These guiding logical principles are not *premises* of inference or argument. They are conditions to be satisfied such that knowledge of them provides a principle of direction and testing. They are formulations of ways of treating subject-matter that have been found to be so determinative of sound conclusions in the past that they are taken to regulate further inquiry until definitive grounds are found for questioning them. While they are derived from examination of methods previously used in their connection with the kind of conclusion they have produced, they are *operationally a priori* with respect to further inquiry. (LW 12: 21, author's emphasis)

In this context, we can ask with Isaac Levi the important question: "How [. . .] can inquiry which has to be evaluated by reference to a standard be itself the source of the standard?" (Levi 2011: 82). For Dewey, the general validity of the logical forms that constitute the general method of inquiry can be grounded in the very dynamics of the natural sciences:

> Moreover, different methods have been not only tried, but they have been tried out; that is, tested. The developing course of science thus presents us with an immanent criticism of methods previously tried. Early methods failed in some important aspect. In consequence of this failure, they were modified so that more dependable results were secured. Earlier methods yielded conclusions that could not stand the strain put upon them by further investigation. It is not merely that the *conclusions* were found to be inadequate or false but that they were found to be so because of methods employed. Other methods of inquiry were found to be such that persistence in them not only produced conclusions that stood the strain of further inquiry but that tended to be self-rectifying. They were methods that improved with and by use. (LW 12: 13–14, author's emphasis)

Accordingly, the question that is central to any constructivistic understanding of the prescriptive force of (epistemic) norms, concerning which actual norms are to become the standard for further normative reflection, is answered in a relatively simple sense that exhibits Dewey's "measured scientific optimism" (Fairfield 2013: 83): natural science has historically proven able to deal with environmental conditions in a manner that has allowed us to maximize our control over them. However, to the extent that it has succeeded in this, the experimental practices and methods of natural science are best situated for becoming the object of the work of the logician: it is on the basis of this success that general logical forms can be prescriptive for other forms of inquiry, such as social inquiry. In short, Dewey's *Logic* can be seen as a theory of the immanent normativity of epistemic practice. In it, Dewey explains both the emergence of epistemic practice as well as its transformative dynamics, while at the same time providing the basis for the validity of this practice by affirming that a certain method has "worked" better than others. Dewey mobilizes the idea of what we could describe as learning processes based on actual confrontation with existential conditions in primary inquiry. Learning processes in this context mean the transformation of methodological requirements in order to fulfill the conditions for successful inquiry. General forms and particular methods are prescriptive to the extent that they are the result of such learning processes.

As announced, Dewey's theory of logical forms as immanent to epistemic practice, and the idea of a general pattern of inquiry, can be especially productive for an analysis that accounts for the possibility of collective learning processes emerging from localized practices dealing with specific problems; hence, epistemic practices, such as testimonio, consciousness-raising, organizing assemblies, visiting citizens door to door, or introducing informal conversations within a workshop, can be seen as highly localized innovative methodologies that, according to my hypothesis, are able to challenge particular hegemonic methods by embodying fundamental operations of experimental inquiry. In order to understand this thesis, central to the present account, we need now to inquire into Dewey's analysis of the general structure of epistemic practice.

THE PATTERN OF INQUIRY

As we have already anticipated, as a general structure, the pattern of inquiry is constituted by the basic operations of particular methods developed in primary inquiries. Despite the fact that they are distinguished in theoretical analysis, fundamental operations of inquiry cannot be separated from each other. Hence, each of the operations within the pattern of inquiry must be seen as part of a functional whole with the goal being to generate knowledge about the world, something for which Dewey reserves the expression "warranted assertibility" (LW 12: 16–17). Since they represent constitutive parts of a relational whole, those changes affecting one operation cannot leave the others unaffected without at the same time generating pathological forms of inquiry. Hence, for example, as we will see in more detail, in actual practice operations involved in the identification and definition of problems should not be disconnected from those involved in hypothesis-formation, since the definition of the problem cannot be made fully in isolation from the search for its solution(s). As a consequence, the pattern of inquiry should not only be seen as prescriptive in that it establishes the set of basic operations minimally required for the exercise of successful epistemic practice; its prescriptive force also concerns the connections and influences among the different basic operations of inquiry.

FACTS AND IDEAS

Before turning to the analysis of the four basic operations of inquiry, we need, however, to address a still more basic distinction that permeates each of them. It concerns the two basic elements that constitute any inquiry: operations with facts and with ideas. Dewey uses several expressions to refer to the two elements of this distinction, sometimes speaking of "factual or perceptual" and "ideological or conceptual material," sometimes referring to them as "data" and "hypotheses" as well as at other times speaking of "existential" or "observed conditions" and "theories" among other expressions. Within the whole of inquiry, facts and ideas constitute the object of different kinds of operation: Dewey talks very often in terms of "observation" of facts on the one hand, while on the other hand ideas are "suggested," "proposed," and "tested."

According to Dewey, the meaning of facts and ideas can only be established from the point of view of the function they play within an operational whole of inquiry. Dewey famously characterizes inquiry as the determination of an indeterminate situation: *"Inquiry is the controlled or directed transformation of an indeterminate situation into one that is so determinate in its constituent distinctions and relations as to convert the elements of the original situation into a unified whole"* (LW 12: 108, author's emphasis). An indeterminate situation is not understood by Dewey to mean a mere cognitive status of the subject toward her environment, it is rather a trait that pervades the very existential whole in which the subject is immersed: "it is the very nature of the indeterminate situation which evokes inquiry to be questionable; or, in terms of actuality instead of potentiality, to be uncertain, unsettled, disturbed" (LW 12: 109).

In this context, facts correspond to those elements of an indeterminate situation that constitute stable or settled points of support for the inquirer in view of the further determination of the situation. As Dewey famously puts it:

> When an alarm of fire is sounded in a crowded assembly hall, there is much that is indeterminate as regards the activities that may produce a favourable issue. One may get out safely or one may be trampled and burned. The fire is characterized, however, by some settled traits. It is, for example, located somewhere. Then the aisles and exits are at fixed places. Since they are settled or determinate in existence, the first step in institution of a problem is to settle them in observation. There are other factors which, while they are not as temporary and especially fixed, are yet observable constituents; for example, the behaviour and movements of other members of the audience. All of these observed conditions taken together constitute "the facts of the case." (LW 12: 112)

Hence, we need primarily to see facts as those operational elements within inquiry that point to the determinate conditions that must be taken into account in inquiry: "fact are such in a logical sense only as they serve to delimit a problem in a way that affords indications and test of proposed solutions" (LW 12: 493). As operational elements, facts play a double role in inquiry, as obstacles and resources for the operations of inquiry, hence

> no existing situation can be modified without counteracting obstructive and deflective forces that render a given situation confused and conflicting. Nor can an objectively unified situation be instituted except as the positive factors of

existing conditions are released and ordered so as to move in the direction of the objective consequence desired. (LW 12: 493)

On the other hand, by the operational meaning of "ideas," Dewey refers to those elements that point to and guide the operations leading to a solution to the problem: "An idea is first of all an anticipation of something that may happen; it marks a possibility" (LW 12: 113). At the same time, "[i]deas that are plans of operations to be performed are an integral factor in actions which change the face of the world" (LW 4: 111). Their action-guiding function becomes particularly evident in experimental operations, hence in this case: "[t]he test of ideas, of thinking generally, is found in the consequences of the acts to which the ideas lead, that is in the new arrangements of things which are brought into existence" (LW 4 109). For Dewey, when thinking about the role of ideas in inquiry we must distinguish between ideas as suggestions and well-defined ideas. This distinction relies again on the basic thesis that we need to regard inquiry as a progressive determination of an undetermined situation, since suggestions must be seen as vague ideas that become progressively determined in the course of inquiry. In this connection he argues that

> ideas differ in grade according to the stage reached. At first, save in highly familiar matters, they are vague. They occur at first simply as suggestions; suggestions just spring up, flash upon us, occur to us. They may then become stimuli to direct and overt activity but they have as yet no logical status. [. . .] The suggestion becomes an idea when it is examined with reference to its functional fitness; its capacity as a means of resolving a given situation. (LW 12: 114)

Hence, we need to see the process of inquiry as one in which out of vague suggestions ideas progressively take shape to the point that they become able to direct action toward the resolution of the problematic situation. Coming back to the distinction between facts and ideas, for Dewey inquiry involves what he calls a "functional correlation" between both. Hence, as Dewey puts it: "In logical fact, perceptual and conceptual materials [i.e., facts and ideas, JSZ] are instituted in functional correlativity with each other, in such a manner that the former locates and describes the problem while the latter represents the possible method of solution" (LW 12: 115). Both elements are functionally involved in inquiry to the extent that they participate both in the elaboration of a problem and its possible solutions.

As has been already mentioned, with the exception of the operations of "reasoning"—which concern only the relation among ideas—each of the basic operations that constitute the whole of inquiry are to be seen as involving a specific form of interplay between facts and ideas. Hence, if there is a sense in which we can talk in prescriptive terms of the different operations involved in inquiry we must consider that their prescriptive force is connected to the "correlation" of facts and ideas which represents a functional requirement for the determination of an indeterminate situation. In other words, the facts–ideas correlation and the organic interconnection of the constitutive operations of inquiry must be seen as the two sides of the same coin.

THE BASIC OPERATIONS OF INQUIRY

a) Problem-identification and problem-definition

It has already been mentioned that Dewey conceives of inquiry has having its beginning in an "indeterminate situation." In Paul Fairfield's words:

> Thinking responds to a doubtful or problematic situation—the unknown, anomalous and perplexing—by posing questions, advancing interpretations and hypotheses, following the course of a given hypothesis to its conclusions, testing it against the available evidence, and looking for specific experiential consequences. (Fairfield 2013: 82)

For Dewey, in its initial stage, inquiry starts when the undetermined situation is identified and progressively defined as a problem to be solved: "[a] problem represents the partial transformation of a problematic situation into a determined situation" (LW 12: 111–112). At this stage, the transformation is only partial because it stands only on the way to its solution, which is taken to be the final determination of the indeterminate situation. However, "[t]he way in which the problem is conceived decides what specific suggestions are entertained and which are dismissed; what data are selected and which rejected; it is the criterion for relevancy and irrelevancy of hypotheses and conceptual structures" (LW 12: 112). The interplay of facts and ideas in problem-identification and problem-definition that is inherent in the pattern of inquiry is here of a double nature: on the one hand, the identification and definition of a concrete problem cannot do without the careful observation of "the facts of the case." On the other hand, observation and discrimination of what facts constitute the "facts of the case" are guided by ideas, which in their turn point to possible solutions. Facts "are selected and described, [. . .] for a purpose, namely statement of the problem involved in such a way that its material both indicates a meaning relevant to resolution of the difficulty and serves to test its worth and validity" (LW 12: 116).

b) Hypothesis-formation or determination of a problem-solution

While in problem-identification and problem-definition operations with facts need to be guided by ideas, in hypothesis-formation facts come to play a controlling or guiding role. Hypothesis-formation consists in the elaboration of the best possible solutions to a problem as it becomes progressively determined. Problem-definitions establish, according to Dewey, the criteria of relevance for the set of possible solutions that come to the mind of the inquirer. Here we need to recall Dewey's distinction between "suggestions" and "ideas." The vagueness of suggestions adds a further dimension to the process of progressive determination of the problem that characterizes inquiry. In this case, suggestions become progressively determined in a process that has as one of its criteria of relevance the problem-definition that remains at its base. However, as we saw, operations of problem-definition cannot be said to preexist those of hypothesis formation, since problems are also defined in light of the view of possible solutions. Here we see how the "correlation" between facts and ideas takes place at a second, more complex level that involves operations of problem-definition and hypothesis-formation:

> Observation of facts and suggested meanings or ideas arise and develop in correspondence to each other. The more the facts of the case come to light in consequences of being subjected to observation, the clearer and more pertinent become the conceptions of the way the problem constituted by these facts is to be dealt with. On the other side, the clearer the idea, the more definite, as a truism, become the operations of observation and of execution that must be performed in order to resolve the situation. (LW 12: 113)

c) Reasoning

As a constitutive part of the operations involving hypothesis formation, Dewey takes into consideration one special sort of operation particularly concerned with proving the coherence of new ideas-hypothesis with other ideas that we already hold. He calls this set of operations "reasoning" and defines it as the operations involved in "developing the meaning-content of ideas in their relations of each other" (LW 12: 115). These inferential operations are an essential part of any inquiry process if its aim is producing "warranted assertibility." In this regard Dewey observes that "[w]hen a suggested meaning is immediately accepted, inquiry is cut short. Hence the conclusion reached is not grounded, even if it happens to be correct" (LW 12: 115). Reasoning operations must be seen as a constitutive part of the inquiry process from the point of view of the progressive determination of its ideological content:

> An hypothesis, once suggested and entertained, is developed in relation to other conceptual structures until it receives a form in which it can instigate and direct

an experiment that will disclose precisely those conditions which have the maximum possible force in determining whether the hypothesis should be accepted or rejected. (LW 12: 115–116)

In other words, the normative epistemic value of the operations of reasoning is to be measured by their contribution to an inquiry-internal learning process: it is part of the larger process of articulation that is involved in the transformation of suggestions to clear ideas. Even if they do not have a direct relation to facts, operations of coherence testing are logically involved in all further operations of inquiry, since the definition of problems, the generation of hypotheses-solutions, and the testing of hypotheses in experimental settings involve the mobilization of ideas as guiding both observation and action.

d) Testing of hypotheses: Experiment and experimentalism

We come now to the last of the four basic operations of inquiry, that of experimental testing of hypotheses. Due to its central role in Dewey's theory of inquiry, it is worth exploring its full characterization in the larger context of a reflection on pragmatism and experimentalism—a characterization that aims at clarifying the sense of the operationalization of Dewey's theory of inquiry in the domain of politics. For pragmatists, experiments represent an essential part of the inquiry process aiming at knowledge, truth, or "warranted assertibility." They represent the moment of an active intervention in the world, a feature that is central to classical pragmatist epistemology, as opposed to classical empiricism and rationalism (Fairfield 2013: 82–83). Pragmatists see experiments as the practical implementation of hypotheses through the intelligent control of environmental conditions with the aim of verifying or revising these hypotheses. For many pragmatists, and particularly for Dewey, the centrality of experiments as practical and intelligent implementations of hypotheses does not represent a monopoly of the natural sciences. Hence, Dewey argued for an extension of the experimental method, not only to social-scientific disciplines, but also to many other dimensions of social life. This extension concerns especially the field of education, since Dewey was fully aware of the prominently educational component of an experimental relation toward the world. Moreover, for Dewey the influence of experimentalism should extend toward our dealing with moral and legal norms, as well as into political decisions and collective plans of action. All of these are to be seen, according to Dewey, as hypotheses to be tested and, if necessary, revised by the consequences of their particular implementation.

As experimentalist, Dewey understands the experimental moment of inquiry as the end point of all basic operations of inquiry. Hence, the latter are defined in reference to the operational role they play in the experimental implementation of hypotheses. The experimental moment of inquiry includes in its turn a set of different operations. Firstly, in the practical implementation of hypotheses, the environment of the experimenter and thereby also the experimenter herself is modified. Modification or manipulation of the environment is guided by ideas that direct the actions of experimenters toward the verification of hypotheses. Secondly, through the manipulation of the environment, that is, through action, new facts arise which are to be seen as consequences of the implementation of hypotheses. These consequences are observed and measured: they function as the test for the validity of the hypotheses. In this context, the "manipulative" moment of the experiment comes to the fore, such that the "result" constitutes not only the verification of the hypothesis but also the acquisition of knowledge about objects and their mutual relations: "the outcome of the directed activity is the construction of a new empirical situation in which objects are differently related to one another, and such that the *consequences* of directed operations form the objects that have the property of being *known*" (LW 4: 70, author's emphasis).

EXPERIMENTALISM IN THE BROAD SENSE

From this background, it is possible to characterize experimentalism in terms of the (re-)connection of facts and ideas along the different phases of the inquiry process as well as, at a higher level of complexity, the functional (re-)connection among the four different operations of inquiry. In other words, experimentalism, in science as well as in any form of social inquiry—which certainly includes the inquiries of any democratic public or social movement—does not only mean organizing experiments in order to produce knowledge and solve a situation—though it certainly also involves that. Experimentalism means, in its broadest sense, the realization of the four fundamental operations in a fluid relation to each other, that is, in a relation in which the development of each of the operations—for example, of how we define a problem—is connected to the development of all the other—for example, how we look for hypothetical solutions for the problem. Certainly, this fluidification of inquiry involves the implementation of experiments that test the hypothesis, since the practical implementation of hypothesis and their testing are themselves a form of making the relation between operations fluid. Hence, even if, in this broad sense, experimentalism cannot be reduced to the institutionalization of experiments functioning as tests for hypotheses, the "experimentalization" of a public culture of inquiry must include this possibility, since it represents an essential form of reestablishing the functional correlation of facts and ideas that represents the most basic feature of inquiry.

As we mentioned, Dewey's broad understanding of experimentalism is not limited to the analysis of the practices of the natural sciences. Social inquiries should, according to him, also be organized according to an experimental method. According to Dewey, social inquiry must be understood in the broad sense as the inquiry into social facts, in contrast to natural facts. Further, social inquiry is not limited to what we find in the social sciences but is also brought into practice by political institutions as well as within the public sphere. Hence, social inquiries take place when citizens, politicians, or judges consider the adequacy of a legal proposition and implementation as well as other administrative decisions and measures. To this extent,

> every measure of policy put into operation is, *logically*, and *should* be actually, of the nature of an experiment. For (1) it represents the adoption of one out of a number of alternative conceptions as possible plans of action, and (2) its execution is followed by consequences which, while not as capable of definite or exclusive differentiation as in the case of physical experimentation, are none the less observable within limits, so that they may serve as tests of the validity of the conception acted upon. (LW 12: 502, author's emphasis)

Thus, Dewey warns us against the risks that accompany a rejection of the experimental method in the identification, definition, and solution of social problems:

> [F]ailure to recognize its experimental character encourages treatment of a policy as an isolated independent measure. This relative isolation puts a premium upon formation of policies in a comparatively improvised way [. . .]. On the other side, failure to take into account the experimental nature of policies undertaken, encourages laxity and discontinuity in *discriminative* observation of the consequences that result from its adoption. (LW 12: 502, author's emphasis)

In this sense, according to Dewey, experimentalism represents a standard that should be adopted in order to enhance the problem-solving capacity of social and political processes of decision-making and deliberation. As I will show later, it is tightly connected to the normative standards of democratic self-government: instead of a government of experts, experimentalism requires the inclusion on equal terms of all those individuals affected by political decisions taken in democratic processes of will-formation and decision-making. Moreover, experimentalism regarding social and political questions does not need to involve treating individuals and collectives as "laboratory rats." In contrast to natural-scientific inquiry, experimentalism must proceed with the agreement and forms of association of those directly involved in the experiment: "Any hypothesis as to a social end must include as part of itself the idea of organized association among those who are to execute the operations it formulates and directs" (LW 12: 496). We will see later how Dewey's idea of experimental social inquiry can be mobilized in the formulation of a systematic epistemic argument for deepening democracy.

Due precisely to both the strong link of experimentalism with democratic norms and values and its central role in the promotion and enabling of collective and individual learning processes, Dewey's experimentalism has had an important reception in political, legal, and social sciences as well as in political and moral philosophy. As Roberto Frega puts it:

> From the standpoint of the wide view of democracy, democratic experimentalism provides not only a fruitful general framework for rethinking democracy in complex societies but, more specifically, also a set of theoretical insights to explain why democracy correlates positively with social innovation. To that extent, democratic experimentalism offers helpful tools to explore the correlation between democracy and efficacy, at a time when the resurgence of authority of expertise seems to rule out democracy as a valid framework within which to think and produce social innovation, and when the trade-off between knowledge and participation sheds its disquieting shadow over the prospects of the democratic project. Democratic experimentalism, with its orientation toward methods of controlling the production and testing of new solutions to existing problems, seems to legitimate a plausible hope for reform in areas of social life in which entrenched obstacles to change seemed to allow none. (Frega 2019: 284)

Here is a short overview of some of the most relevant political applications of Dewey's experimentalist approach. In his edited book *Demokratischer Experimentalismus* (1998) Hauke Brunkhorst has brought to the fore of German political-philosophical discussion Dewey's intuitions on the experimental nature of modern democracies. For Brunkhorst, the essential connection of democratic societies to experiments and experimentalism requires, on the one hand, the continuous cooperation between science, the press, and public opinion. On the other hand, democratic experimentalism must be conceived of in connection with notions such as evolution, progressivism, and hope, such as Dewey did. In his turn, Matthias Kettner develops in the same book the notion of a consequentialist public sphere to test in actual conditions. For him it is a central Deweyan intuition that the self-organization of a democratic community is necessary a

> science committed to coping with social problems" whose "experimental character [. . .] focuses on the active, searched and wanted expansion of the gained experience as well as on a non-violent and undogmatic handling of disagreements. (Kettner 1998: 64)

On the other side of the Atlantic, Charles Sabel and Michael C. Dorf have developed in recent years a theory of political institutions they have labeled "democratic experimentalism." By developing such a theory, they aim at providing an answer to the political-institutional problems generated by the rising complexity of societies (Sabel & Dorf 1998, see also Sabel 2012). According to the theory of democratic experimentalism, government institutions and administrations must become strongly decentralized agencies of problem-solving, profiting from local knowledge of citizens, who in their turn directly participate in the definition and resolution of their problems. At the same time, democratic experimentalism promotes the coordination of local—public and private—agencies at the national and global level through the pooling of information and reciprocal learning (mutual monitoring). Furthermore, Sabel and Dorf's democratic experimentalism looks to account for the primary indetermination of abstract fundamental rights by pointing to institutional mechanisms that promote the experimental implementation of those rights. By doing so, their goal is to go a step beyond Dewey, who held back from exploring in detail the institutional mechanisms of democracy.

Within the context of epistemic theories of democracy, Elizabeth Anderson (2006) has recently developed a Deweyan alternative to existing epistemic approaches, thereby proposing an experimentalist understanding of politics. For Anderson, a Deweyan approach to democracy involves introducing the experimentalist and fallibilistic method of natural science by understanding political institutions and practices as experimental mechanisms:

Most importantly, Dewey's experimentalist model of democracy helps us see the epistemic import of several democratic institutions that sustain its dynamism, its capacity for change: periodic elections, a free press sceptical of state power, petitions to government, public opinion polling, protests, public comment on proposed regulations of administrative agencies. In Dewey's model, these are mechanisms of feedback and accountability that function to institutionalize fallibilism and an experimental attitude with respect to state policies. They push governments to revise their policies in light of evidence—public complaints, as expressed in both votes and discussion—that they are not working, or expected not to work. On Dewey's model, votes and talk reinforce one another, the votes helping to insure that government officials take citizens' verbal feedback seriously, the talk helping to define and articulate the message conveyed by votes. (Anderson 2006: 14) Next to pointing to the epistemic benefits of feedback and revision, the Deweyan model of democracy is also able to account for the epistemic benefits of disagreement, which are present at different stages of an "experimentally conceived" democratic process: "during deliberation, at the point of decision (voting), and after a decision has been made." (Anderson 2016: 15) These two sets of "epistemic benefits," make an epistemic justification of democracy on the basis of Dewey's experimentalism particularly productive. Furthermore, it is not merely about justifying existing democratic institutions but also about transforming them in this experimentalist dimension.

These experimentalist approaches are oriented toward the analysis of institutionalized democratic practices. Only, with a few exceptions, Deweyan experimentalism has not been explored in a way to characterize the epistemic practices of social movements.

INQUIRY AND ARTICULATION—THE LINK BETWEEN CRITICAL THEORY, PRAGMATISM, AND HERMENEUTICS?

The present attempt to provide a pragmatist account of the epistemic practices of social movements, drawing on Dewey's idea of inquiry, mobilizes at different stages of its argumentation motives that have a more explicit formulation in another important theoretical tradition of the nineteenth and twentieth centuries such as philosophical hermeneutics.

With this tradition, Dewey shares the idea that inquiry represents a process of articulation (Jung 2009). From the point of view of social inquiry, one could say that inquiry articulates the social world by giving it a specific shape. By understanding inquiry as articulation, Dewey approaches the expressivist tradition of Herder, Hegel, and more recently, Charles Taylor (1977, 1985, 1990) and Robert Brandom (2019). In its political version, the notion of articulation points to the basic intuition that many of the realities—emotions, collective identities, public problems—that are part of political life are not fully independent of the very process by which citizens account for them. Understanding democracy as articulation means acknowledging that the apparent descriptions and evaluations in our democratic debates and decision-making processes are, at least partially, the result of constructive processes. In the available literature, the notion of articulation has rarely been mobilized in approaches to democracy. Radical democrats such as Ernesto Laclau (2005) represent an exception to the rule. However, their view of articulation of populist identities is purely constructive, leaving aside the "objective side" (Jaeggi 2014: 184) of articulation, that is, the fact that problems are only partially constructed, since any definition of a problem does draw on certain facts that characterize a vague situation.

Drawing on the tradition of Romantic expressivism, Charles Taylor has developed this notion in order to account for subjective processes involved in "becoming one-self" (Selbstwerdung) (Jaeggi 2014: 184). Rahel Jaeggi has stressed the particular use of the notion of articulation to account for an essential aspect of subjectivity, namely, the question about "the relation between what is previously given and what is constructed or made" (Jaeggi 2014: 184). Hence, "the interesting point, then, is that in a certain respect articulation must accomplish two things: it makes or creates what is articulated, but it must simultaneously correspond to what it finds before itself as unarticulated (the material, as it were, that it deals with)" (Jaeggi 2014: 184). Certainly, Charles Taylor develops the notion of articulation in a very different context from that of a theory of inquiry. However, Dewey's definition of inquiry shows interesting resemblances with Taylor's idea of articulation. These resemblances become particularly evident if we recall Jaeggi's own reconstruction of Dewey's notion of inquiry as a process of problem-solving where problems are "at once given and made" (Jaeggi 2014: 142). Hence, according to Dewey, "Although the problems arise 'from the world,' at the same time this world (i.e., the situation) is not independent of us. It is, as Heidegger puts it, 'round about us' [um uns herum]; as a practical nexus, it is related to us" (Jaeggi 2014: 185).

Apart from well-known idea that inquiry represents the progressive determination of a partially vague situation, which can be understood in terms of articulation, we can find at least two more senses in which inquiry may be called an articulative process. The first one has to do with what Dewey characterized as the progress from suggestions to ideas. Hence, as we saw, Dewey understands suggestions as "vague" ideas which are progressively determined during inquiry. This progressive process of determination takes place, first, by putting suggestions in relation with other ideas, thereby exploring their potential meaning in relation to existing views, knowledge, rhetorical possibilities, and so on. Second, they are determined by being put in an operational relation with this search for facts that help at defining a problem and the generation of new facts in experimental settings meant to test solutions to that problem. For Dewey, the articulation of suggestions represents a particularly creative moment of inquiry, hence, at the beginning, suggestions involve a wide range of meaning possibilities that will be narrowed down within the process of inquiry. Finally, inquiry is articulative to the extent that it is responsible for the articulation of the identity of the inquirer, be it an individual or a collective. Hence, in her intelligent interaction with the environment, the experimentalist inquirer is able to enter into a relation with herself that must be also seen as a process where identity is "at once given and made." This third dimension of inquiry's articulative nature will be developed in detail in chapter 8, where I outline Dewey's theory of social movements as embodying learning processes that are able to articulate collective identities(s). Hence, it is essential for understanding social mobilization as an expressive process in which the identities(s) of struggling groups also go through a learning process that leads to an adequate articulation of injustice.

EXPLORING EXPERIMENTALISM'S
COUNTER-HEGEMONIC POTENTIAL
I: DEMOCRATIC DEEPENING

Having presented Dewey's experimentalist approach to social and political inquiry as including (1) the idea of a fluid and mutually dependent relation between fundamental operations of inquiry and (2) the articulation of vagueness into determination regarding situations (problems), ideas, and identities, it is time now to explore and fledge out in more detail the reasons why I attributed to experimental inquiry a double counter-hegemonic potential. To recall, experimentalism should provide, on the one hand, the cognitive conditions for the emergence of an oppositional consciousness such as the one we find in feminist, ecologists, or worker's struggles. In other words, by adopting experimentalism as the method underlying their normative inquiries, social movements develop important cognitive conditions necessary for the development of counter-hegemonic views on social problems and their solutions. On the other hand, the adoption of experimentalist epistemic practices should contribute—in the disclosive sense I have exposed in part I—to deepening the meaning of our democratic ideals and norms. In part I, I have characterized this "deepening" as involving a political learning process with at least two dimensions: (1) the extension of the range of the practices that can count as democratic, (2) the deepening of the inclusive nature of specific interpretations of democratic norms and values, As in part I, here I propose to focus again on the second. However, in the conclusion I will have a bit more to say about first.

To recall, the aim of part I was not to provide a systematic epistemic justification of democracy but rather to explore the sense in which Dewey conceives of the cooperation between democracy's intrinsic and epistemic values. However, my analysis assumed the possibility of such a systematic epistemic justification. At the present stage, the link we are progressively establishing between the pattern of inquiry and the political power of the epistemic innovations that take place in social movements puts us under a stronger justifying pressure: to what extent should we understand those innovations and operations reconnecting facts and ideas, that is, the "experimentalization" of public cultures of inquiry, as promoting the deepening of our understanding of democracy and democratic practice?

In my view, we can offer an answer to this question by developing a Deweyan justification of democracy. This is so because an epistemic justification of democracy shows that democracy represents a necessary requirement for the epistemic success of the political practices at hand. In this case, epistemic success refers to the capacity of epistemic practices to generate the cognitive conditions for the formation of an oppositional consciousness. That

Dewey provides the theoretical means for formulating an epistemic argument for democracy has been stated by different authors (Putnam 1990; Anderson 2006; Honneth 1998; Festenstein 2018), while others have denied the possibility of such a strategy on various grounds (Hartmann 2003). As I aim at showing, a Deweyan justification of democracy that draws on the notion of experimental social inquiry has the potential not only of justifying democratic norms of inclusion and equality but also of disclosing deep understanding of these norms, in a way that they challenge existing understandings, thereby expanding the limits of our political imagination in the sense social movements have historically done so.

To start, I need to mention that there is not only one possible epistemic strategy for justifying democracy in Dewey's work. Furthermore, while most epistemic approaches have drawn on Dewey's view of inquiry, understood in a broad sense that includes physical as well as social inquiry, I believe that by drawing on the latter we can outline a relevant argument that has remained fully unexplored in the literature up to this day. Social inquiry represents a form of inquiry that Dewey analyzes in a separate chapter of his *Logic* and which has its own specific features distinguishing it from natural sciences. In my view, by drawing on Dewey's notion of social inquiry, we can find a justification of democratic practice that strengthens the meaning of democratic inclusion and equal participation in a deeper sense than its "physical" versions. To this extent, the idea of "deepening" democracy is the requirement of experimental inquiry seems to be more substantially grounded if we take into consideration that political processes represent particular instantiations of social inquiry. But let's take a look first at this distinction between natural and social inquiry in order to see why by drawing on the latter we may provide an argument for inclusion and equal participation that has the potential of deepening well-established interpretations of these political norms.

To recall, in *The Theory of Inquiry* Dewey distinguishes between two main kinds of inquiry: physical and social inquiry, which correspond to the kinds of facts as well as to the kinds of problems inquiry needs to deal with in each case: social natural and social facts, that is, problems emerging from our interaction with nature and, secondly, problems emerging from social interaction. In the present context my aim is to explore the specific elements of social inquiry, since the latter represents the kind of inquiry that is mostly involved in political decision-making as well as in social mobilization. This should, however, not be understood as implying that social movements cannot generate methodological innovations regarding methods of natural-scientific research: AIDS activism represents a good example of the physical-epistemic potential of social mobilization (Bohman 1999). To the extent that physical-scientific practice represents a social practice dependent on collective values (see Putnam 2002; Longino 2002; Kitcher 2001), social movements can throw new light on those values and hence contribute to change the particular practices and methods at work in the study of natural and technical realities.

In Chapter 24 of *The Theory of Inquiry* called "Social Inquiry," Dewey articulates in the logical terms we have previously presented, a critique of actually existing social inquiries. Dewey uses the term "social inquiry" in a wide sense, including not only the formalized practices of what we usually call "social sciences" but also those of the media, state-administrators and— most importantly for the present argument—those of the public(s). In fact, Dewey's view of what he called the "state of social inquiry" of his time can be found in many of his major works dealing with various disciplines: according to Dewey, while inquiry into natural facts had achieved a high degree of development in their capacity to resolve problems, social inquiry in its different forms had remained unable to "satisfy the logical conditions that have to be satisfied in other branches of inquiry" (LW 12: 481). Dewey characterizes this crisis in the terms I have been using in the previous sections, that is, in terms of the relation between facts and ideas:

> But the failure to satisfy the requirement of institution of factual and conceptual subject-matter in conjugate correspondence with each other is such a marked characteristic of the present state of the social disciplines [. . . .] that is necessary to make the point explicitly. (LW 12: 485)

In fact, for Dewey the establishment of a situation of "conjugate correspondence"—in my own words: fluidity—of the two poles of inquiry represents the most central task to be accomplished if society is to be able to take its fate into its hands:

> For if there is one lesson more than any other taught by the methods of physical sciences, it is the strict correlativity of facts and ideas. Until social inquiry succeeds in establishing methods of observing, discriminating and arranging data that evoke and test correlated ideas, and until, on the other side, ideas formed and used are (1) employed as hypotheses, and are (2) of a form to direct and prescribe operations of analytic-synthetic determination of facts, social inquiry has no chance of satisfying the logical conditions for attainment of scientific status. (LW 12: 45)

Even if Dewey's reformist agenda goes hand in hand with an "experimentalization" of the social sciences as well as of other spheres of social inquiry, he also provides a characterization of social inquiry which contrasts to that of physical inquiry. Thus, it is in the specific features Dewey attaches to social inquiry that, as I mentioned, we can find a systematic justification of democratic participation based on the epistemic need of "deepening" existing political norms. Contrary to what some philosophers of science may think, social inquiry and natural science do not differ regarding the presence or not of values in their respective enterprises (LW 12: 161–181). Hence, physical inquiry is embedded in a context of values which give direction to the different operations of inquiry (Putnam 2004; Kitcher 2001). For Dewey, the differences between social and physical inquiry primarily regard the nature of the facts as well as the problems both kinds of inquiries have to do with.

Social facts and problems differ from physical facts and problems at least in three different senses, of which the third one is particularly interesting for the present argument. First of all, social facts have an "intricate" nature that makes them, as well as their study, particularly dependent on "physical" facts: "[f]or the essential conditions which from the physical environment enter at every point into the constitution of socio-cultural phenomena" (LW 12: 485), hence "[n]o individual person and no group does anything except in interaction with physical conditions" (LW 12: 485). Therefore, "[w]ithout physical knowledge [which includes biological knowledge, J.S.Z.] there are no means of analytic resolution of complex and grossly macroscopic social phenomena into simpler forms" (LW 12: 486). Apart from this first trait, Dewey mentions a second one, namely, the particular "historical" nature of social facts. The historicity of social facts points to its continuity with other social facts. Hence, according to this historical nature, any attempts to isolate them from the larger context in which they are embedded should be seen as artificial:

A physical fact may be treated as a "case." Any account of, say, the assassination of Julius Caesar assuredly involves the generic conceptions of assassination, conspiracy, political ambition, human beings, of which it is an exemplifying case and it cannot be reported without the use of such general conceptions. But treatment of it as just and merely a case eliminates its qualities that make it a social fact.

Hence, although observation and assemblage of materials in isolation from their movements into an eventual consequence may yield 'facts' of some sort, the latter will not be facts in any social sense of that word, since they will be not historical. (LW 12: 494–495)

Finally, we come to the last defining trait of social inquiry, one that is particularly relevant for the present argument; hence, social inquiry is characterized by a specific condition of the validity of the hypotheses generated for the resolution of social problems. This specific condition concerns the role played by "associate activity" of the inquiry process. This becomes clear by comparing the activities and kinds of agreements that are logical conditions of validity for physical and social inquiry:

> In physical matters, the inquirer may reach the outcome in his laboratory or observatory. Utilization of the conclusions of others is indispensable, and others must be able to attain similar conclusions by use of materials and methods similar to those employed by the individual investigator. His activity is socially conditioned in its beginning and close. But in physical inquiry the conditioning social factors are relatively indirect, while in solution of social problems they are directly involved. Any hypothesis as to social end must include as part of itself an idea of organized association among those who are to execute the operations it formulates and directs. (LW 12: 465)

For Dewey, the validity test of physical inquiry is, on the one side, to be found in the capacity of the proposed hypotheses to be repeated by other scientists. Repeatability in a larger social context that involves communication among scientists and sharing of methods and results represents then the condition fixing our beliefs. Together with the idea that people differently situated may contribute to provide new information, new facts and ideas, the former view on the sociality of scientific practice is usually mobilized within the context of epistemic justifications of democracy (Putnam 1990). However, one may wonder if the epistemic process may not have stronger communicative and cooperative requirements, more than those of a community of physical scientists, since even Dewey conveys that in the latter case the "conditioning social factors are relatively indirect." This in my view is the case with social inquiry, where such factors are "directly involved." Hence, as the previous passage points out, from a logical perspective the validity of social hypotheses such as the implementation of certain policies cannot be established without the de facto agreement of activities of those who are involved in the latter, something that generates stronger social requirements for inquiry:

> This difference [i.e. the difference between the subject matters of physical and social inquiry, J.S.Z.] makes a great practical difference in the conduct of inquiry: a difference in the kind of operations to be performed; these associated activities enter into the idea of any proposed solution. The practical difficulties in the way of securing the agreements in actual association that are necessary for the required activity are great. (LW 12: 497)

This stronger version of the sociality of the epistemic process as requirement for the effective solution of social problems can be mobilized for an epistemic justification of democracy. Hence, the "agreements in actual association" that "enter into the idea of any proposed solution" can only be secured through the inclusion in the epistemic process of the wills, perspectives, and experiences of those who are to participate in those associations. In other words, the identification, definition, and resolution of social problems involves direct and stronger forms of social cooperation among those affected by the problem-solving activity since this is the only way to secure the agreement of activities that constitutes the logical condition of any social problem-solution. Furthermore, the ways of understanding inclusion in inquiry must remain open to the interpretative activity of the affected, since only through their interpretative work can inclusion become a means to securing the necessary agreement in activities in which they are involved. It is therefore from the perspective of social inquiry that our argument about the deepening potential of social movements can actually be systematically argued for. While classical interpretations of Dewey's epistemic argument for democracy rest on his idea of physical inquiry, I believe that the features characterizing social inquiry that I have identified can play a role in explicating deeper senses of democratic inclusion.

Both the idea that deepening democratic cooperation represents a requirement for the effective resolution of social problems, and that experimentalism represents a particularly deep form of democratic cooperation that includes the activities by which citizens identify and define problems generate hypothesis, implementing and testing them represents a central pole of the normative argument deployed in this book. Hence, its central normative thesis is that the adoption of experimentalism as the set of epistemic conditions that are particularly helpful in building an oppositional consciousness that is able to effectively fight injustice and promote justice goes hand in hand with the deepening of the democratic cooperation among members of social movements. We can say that deepening democracy and building counter-hegemonic consciousness must be considered to be two sides of the same experimentalist coin.

EXPERIMENTALISM AND THE BUILDING
OF OPPOSITIONAL CONSCIOUSNESS:
ADORNO AND DEWEY

After having developed an argument not only for inclusion and equal participation, but for deepening the ways in which both norms are realized based on the idea of experimental social inquiry, it is now time to explore the other side of the coin, namely, the idea that experimentalism, understood as fluid and articulative inquiry, can contribute to the generation of an oppositional consciousness. I propose to undertake this exploration, by examining the notion of "non-reified" thinking by putting into discussion Theodor Adorno and John Dewey. According to Adorno's lectures on reified thinking (2017 (1958), thinking is reified when it is not able to go beyond the concepts and facts that appear to us immediately in our everyday experience. These ideas and facts are usually so organized that they tend to reproduce and hide existing power structures. As a consequence of this limitation, reified thinking contributes to the confirmation and further reproduction of the status quo. In my view, experimentalism represents a paradigmatic form of nonreified thinking that, due to its fundamental features, is able to reconfigure our views in ways that challenge existing power relations. Hence, experimentalism does not only promote deeper forms of inclusion of individual perspectives which are essential for the generation of counter-hegemonic views on social problems. More importantly, it also makes fluid the connection between individual experiences and the symbolic means that are meant to account for those experiences. To this extent, experimentalism provides the logical conditions for articulating of social suffering and vague feelings of injustice (Renault 2008, 2019) in a way that challenges existing ideological constructions. Let's explore this idea in more detail.

ADORNO'S CHARACTERIZATION OF REIFIED THINKING

It should be noted, first of all, that when Adorno criticizes in his lectures the reified thinking of his time as hiding power relations, he has in mind the sociological research of his time. However, as he himself sometimes admits in his lectures, his characterization is also valid for what Dewey would call "habits of mind" of his contemporaries, sociologists or not. Hence, for Adorno, the tendency to reified thinking is not only something that affects sociology but it is also a more general feature characterizing contemporary minds—not the least due to the pervasiveness of culture industry.

In his critique of reified thinking, Adorno discusses what he takes to be its two main paradigmatic forms: one is rationalism and the other, "positivism." Through the evident differences lying between them, both ways of thinking have in common a central premise, namely, that knowledge has its ultimate basis on some instance that works as absolute and which provides a source of certainty in inquiry. Here it is difficult not to point already to Dewey's *Quest for Certainty* (1929), where he depicts a story of the emergence of the human need for certainty in an uncertain world, which he takes to be at the root of many social ills of contemporary societies (see also Westbrook 71–77). But let's come back to Adorno's critique of positivism: in this case, the place of the absolute, ultimate instance is filled by what positivists commonly call the "observed facts." Observed facts are taken to be the last instance of knowledge. This means for Adorno, that for reified inquiry into social phenomena, there is no sensed need to go beyond those facts which appear as certain and immediate to experience. However, as Adorno shows through examples from his own research, immediately experienced facts always often hide another dimension which cannot be perceived by common empirical procedures. This dimension corresponds to the general structures that are at the basis of individual behavior and experience, which somehow must be brought by thought from outside of the object of inquiry. Reified thinking is unable to point to these general structures since it only sees in the given facts the confirmation of established ideas. This experience of fixation (Verfestigung) and solidification (Verhärtung) is not only something that happens to the reified approach to facts in sociological inquiries. It also affects concepts put at play in inquiry as incapable to be transformed, just as we can find in Max Horkheimer's description (1992) of what traditional theory is against critical theory. Hence, in Adorno's own words:

> And it is certainly most important, as a thinking individual, resolutely to resist any mechanical application of one's own categories—in other words, to reflect constantly upon these categories, to examine whether they are still indeed appropriate to the things which are being thought under them. (Adorno 2017: 92)

In short, the main feature characterizing reified thinking in social inquiry is that it stops at the precise moment when it should go further into the veiled dimension of practice and experience but also into the exploration of the adequacy of established categories or concepts to the things they are supposed to account for. By interrupting the process of thinking on the side of facts or on the side of concepts, it remains in a stage in which its only epistemological and practical achievement consists in confirming and reproducing the status quo.

DEWEY AND ADORNO ON NONREIFIED THINKING

There are important differences between Adorno and Dewey regarding the question of what it means for thinking to not to be reified. However, comparing both views at a logical level seems to be a promising task since it evidences the possibility of having alternative models of nonreified thinking. First of all, as we have seen in the previous section, for Adorno but also for Dewey it is wrong for social thinking to assume that there is any kind of absolute instance that represents the basis of knowledge. As a consequence, there is not sensed need to stop thinking when it actually should not stop.

On the contrary, inquiry stops only when a social phenomenon is unmasked (Adorno) or when a problem is solved (Dewey). But even in these cases, thinking should not actually "stop" since the very thing that is thought about is in constant change so that further thinking is always needed. This has, secondly, a direct translation into the relation between facts and concepts. Hence, we have to think of it as a fluid relation, one in which facts may contribute to change our concepts, categories, or ideas and in which our concepts, categories, or ideas may contribute to discovering new facts or interpret them differently. However, for each author this fluid relation of mutual influence between facts and concepts has different ontological sources and shapes. For Adorno, fluidity has its roots in the very contradictory nature of thought and reality: it is a dialectical fluidity. So, for example, in his famous sociological study about citizens from Darmstadt, sociological inquiry brought the general idea of class into the picture once it has empirically established that there is a contradiction between two empirical facts: people's hatred against state workers and their few bad experiences with them. Surely, this contradiction can only be perceived if thought has been trained for critical-dialectical thinking so that we need to talk about a double source of fluidity: some kind of trained predisposition to critical-dialectical thinking and social reality itself as a source of contradictions. For Dewey, fluidity between facts and concepts also means that the observation of facts and the transformation of concepts mutually influence each other in social inquiry. However, this fluid dynamics is not rooted in the contradictory nature of social reality but on the very experience of problematic situations as situations that need to be progressively determined in inquiry. For Dewey, social problems may involve conflicts, and conflicts may be rooted in contradictions, but contradictions are not the only source of social problems.

Finally, and thirdly, both critical thinking and intelligent inquiry point to the transformation of existing social relations. Dewey's notion of inquiry expresses this idea positively in the idea of experiment: any intended transformation of social relations should be taken as an hypothesis to be tested in experience. For Adorno, the transformation of social relations represents the pretheoretical goal of critical-dialectal thinking. Surely, critical-dialectical thought is more concerned with the critique of existing relations than with the positive proposal of practical hypothesis as in Dewey's case. However, it sees itself confronted with the need of transforming the social world, even if only from a negative point of view of avoiding injustice. In any case, this social-transformative feature is also logical in the sense I am using this expression here because it concerns both facts and concepts in their capacity to influence one another. Hence, transformation (positively or negatively understood) is about transforming facts in virtue of concepts and to transform our concepts in virtue of facts.

Summarizing, we can speak of three features characterizing nonreified thinking: Lack of a last instance that works as an absolute, fluid relation between facts and ideas that I have and transformation of the (social) world as the vanishing point of thinking. As we saw, these features are shared both by Adorno's view of dialectical thinking and Dewey's notion of experimentalism. Hence, they are aspects that we have previously seen in the analysis of the fundamental operations of inquiry, even if we have used different terms to discuss them. Through the comparison with Adorno's critique of reified thinking we can understand now, however, in what sense experimentalism can promote the generation of counter-hegemonic views that are able to challenge the status quo. Hence, experimentalism is a form of nondogmatic thought that does not look for absolute certainties, but rather is open to revision through the new experiences of those included in the inquiry process. At the same time, experimental inquiry points to social change through the experimental implementation of hypothesis and relates, due to the internal correlation between the different operations of inquiry, problem-solving to problem-definition. This does not mean that only those problems that can be easily solved can come to be seen as problems. But it does mean that the projection of alternatives of the social world goes hand in hand with the intelligent consideration of possibilities for action. Both in the framing of a situation as unjust and in the projection of more just social relations the possibility of going beyond hegemonic understandings is enabled by both, the maximally inclusive character of experimental methods and the nondogmatic, fluid and practical nature of nonreified, experimentalist thinking.

INQUIRY AND THE FEELING OF INJUSTICE

Another productive way of making the experimentalist view of epistemic practices productive for an analysis of the counter-hegemonic power of social movements consists in showing how they can account for the cognitive processes involved in what Emmanuel Renault has called the "experience of injustice" (2019, see also Honneth 1995 and Pappas 2016). This involves including the idea that very often counter-hegemonic inquiries represent the articulation of the cognitive content that is present in negative political emotions like suffering and rage. More particularly, the identification of an articulative dimension of inquiry expressed in the idea of the correlation among basic epistemic operations makes Dewey's model particularly fit for accounting for the normative-cognitive dimension of people's efforts to make sense of situations that they primary sense as involving an indeterminate moral grievance. As Renault shows, in many cases we must see the processes leading to the generation of a "frame of injustice" (cadre d'injustice) from a first, vague, impression or feeling of injustice (sentiment d'injustice) as one of progressive determination of the cognitive content embodied in the latter:

> the negative feelings involved in the experience of injustice, like shame or indignation, have a specific cognitive content, an "opportunity for moral insight"[48] that, in certain conditions, can lead individuals to a clear awareness of the injustice that they endure. (Renault 2019: 51)

In his characterization, Renault draws on some central insights in Honneth's *Struggle for Recognition*, which he understands as an outline of the moral grammar underlying the normative conflicts of our modern societies. According to Renault, we must see in the feelings of injustice the negative experience of a denial of a more or less implicit expectation of recognition. The passage from this feeling to a more adequate understanding of the injustice involved in the denial of recognition represents, however, more than a process of explication of this moral grammar. Renault characterizes it as a process of articulation that has two main interrelated dimensions: on the one hand, any experience of injustice has at its base a referential dimension, that is, a "situation of injustice." This idea plays a central role in his social-critical project since it points to the contextual nature and particularity of the experience of injustice:

> In fact, individuals always associate their feeling of injustice with particular social interactions or contexts, and it is likewise always against the latter that they direct their complaints concerning justice. To be sure, one can have a diffuse intuition of a structural injustice (for example, of the universally unjust character of a structurally inegalitarian society), but the crystallization of such an intuition into a feeling of injustice is always occasioned by a situated injustice, and it is beginning with such feelings that the consciousness of structural components of injustice can then be reflectively articulated. (Renault 2019: 37)

On the other hand, an experience of injustice involves the articulation of the principles, the norms and values, that allow for a characterization of a problematic situation as unjust. According to Renault, when "social experience contains within it an element that could thwart the framing of experience, as well as affective and cognitive resources capable of entailing a transformation of the frame of experience" (Renault 2019: 52). In light of the normative expectations that are disappointed in the concrete situation, the epistemic need arises for the generation of a new frame that characterizes the problematic situation. The experiences of injustice as a cognitive reaction to the nonfulfillment of normative expectations involve a reflexive return to the very normative expectations that constitute the normative ground for mobilization.

According to Renault, both the determination of a situation as one yielding injustice and the reflexive return to the normative expectations that are at the origin of the moral feelings motivating social struggle are to be seen as articulative processes in a sense similar to Dewey's notion of experimentalism. This becomes particularly clear in the case of what Renault calls, with Jacques Rancière, the "experience of wrong" (l'experiènce du tort), which constitutes one of the paradigmatic objects of Renault's study:

> In the case of a wrong, the feeling of injustice is accompanied by a reflexive effort aimed at the explication of what is at play in this feeling, an effort that stumbles upon the lack of an adequate justification and does not necessarily lead to the formulation of alternative justifications. The theory of recognition extends this reflexive moment by making explicit the different kinds of normative expectations that are at stake in the experience of injustice. And it attempts to complete this imperfect hermeneutic of injustice by integrating these normative expectations within the definition of justice. (Renault 2019: 54)

The experience of tort represents only one of the possible forms in which the injustice of a situation may be experienced. According to Renault:

> the experience of injustice can take three different forms. A feeling of injustice could be based upon an assessment that the principles of justice established in the political public sphere or in particular institutional arenas have been violated. It could also be based upon the feeling that these principles are understood in a too-restrictive sense, because their interpretation in fact excludes groups of individuals from the rights that they define. Finally, it could be based upon the feeling that these principles are false because they are consistent with injustices that are as grave as they are inexpressible in the established normative language. (Renault 2019: 45)

While in the first case the epistemic practices of mobilized groups have merely to do with the identification of a situation as not fulfilling certain normative principles which are clearly formulated, in the second and third cases the deployment of the cognitive potential of an experience of injustice involves a work of interpretation of the very principles that are to be applied in the characterization of the situation. In my view, Dewey's idea of experimentalist inquiry not only can account for the epistemic activity involved in each of these different ways of experiencing a situation as unjust. Moreover, it provides a set of basic requirements that are to be fulfilled by those epistemic processes if they are to generate "adequate" frames of injustice. As we saw, these criteria do not only concern the inclusion of the maximal number of individuals involved in the situation but more fundamentally, the very methods by which situations are described and normatively judged, norms are collectively interpreted and new categories are generated.

HYPOTHESIS-FORMATION: THE WORK OF IMAGINATION

Finally, as we have pointed, from an experimentalist point of view, the generation of a frame of injustice that is able to account for particular situations must go hand in hand with the consideration of possible solutions and the means for attaining them. This is due to the fact that experimentalism involves the (re-)connection of operations of inquiry so that no operation takes an autonomous role, thereby blocking the necessary mutual relation between facts and ideas in inquiry. In this regard, the progressive determination of a feeling of injustice must be accompanied by a positive understanding of better social relations. In principle, this understanding of a more just society can assume different degrees of determination, be abstract or more concrete. As we saw, disconnecting operations of problem-definition from the elaboration of hypotheses involves the loss of an important protection against the artificiality of social problems. Since the artificiality of a problem has to do with the rejection of its "objective" dimension, we must see hypothesis-formation—so long as it remains connected to the other operations—as contributing to an integration between the given and made aspects of social inquiry. However, the anchorage in "reality" promoted by hypothesis-formation does not involve a rejection of the major role played by imagination in all stages of inquiry, and most particularly in the "projection" of a transformation of a situation of injustice.

For José Medina (2012), one specific aspect that characterizes the counter-hegemonic power of mobilization is the capacity of collective epistemic practices to promote and integrate individual creativity in the formulation of what Dewey calls hypotheses, solutions, or plans of action. Medina uses the expression "resistant imaginations" to explore the counter-hegemonic power of this dimension of human cognition. While social imagination can often work in oppressive ways by opening up possibilities for some and foreclosing them for others, imagination can also be mobilized in emancipatory forms. In Medina's words: "resistant ways of imagining can contest exclusions and stigmatizations, and they can help us become sensitive to the suffering of excluded and stigmatized subjects" (Medina 2012: 252). Medina connects the possibility of developing resistant imaginations to the following conditions: "our imagination has to become pluralized, polyphonic and, experimentalist" (Medina 2012: 252).

For Medina, the possibility of resistant imaginations is linked to the pluralization of epistemic practices, which goes beyond deliberation:

> Unlike the deliberations of cold hypothetical reasoning where we remain mere spectators and contemplate situations that are simply given to us, the dramatic imagination presents us with counterfactual scenarios in which we are effectively and morally implicated and, as a result, we may be willing or unwilling to entertain such scenarios in the terms given to us. (Medina 2012: 255)

In my view, Dewey's thesis of the openness of the process of idea- or hypothesis-generation, as involving a characterization of the progressive determination process that goes from suggestions to ideas, can accommodate the emancipatory potential of what Medina calls resistant imaginations. Moreover, the characterization of experimentalism as embodied in different practices and involving different basic interrelated operations promotes the "resistant" use of imaginations in at the different stages of inquiry: that of the determination of social problems, that of the practical implementation of hypothesis through an experimental setting, and so on. According to this model, imagination becomes resistant when it is integrated in the interplay between ideas and facts, but also when it contributes to this interplay by promoting the generation of methodological innovations, thereby contributing to polyphony and the pluralization of methods involved in an experimental culture of public inquiry.

CONCLUDING REMARKS

In this chapter I have explored Dewey's notion of experimental inquiry in its double quality to promote the articulation of unjust situations as well as the creative search for justice, and to expand the meaning of democracy by promoting deeper forms of inclusion and equality of participation. As we saw, the fundamental operations of experimental inquiry can be embodied in a plurality of ways. It is precisely through the pluralization of epistemic practices that participants are able to embody the basic operations of inquiry. This will be clear in the next chapter, when we see how the development of many different forms of epistemic practice can be described from the point of view of the introduction of experimental inquiry. The present exploration has taken us through a long way of examination of Dewey's theory of experimental inquiry. I hope to have shown that experimentalism represents a plausible account of the basic structure collective inquiries need to have if they are to enable the generation of counter-hegemonic innovation in conditions of ideological hegemony. Hence, due to its features as a pluralist, inclusive, articulative, fluid, praxis-oriented, and creative process it seems to be well positioned to overcome the kind of pathologies underlying hegemonic public inquiry, which I have characterized with the Adornian term "reified thinking." In other words, the adoption experimentalism provides a plausible explanation why social movements are sometimes able to overcome the symbolic burdens imposed by hegemonic cultures and provide alternative view on injustice and just social relations. At the same time, adopting experimentalism also means promoting democratic advancement. This would explain why, as the case of consciousness-raising paradigmatically shows, some social movements have been able to develop more democratic forms of political practice. These practices have proven to be more inclusive and equal, and they have become historically standards against which the democratic quality of other practices has been evaluated. As I will develop in the coming chapters, my empirical hypothesis is that consciousness-raising represents a particular way in which experimentalism has been put in practice by social movements. What once emerged from the attempt to account for the life experiences of women in a way that challenges their hegemonic interpretation represented, in virtue of its epistemic requirements, a way of deepening our interpretation of what it means to practice democratic inclusion and equality.

As I made clear in the introduction of the book, by developing a broad notion of experimentalism in social matters and pointing to its double counter-hegemonic potential, my aim has been to present a plausible candidate that explains why, in many cases, social movements that struggle against injustice and for more just social relations, are able to advance democracy, even if the latter may not be their main priority. My first point is that experimentalism might be able to explain (1) why some social movements have been able to articulate experiences of injustice in ways that, retrospectively, can be seen as moral advancements, such as the emergence of the notion of "sexual harassment" in the feminist movement. My second point is that (2) experimentalism explains why those epistemically successful processes have also contributed to changing our understanding of politics in a way that deepens our understanding of basic political norms. By "deepening" democracy I refer, as Honneth does, to the idea that democratic practices become more inclusive and cooperative. The Deweyan epistemic justification of democracy I have developed intended to show to what extent the success—namely, the fact that they can be retrospectively seen as contributing to moral advancements—of the epistemic practices of social movements is linked to the conditions that deep forms of democracy are put in practice, forms that usually challenge hegemonic understandings of what it means to participate in democratic life.

Chapter 6

Experimental Epistemic Practices in Social Movements

In the previous chapter I have examined Dewey's notion of experimentalist epistemic practices in order to account for their double counter-hegemonic capacity: to promote the emergence of an oppositional consciousness and to advance democratic transformations. Experimentalism constitutes thereby the core of the argument deployed in this book: it establishes the connection between the epistemic needs experienced by those groups struggling against unjust social relations and their capacity to promote and deepen democratic practice. As I have shown, the double counter-hegemonic capacity of experimentalist practices is mainly due to two features: their capacity to make fluid the relation between the fundamental operations of any inquiry, and more concretely, the relation between facts and ideas, and its expressive form, that is, its capacity to acknowledge the vagueness of problems and to articulate them in an inclusive way. Both can be realized in actual inquiry in very different ways, ranging from the introduction of story-telling, the promotion of imagination, artistic expression, to the implementation of real life experiments. It is now time to explore in what terms the idea of experimentalist epistemic practice can be useful for understanding the activities of inquiry that take place in social movements.

Note that my aim is not to argue that all social movements, in virtue of the fact that they organize as movements, are able to put in practice experimentalist practices. As we will see in chapter 8, this capacity depends on social factors promoting or blocking experimentalist inquiry. Rather, my thesis is that experimentalism, as I have characterized in the previous chapter, provides a promising tool for accounting for certain achievements in social movements. These achievements include, on the one hand, the capacity of a social movement to produce counter-hegemonic perspectives: new categories, new concepts, alternative forms of social classification, new self-understandings and interpretations of values and norms, in general, the cognitive conditions for the generation of an oppositional consciousness. On the other hand, the capacity to generate new forms of political organization, new forms of communicating and listening, new ways of sharing information and experiences, of interacting with one another, of communicating with other actors such as media, state institutions, or groups opposing them. In many cases, parting from experimentalism allows us to grasp the connection between the generation of counter-hegemonic output and counter-hegemonic forms of democracy that emerge in social movements. Hence, as I have shown in the previous chapter, experimentalism only grants its epistemic success by deepening the democratic nature of the inquiries that take place in social struggle.

We can find in the literature many analyses of the presence in social movements of practices aiming at changing and transforming hegemonic, power-stabilizing views on social reality. In the course of the preceding chapters, we have had the opportunity to mention some particularly well-known examples, such as consciousness-raising meetings and testimonio practices. Next to these well-known and well-studied practices, many other forms of methodological innovations have been studied in sociological literature. Thus, as we saw in the previous chapter, while the collective articulation of particular needs and points of view can take the form of a consciousness-raising meeting, the formation of reading publics, the development of artistic movements, the celebration of citizen assemblies on the squares of big cities around the planet, and so on, might also be seen as forms of organization of epistemic practices that try to respond to the logical needs of social inquiry under the limited conditions of the given social and natural environment. In so doing, they also make a contribution to enhancing the quality of public discussion and democratic will-formation. Below some examples of epistemic practice will be outlined with a view to stressing the link of the innovative, democratizing features of these practices with the very epistemic goal(s) they are meant to respond.

CONSCIOUSNESS-RAISING MEETINGS

Consciousness-raising groups represent a paradigmatic example of what we mean by an experimentalist practice with double counter-hegemonic potential. We will have the opportunity to discuss consciousness-raising in more detail in chapter 7, since I will take as an example for showing the theoretical advantages of our focus on the fundamental operations of inquiry for the analysis of epistemic practices in social movements. However, some initial remarks can be of help at this point, particularly in order to see it as a particular form of epistemic practice which, like others, is able to put at work essential aspects of experimental inquiry. If we follow Charlene Haddock Seigfried, we should understand the emergence of consciousness-raising meetings as a development responding to the cognitive needs of feminist struggles of the second wave. Seigfried describes this historical development in the following terms:

> In the sixties and seventies, through consciousness-raising sessions and critical reflections on personal experience, it became possible to recognize, name, and criticize the web of social, cultural, and political structures within which experiences took on the particular oppressive dimensions they did. (Seigfried 1996: 153)

These groups also "generated a sense of sisterhood and conviction that their political analyses truly named, and provided a remedy for, the felt oppression" (Seigfried 1996: 153). For Seigfried, this sense of sisterhood was, at the beginning, mainly due to the very homogeneity of the participants in consciousness-raising groups, namely, white, middle-class, heterosexual women. Seigfried depicts how over time other groups of women were included in the meetings, showing thereby the one-sidedness of the previous views on oppression the first participants had developed. For Seigfried, however, "the wrong position was not simply replaced by the right one but [. . .] gradually each modified her initial stance as she assimilated different ways of naming the contested experiences" (Seigfried 1996: 154–155). Seigfried's approach is illuminating since it not only portrays consciousness-raising practices as "truly" naming felt oppression—thereby going beyond a mere disclosive function (see Bohman 1998)—but also as experimental epistemic practices that were able to promote the progressive integration of experiences of different social groups, even if this process was not a conflict-free one.

In a different context, that of the development of the notion of epistemic injustice, Miranda Fricker (2007) similarly conceives of consciousness-raising groups as responding to a cognitive need: the articulation of experiences in a way that overcomes the conceptual limitations to be found in what she calls "the common hermeneutical resource," which refers to the general stock of conceptual resources available to individuals in a given time and place for making sense of their own experiences. According to Fricker, consciousness-raising meetings respond to the need to correct gaps in conceptual resources by trying to make sense of women's own experiences. As an example of what we could here call an "epistemic achievement" in consciousness-raising meetings, Fricker points to the emergence of the notion of "sexual harassment" which, among many other things, proved to be useful in describing the experiences of many women at the workplace. Drawing on Seigfried's and Fricker's accounts, we can observe that the particular forms of the organization of communicative practices, the atmosphere of "cognitive confidence" created in the communicative contexts, the concrete forms of organizing discussion, and so on, constituted an innovative way of involving women in sharing and collectively reflecting upon the value and meaning of their life experiences.

What we should retain is that, arising from the cognitive needs of accounting for woman's situated experience, these new methods challenged the hegemonic ways of organizing operations involving the collection of what Dewey calls "experiential material" and the formulation of (hypothetical) solutions to women's problems. They did it by opening up their inquiries to include the expression of women's experiences, for example, by introducing story-telling in their discussions. Hence, introducing story-telling can be seen, in many epistemic contexts, as a way to make people's inquiries more experimental. This is so because story-telling, as many other "methods of inquiry," can play in certain contexts a rearrangement of ideas through the introduction of new experienced facts. Surely, story-telling, as any other form of collective inquiry, can be reified, thereby adopting fixed patterns of inquiry, separating fundamental operations (problem-definition, problem-solution, etc.) from each other, excluding perspectives and reproducing the views of the powerful. Reification is a risk that can affect any form of communication and practice, including, as Young has shown, the mutual exchange of reasons. However, we can see how, in certain situations, story-tellers are able break with previously existing, "pathological" patterns of inquiry in public debate. This is why experimentalism constitutes a productive perspective from which we can assess the quality of epistemic practices: it is able to point precisely to the moments where inquiry is not reified, but is kept fluid and articulative. In the same experimentalist spirit, participants in consciousness-raising also did an enormous effort of creativity by coming up with new terms and categories that were able to account for their life experiences in ways that were fair to them.

We can see that the epistemic potential of social movements might consist in offering new ways of providing alternative, counter-hegemonic methods of inquiry capable of overcoming the exclusionary effects generated by dominant ones in virtue of their experimentalization. At the same time, through this epistemic innovations such as the introduction of story-telling or the creative dealing with social categories, feminists consciousness-raising groups contributed to the generation of counter-hegemonic democratic cultures, pointing to alternative ways of relating to each other that could be appropriated as deeper realization of the democratic ideal.

TESTIMONIO

According to Iris Marion Young, practices of testimonio have, come to the represent, next to consciousness-raising, a paradigmatic example of the "political function of storytelling" (Young 2001: 71):

> Some resistance movement leaders in Central and South America narrate their life stories as a means of exposing to the wider literate world the oppression of their people and the repression they suffer from their governments. Often such testimonios involve one person's story standing or speaking for that of a whole group to a wider, sometimes global, public, and making claims about that public for the group. (Young 2001: 71)

Practices of testimonio have had a strong impact in the public life of many Latin-American countries. They have not only contributed to a visibilization of injustices and crimes committed under Latin-American dictatorial regimes, but they also have been enacted by the participants in social movements of resistance themselves, thereby contributing to a reflective elaboration of the experiences of success and defeat linked to those movements. Furthermore, testimonio has become a literary genre with fictional and nonfictional elements that stays at the threshold between literature and politics (Beverly 2004). In testimonio, the moment of articulation of indeterminate situations becomes particularly apparent. Hence, story-telling is not about making visible given "facts" to the general public, but also to provide them with a new meaning, one given by the experience of the story-teller. It is also about articulating lived experiences by elaborating inclusive narratives and categories which are able to account for forms of individual and collective suffering (Smith 1998).

In testimonio practices, participants deepen the meaning of democracy, which is now understood in its expressive, narrative, and cooperative radicality. From the perspective of testimonio, doing politics does not only mean giving one's vote, nor exchanging arguments in a neutral atmosphere. It also means explaining stories, sharing experiences with fellow citizens. These practices are counter-hegemonic because they contradict the dominant norms of political practice. They go beyond strictly rationalistic interpretations of the norms of public debate, limited to the exchange of rational arguments. Thus, according to Tully (1995), the use of narrative techniques in public discussion generates new forms of deepening social cooperation. It enhances the capacity to see our own views as strange and unfamiliar. We take distance from them and develop a critical attitude toward them (Tully 1995: 206). In other words, in testimonio we assist to the development of collective inquiries that make possible the revision of one's perspectives thanks to the sympathy that is born in sharing experiences. To use the epistemological terms that I have been using here: Narration is a method of fluidification of the fundamental operations of inquiry and articulation. It allows for revising one's own ideas in light of new "experienced facts" and ideas thanks to elements such as sympathy and aesthetic quality. Again, this capacity to make inquiry fluid makes of story-telling one kind of experimentalist epistemic practice with double counter-hegemonic effect: the capacity to generate new perspectives which challenge existing power relations and, the capacity to deepen the social meaning of political practice, into a more expressive and cooperative one.

RECATEGORIZATION WORK IN THE
CHILEAN DICTATORSHIP

A particularly interesting expression of experimentalism's fluid relation between facts and ideas concerns the way in which social movements are able to change the categories with which we understand the (social) world (see Cefaï & Terzi 2012). Pierre Bourdieu (2001) has provided a variety of analysis regarding how social categories contribute to the reproduction of social relations and how the "symbolic work" of certain individuals—that is, their inquiries—is able to challenge them, thereby undermining the concepts that promote the perpetuation of power relations. But, to what extent does this counter-hegemonic symbolic work express what I have called the fluidification of facts and ideas? In a very different context, Paola Diaz has examined the history of the progressive (re-)categorization of the crimes committed in the context of the Chilean dictatorship by the Asociación de Familiares Detenidos Desaparecidos. Her perspective reveals the counter-hegemonic power of epistemic operations that we have attributed to experimentalism, as well as the difficulties standing on the path to experimental innovation.

Diaz is particularly interested in the variations of the categories employed in the identification of the crimes and the status of the victims over time. More specifically, Diaz describes the struggle of the relatives (mostly wives and mothers) of the victims of the crimes of Pinochet's dictatorship from the point of view of the categories employed to refer to those who disappeared under suspicious circumstances. When doing so, she distinguishes different periods. In the first period,

> [t]hese women called their arrested relatives simply "detainees" and they only considered their possible arrest within the framework of routine and legal procedures.

After months of unsuccessful searches and efforts by the available legal means [. . .] they began to call their parents "not found detainees" (detenidos no encontrados)

From 1975, the grouping Group of families of prisoners gradually replaced the category "missing prisoners" (detenidos desaparecidos) for that of "prisoners not found," and changed its name to "Association of families of missing prisoners." (Diaz 2012: 327, my translation)

Particularly interesting is Diaz's description of how this latter change of name of the relatives' association took place:

The change in categories occurred gradually, in connection with a series of events. First, in 1975 there were press articles [. . .] publishing a list of 119 Chileans who died in clashes between guerrillas. This list of names corresponded to one hundred and nineteen "detainees not found." Then, in 1976, prisoners from the concentration camps were released, but the "detainees not found" were not there. Finally, in 1978, the remains of fifteen peasants previously reported as "detainees not found" were discovered south of the city of Santiago in the locality of Lonquén.

These events and the collection of testimonies from prisoners who passed through the same clandestine detention centers helped to reconfigure the situation. These were no longer "traditional" detainees who could be released, but "missing detainees." (Diaz 2012: 328, my translation)

Diaz's study is interesting in many ways as an example of experimentalist epistemic practice. Hence, it shows how the adoption of an experimental attitude was responsible for the kind of learning process involved in the transformation of the categories that allowed for a better public and legal apprehension of the crimes of the Chilean dictatorship. On the one hand, she shows how the unearthing of the horrible facts of the Chilean dictatorship's crimes—not least with the testimonies of its victims—contributed to articulate the new categories while at the same time these new categories promoted the investigation of new "facts" along with the revision of old facts in a new light. Furthermore, she shows how the adoption of different categories was bound up with different strategies for solving the problem of unjust silencing of those crimes such as the search for legal paths or activities of publication of the crimes. Here we see again what I have called an experimentalist fluidification of inquiry: the categories used in the definition of the "problem" of the crimes of the Chilean dictatorship were put in direct connection with the "problem-solving" strategies oriented toward a just legal and public processing of the crimes. They both served to adequately name those crimes and to efficiently struggle for justice regarding the legal and public consequences of those crimes. Certainly, epistemic practices were taking place in a context of extreme repression where the discovery and public articulation of these new categories was not merely an epistemic issue (Orellana & Hutchison 1991). However, their activities of recategorization in light of new facts and developments, and their (re-)connection of problem-defining categories to the ends of justice as a "solution" represented important means for promoting further public inquiry into facts (about the victims and those responsible for the crimes) as well as for framing the possible actions to be taken.

THE "CONSENSUS-PROCESS"

Casas-Cortés reports about her experience as an engaged social analyst in the Chicago Direct Action Network (DAN). The Chicago DAN was from 1999 to 2002 a global and local resistance network that combined different targets in accordance with a critique of global capitalism. Casas-Cortés's analysis is particularly interesting in this context, since it points at the strong link between the radicalization of democratic understandings and the organization of epistemic practices. A central practice that characterizes the network was the organization and participation in what DAN members called the "consensus process." It is worth quoting a long passage describing this complex set of knowledge-practices as promoting new understandings of democracy:

> Meetings were one of the most important sites for engaging the rules of consensus-process in the Chicago DAN. By following specific prescriptions, these weekly gatherings acted much like experiments in a lab working on generating co-operative and non-authoritarian relationships as the basis of a rethought understanding of democracy. Some of these basic rules were: becoming a good listener; not interrupting people who are speaking; getting and giving support; not speaking on every subject; not putting others down; being explicit and calling attention to oppressive behaviours based on gender/class/race/national origin; and finally the very fact of setting aside time to deal with process. The latter was called a "point of process" and could interrupt the discussion at any point during its course in order to address any question related to procedures. Also, at the moment in which a group decision needed to be made, different steps were taken: clarification, discussion, synthesis and proposal. The engagement of the proposal tried to avoid conflict-reducing techniques such as majority vote, averages, or coin-tossing, embracing the creative production born from disagreements and diverse participation. There were techniques to express differences

and avoid the imposition of a false homogeneous face onto the group. This was done through hand signals that could mean agreement, non-support, standing-aside, withdrawing or blocking the proposal being set forth. We were all so excited and serious about the process! It often mattered as much as the very topic we were discussing. Here, the long tradition of consensus-decision-making practised by movements at different times in U.S. history, ranging from anti-nuclear activists or the Quaker Friends' meetings, was actualized in our weekly meetings. Most of us were learning the procedures for the first time, although a few of the participants had used consensus-based discussions in other settings.

All the great analyses and actions organized during that time shared an important component: the way in which each was organized. While perhaps this is not so obviously a form of "knowledge," it definitely implies a relearning of how to act and think about democracy. Even though we were familiar with representative democratic procedures, these rules were substantially distinct. Engaging them was challenging, since normally, in many social settings, one is not supported to think and live in ways geared towards equal participation, anti-authoritarianism, radical diversity, nonsupremacist behavior, and ultimately, democratic collective action. What mainstream schools teach us to write together or even "think collectively?" (Casas-Cortés, Osterweil & Powell 2008: 35)

Casas-Cortés and colleagues characterize consensus practices as loci for the exercise of democracy, an exercise that involves learning about new micropolitical forms, thereby generating knowledge about forms of democratic organization. Here it is particularly interesting to note that, contrary to the rest of examples we are providing, the "consensus process" is a democratic practice that has itself as an object of epistemic consideration. In other words, democratic practice is seen as an epistemic requirement for producing knowledge about democracy itself. Hence, democratic practice can certainly become a problem to itself and approach in a reflexive way both its intrinsic and epistemic roles.

CONRICERCA AND INCHIESTAS

In the same study, Casas-Cortés and colleagues report on what they take to be another set of knowledge-practices put at work in the context of the so-called Movimento dei movimenti, a movement of movements that met in Genoa in 2012, one year after the death of the activist Carlo Giuliani in the protests against the G8 of the previous year. The authors describe how these movements made use of various Italian and Latin American cultures of inquiry, such as the "conricerca" and worker "inchiestas." These practices "were historically used on the factory floor to come to a mutual understanding

about the working conditions," and building on them "activists and collectives have recently worked to update these research tools in order to try
to make sense of the more diffused struggle in the less delimited space of
contemporary cities" (39). The authors point to the fact that the adoption of
these new practices followed from the collective sense of uncertainty, which
is expressed in the following passage of their Conscienzapolitica website
2003 post:

> So many questions, no given certainty: we need new lenses with which to read
> reality, new forms of collective action to transform it. Ambitiously we speak of
> "conricerca" to point to a process of production of know-how [conoscenza] and
> other knowledges [saperi], of experimentation in new forms of social and politi-
> cal cooperation, of the construction of languages and communication, . . . of
> opening spaces of self-formation and counter-formation. . . . Insofar as they are
> non-conclusive, open and transformative, conricerca is really an open-source,
> non-patentable and constitutively contrary to any form of copyright! (Quoted
> after Casas Cortés, Osterweil & Powell 2008: 39)

In any case, the Movimento dei movimenti is a particularly interesting
example to the extent that its participants were able to recover and reenact
old cultures of inquiry that belonged, for example, to the proletarian tradition. Hence, the mutual epistemic influences and learning processes that we
believe to be a constitutive part of public life take place both in a synchronic
and diachronic sense.

But let's turn to conricerca, since in my view also represents an example
of experimentalist inquiry. Conricerca was a method of political research
promoted both by sociologists and workers in the factories of Italy's industri-
alized north in the 1950s. In contrast to the previous examples, this form of
epistemic method did not arise directly from worker's epistemic needs, but
it was the product of methodological and political reflections about the role
sociology should play in the struggle against capital. Conricerca was meant
to unveil the negative social developments generated in the capitalist order
but also to contribute to effective political organization in workers' collective
struggles.

What is particularly interesting in the context is that in conricerca the radicalization of the democratic quality of workers' organizations was seen as a
condition for its epistemic success. This radicalization involved, according
to Roggero (2011), the promotion of horizontal relations between experts
(sociologists) and workers as knowers. Borio et al.'s characterization is particularly interesting in this context since it focuses precisely on features of the
conricerca that clearly point to fundamental aspects of experimental inquiry
in the way we understand it here:

Conricerca is in contrast, always critique and problematization. It does not allow us to stand idly by on mummified certainties. Conricerca has it that certainties must be acquired in the field, so that we can constantly question them and formulate new hypotheses. The slippery question of identity must be confronted from a similar perspective. We form our identities by critiquing and opposing ourselves to that which exists, and by activating processes that construct alternatives. In this way, identity enables us to recognize ourselves and make ourselves recognized: it is a process, and we cannot allow it to survive unchanged by the dynamics that nourished it, lest it become a deadweight. (Borio, Pozzi & Roggero 2007: 164)

The authors continue to characterize conricerca in contrast to what they call "inquiry." However, it would be wrong to confuse their understanding of "inquiry" with experimental inquiry. On the contrary, their characterization of conricerca seems to be very much in line with the kind of pragmatist experimentalism that we have in mind:

On this basis, we can say that inquiry and conricerca are not the same thing. There are at least three major differences between the two. Inquiry, first of all, is extemporaneous—that is, it lasts for a predetermined time and then stops. This locates it in a medium- to short-range perspective. Its articulation results more than anything else in the rooting of a militant figure who is capable of expressing and allowing for the growth of a knowledge of political intervention. Inquiry gathers data about the political elements of social reality and behaviours; about specific processes of struggle; about the composition of conflict; and about the site where it has located itself. Conricerca, in contrast, configures itself as an open process, a "spiral becoming" that constructs new levels of knowledge and practices, from which one can always start again in order to build others. Second, inquiry is mainly cognitive in its dimensions, whereas conricerca is the concrete activity of transformation of that which exists. It locates itself in a medium range perspective and has a planning horizon. Third and finally, inquiry presupposes a separation between the production of knowledge and the construction of a political path, whereas in conricerca, elaborations of strategy and choices of practices are internal rather than external to the field of cooperation of the co-researchers, in terms of flexible goals, purposes, and trajectories. Often, conricerca is important as a space for the political counter-formation of militants more than for the results. (Borio, Pozzi & Roggero 2007: 168–70)

The three features of conricerca correspond to the idea of experimental inquiry. The third feature is particularly interesting in the present context, since it points to the relation between worker's inquiries and the generation of a political culture among them. This culture is one of "cooperation of the co-researchers, in terms of flexible goals, purposes, and trajectories." Here we see again how an experimentalist culture of inquiry generated in light of an epistemic goal—namely, setting the cognitive conditions for the generation of an oppositional consciousness—cannot be separated from the emergence of a culture of strong cooperation among workers and scientists. The idea, however, that conricerca is often more important for the "political counter-formation of militants more than for the results" does not need to contradict the idea that conricerca is born out of and pursues epistemic needs. It just points to our idea that, once epistemic innovation has taken place, it can be appropriated by agents as a better realization of political practice and be valued as such.

THE HUMAN MICROPHONE

Sociologists, anthropologists, and political theorists have in recent years attempted to grasp the specific features of the cycle of protests that followed the aftermath of the crash of Lehman Brothers in 2008. From a strictly pragmatist perspective, Michael Dorf has suggested that the Occupy Wall-Street movement be seen as possessing the (possibility) of realization of democratic experimentalism, a Dewey-based approach to private organizations that stresses the learning effects of local, experimental inquiries (Dorf 2012). Dorf points particularly to the "democratizing effects" of this movement:

> Part of the misunderstanding of Occupy has been the search of goals for substantive policy, when all along, much of the movement has been about fostering direct deliberation. "General meetings" operate by consensus. The "human microphone" born by necessity when the authorities forbade electric amplification may be thought to serve as a metaphor of the movement as whole: the voice of any one speaker depends on the willingness of the others to amplify it. (Dorf 2012: 267)

For Dorf, the idea of "human microphone" as well as its metaphorical extension represents more adequate realizations of democracy than actually well-established political forms:

> It would be easy to dismiss the human microphone or the communication of views via the waving of fingers as the precious affectations of a movement of arrested adolescents. But such a dismissal would be a demographic oversimplification and largely unfair. Direct deliberation under a rule of consensus is

democratic. What we have come to accept in its stead—representative govern-ment—is, even at its best, only an approximation. (Dorf 2012: 268)

Dorf is particularly interested in seeing these innovative practices as imme-diate ways of enacting a radical understanding of democracy. However, even while the immediate goal of these practices is not to generate "sub-stantial" policies, these mechanisms of deliberation were nonetheless enacted in contexts where different sorts of knowledge (about what and how is to be done by the group, about the injustice of the 1%, about the problems attached to representative democracy, about feminist politics, etc.) needed to be produced.

ASSEMBLIES AS EXPERIMENTAL SETTINGS

We have seen already in the case of the "consensus process" how some move-ments are able to organize experimental situations thereby promoting collec-tive learning. Regarding the protests of the indignados or the 15M movement in Spain, sociologists Estalella & Corsín (2013) have also proposed that we understand citizen assemblies as experimental settings. The authors have provided a detailed analysis of the dynamics of assembly practices by taking as a reference the experimentation theory of Hans-Jörg Rheinberger (1997). Rheinberger conceives of experimentation as a method to generate "a space of novelty and controlled surprise, a domain that keeps a productive ten-sion between that which is stable and what is not" (Estalella & Corsin 2013: 63). Assemblies are conceived of as places of political experimentation in the Rheinbergian sense, that is, as forms of reorganization that consciously generate the conditions for the emergence of novelty, and which find support in such things as the regulation of temporal rhythms—which, for example, makes possible unexpected interruptions of assemblies—and practices of care—which assure the protection and the inclusion of those participating in the assembly practices.

HORIZONTAL DEMOCRACY AND
EFFICIENCY IN A CLIMATE CAMP

A major concern in many social movements regards the compatibility between their radical democratic ideals and their everyday needs to effi-ciently take decisions that are good and fair for all. In an empirical study I personally pursued together with Lisa Herzog, I could observe how the members of a social movement are able to mediate between the two by adopting an experimentalist attitude that shares important features with Dewey's notion of experimental inquiry. This experimentalist attitude could be observed in many of the cooperative activities that took place at the camp: from cooking pizza for hundreds of participants, building a well-working water system to organizing space according to functional, justice-, and care-related criteria. In each of these cases, the promotion of radical horizontality among those who knew how to build a water system and those who did not was only possible by implementing the experimental method: testing new hypothesis instead of merely implementing old solutions, opening design of the tasks to be done to discussion, promoting trial, error, and revision, among other operations. Realizing these operations in the most inclusive possible way involved different forms of practice, sometimes including very subtle elements such as avoiding eye contact when someone asked for "orders," or keeping silent in an assembly when one has already talked for too long.

What was particularly interesting to observe was how the adoption of inclusive experimental practices that promoted horizontality came to be seen by many participants as a condition for the "organizational success" of the camp. Hence, many interviewees in our study pointed to how surprisingly well things worked out when they were organized in such cooperative and experimental ways. Lisa Herzog and I realized that in fact, the democratic organization of cooperative activities generated a sort of efficiency, that, in contrast to standard understandings of efficiency, was based on stable cooperation and strong communicative networks which made it easy for nonexpert individuals to spontaneously jump in. In any case, the adoption of an experimentalist method seemed to be a particularly relevant way in which participants promoted both their radical democratic ideals on the one hand, and efficient cooperation promoting fair results. Surely, the idea that radical democracy was valuable did not directly emerge from their epistemic concerns. Rather, participants valued democracy intrinsically and actually doubted that democratic organization could have positive effects in efficiency and fairness of the decisions of the group. However, the fact that they imported their democratic ideals from a previous activist culture does not mean that their local inquiries represented a moment for experimentation, disclosure, and deepening of the meaning of those ideals. In this process of disclosure, the need to cook pizza efficiently for hundreds of people played certainly a stimulating role since they could experience how certain forms of decentralized decision-making, of interpersonal communication and mutual help, were a condition for the efficiency of the pizza bar.

CONCLUDING REMARKS

The previous analysis aims at opening up a new perspective from which to approach social movements as double counter-hegemonic innovators. In the collective attempt to articulate injustices and project and implement just social relations, social movements are required to develop innovative epistemic practices, practices that challenge the immanent epistemic norms of hegemonic forms of public inquiry. As methodological requirements of social inquiry these norms can make a deeper understanding of democratic practice appear necessary. They can also support those democratic achievements that have been previously developed through other, nonepistemic political learning processes. Hence, in their radical-political function, innovative epistemic norms interact with democratic norms through the stimulation of practices that exceed the limits of established understandings of democratic inclusion and equal participation. Thereby, they reconfigure political norms by deepening their specific meaning. As we saw, they also contribute to expanding the repertoire of the activities that count as political practice (and which must thereby be regulated by political norms).

At the most basic level, in virtue of their experimentalist dimension, many of these innovative practices are able to counteract existing forms of epistemic exclusion. To recall, one can see as epistemically excluded voices that remain irrelevant for collective inquiry, even when those voices can be raised and be listened to, and even when identity prejudice does not bring citizens to consider those voices as less authoritative. Epistemic exclusion concerns the quality of the methods by which people collectively inquire into public problems. Dewey believes that experimentalism in its broad meaning provides the most adequate characterization of the set of epistemic norms that overcome epistemic exclusion. To recall, epistemic norms accrue from people's actual efforts to resolve problems and can be seen as valid and as a priori requirements of inquiry so long as they do not prove to be an obstacle for their main epistemic task. Furthermore, since experimentalism may be realized in an indeterminate plurality of ways, by taking it as an epistemic normative standard put at work in mobilization, we do not need to accept any static consequences for a conception of political practice: epistemic inclusion may always require new methods in light of new instruments at disposal, new blocking mechanisms, and new public environments. Finally, to the extent that it complements and is embedded within a normative dynamics that Honneth describes as promoting further inclusion and generalization, the formation of experimentalist habits on the side of struggling groups can be considered to contribute to political progress. Hence, it is not (only) about correcting the excess or the lack of political equality through the introduction of an epistemic dimension, as Peter would affirm, it is about considering how the epistemic normativity of experimentalism contributes to an always more inclusive understanding of political values. To the extent that experimentalism contributes to promoting political progress by challenging well-established understandings, we can talk in terms of the counter-hegemonic power of the epistemic dimension of mobilization: the power of reconstructing democratic practice.

This has however not been the only sense in which I have been talking about the counter-hegemonic force of the epistemic dimension of political practice. The second sense corresponds to the actual capacity of movements to generate new categories and counter-frames and plans for action in their attempts to identify situations of injustice and promote their abolition. That experimentalism is counter-hegemonic in this content-based sense has been shown in the preceding chapter. Experimentalism in social matters is counter-hegemonic, firstly, because it considers inclusion of the maximal number of voices to be a logical requirement of inquiry. This is due to the fact that the solution of social problems requires an agreement in social activities that can be best secured through the inclusion of social actors in the inquiry process. Secondly, experimentalism has a counter-hegemonic potential because it is able to include and articulate people's voices and experiences through an indefinite variety of practices. Hence, it represents the set of most basic operations that work against epistemic exclusion: here people's experiences are integrated and reflectively appropriated in their factual-ideological connection. Guiding ideas do not block other ideas or experienced facts but are logically dependent on them. Facts are experienced depending on the play of ideas and their practical implementation in reality.

Both the extensive and intensive radicalization of democratic practice promoted by this view of experimentalism cannot be exhausted by Habermas's argumentative view of deliberation as the normatively higher form of democratic practice. Hence, the normative prominence of argumentative discourse in public life may not only generate prejudice-based forms of internal exclusion as reactions of the dominant against groups that are not able to master the logical requirements of deliberation. Even if it may be an important one, deliberation is not the only form of public procedural rationality that promotes the correlation of facts and ideas as well as the interplay among the latter. We may find other forms, such as the "effeminate" communicative practices Kant rejects as part of the emerging public spheres of his time which are able to better perform regarding this essential function of inquiry. In fact, we may venture the thesis that only through the interplay and tension of different forms of communication the epistemic normativity of experimentalism can be realized in political practice. This latter idea represents the normative core of a Frasean view of public life that takes the idea of "counter-hegemonic" practice seriously into account. According to it, epistemic practices, methods, and cultures of inquiry must be seen as constitutive elements of public life open to conflict, mutual influence, and mutual learning. A practice-based critical theory of the public sphere must also focus its attention on the different collective methodologies developed in the course of public inquiry as well as on their mutual interactions. Finally, experimentalism as a counter-hegemonic method promotes the "intelligent" nature of the transformative projects and activities of the mobilized. By doing this, it avoids typical pathologies of inquiry such as the formation of dogmatic habits, forms of conceptual rigidity as well as the artificiality of formulated problems and their proposed solutions or the disconnection of actions from the anticipation of their consequences.

Based on these ideas, I have attempted to understand cognitive innovations in social movements such as the generation of new social categories, of new forms of framing problems and projecting political action and reform as presupposing the development of inquiry operations that embody the basic elements of an experimentalist epistemic normativity. In other words, experimentalism and the specific practices that embody its epistemic normativity represent a methodological response to the cognitive needs that cannot be fulfilled under current forms of public rationality and which, in their most immediate form, can only be "sensed" and progressively articulated in local epistemic contexts of mobilization. The contribution of social movements to political life cannot therefore be reduced to the situated perspectives they can offer to an epistemically static public life but must include the very capacity of producing new practices which, by immediately responding to epistemic requirements, are able to exceed and reformulate the meaning of hegemonic immanent norms of political practice. As the examples of Casas-Cortés, Osterweil, and Powell show, experienced cognitive needs do not necessarily concern nonpolitical forms of justice/injustice. On the contrary, democracy, both in its intrinsic and its epistemic dimension, can become a problem to itself that in its turn can only be confronted with a transformation of political practice. As embodying values of self-determination and cooperation, the methodological innovation must be able to address the needs involved in the identification and articulation of relevant normative values as well as in the judgments concerning a situation from the perspective of "politically unjust" nature. As an instrument for the abolition of injustice and the promotion of just social relations, the democratic method becomes an object for itself: how should we conceive of political practice such that it can learn from its own experience as a problem-solving method?

Part III

EXPRESSIVISM AND SOCIAL MOVEMENTS

COLLECTIVE SELF-APPROPRIATION AND ARTICULATION

Chapter 7

Consciousness-Raising Meetings as Experimental Inquiries

The generation of innovative practices that are able to fully or partially embody the epistemic normativity of experimentalism and thereby promote democracy and democratization is for many social movements not an obvious development. In many cases, not only the inertia of hegemonic habits of public inquiry but also more profound blocking mechanisms seem to stand in the way of an adequate response to the primary "sensed" need of articulating situations of injustice. A systematic exploration of the different mechanisms blocking the possibility of collective learning processes leading to an experimental attitude on the side of the oppressed would exceed the theoretical goals of the present study. Instead of providing such exploration, I will explore some of the central theoretical tools Dewey can provide for understanding the course of those learning processes as well as the general character of the conditions and blocking elements that may be at play.

Before turning into an exploration of Dewey's theory of collective learning processes characterizing the struggles of the oppressed, the present chapter comes back to the question about the applicability of Dewey's experimental model to a theory of social movements. In the present case, my aim is, drawing on the case of consciousness-raising meetings, to further characterize the situation of ideological hegemony that often characterizes the initial stages of many social struggles. Moreover, my goal is to show how the experimentalist approach offers an interesting complement to Miranda Fricker's characterization of the epistemic advantages of consciousness-raising (2007). Fricker has argued that social groups suffer hermeneutical injustices when the symbolic or conceptual resources they have at disposal are unable to account for their own experiences in a way that is satisfactory for those who have them. In this context of ideological hegemony or symbolic domination, Fricker points to the possibility of overcoming hermeneutical injustice by generating innovative practices such as consciousness-raising meetings. Raised within the larger context of a discussion about the meaning of "epistemic injustice," our analysis will focus on the theoretical advantages that follow from the experimentalist approach to epistemic practice we have proposed to follow here. More concretely, Fricker's depiction of the "overcoming" of situations of hermeneutical injustice as involving the local generation of counter-hegemonic notions such as "post-natal depression" and "sexual harassment" within practices that generate "cognitive confidence" will be complemented with the view that makes of the epistemic status of fundamental operations of inquiry a condition of emergence of counter-hegemonic categories.

This chapter provides a first look into Dewey's theory of social domination taken from an epistemic point of view. Hence, Dewey characterizes a situation of social domination as involving different forms of epistemic disadvantage both for the oppressed and the dominant groups. It is from the point of view of this primary situation of epistemic disadvantage—characterized as involving different epistemic pathologies—that we can explore the possibility of collective learning processes, considering the factors involved in overcoming the epistemic pathologies of the inquiries of the dominated. After this first approximation, chapter 8 will focus on the very possibility of generating a counter-hegemonic, experimentalist culture of inquiry in contexts where pathological habits of inquiry dominate public life. Dewey develops a theory of social conflict between dominated and dominant groups that outlines a model of collective learning on the side of the dominated involving the local development of experimental cultures of inquiry. As we will see, the aesthetic notion of "act of expression" can be mobilized in this context as providing an interpretative key that makes sense of the different stages and factors involved in Dewey's depiction of social struggle as they are depicted in his *Lectures in China*. The "expressivist" understanding of collective mobilization that follows from this reading does not only provide an original view on the internal aspects of collective learning processes in social struggle, but also provides central theoretical resources for thinking about social conditions and blocking mechanisms at play. Hence, even if one does not need to agree with the detail of Dewey's phenomenology of mobilization, the idea that collective learning processes of oppressed groups have an expressive or articulative dimension represents, in my view, a major contribution of Dewey's work to an actual theory of social movements.

Primary related to progressive self-appropriation of collective capacities and aims, the notion of "act of expression" comes very close to that of articulation as it has been presented in the context of Dewey's theory of inquiry. There "articulation" referred to the idea that (social) problems have both a "given and made" character, that is, that problems refer to a preexisting or "given" reality even if the latter has not the last word about the exact nature of the problem. To the extent that operations of identification and definition of problems not only have a receptive but also an active dimension on the side of the inquiring subjects, inquiry presents a central hermeneutical element that fits with all those Fairfield identifies in his own analysis such as the strong role played in inquiry by the context in which objects are embedded as well as by language. Hence, they all point to the progressive determination that goes hand in hand with the interpretative dimension of all inquiry. In relation to the sort of problems that constitute the object of our analysis, problems of injustice, the articulatory nature of inquiry points both to the kinds of norms or values at play in their progressive specification as well as the determination of the elements of a situation that allow for a characterization in terms of injustice. In the context of Dewey's conception of social struggle, the notion of "act of expression" also refers to the further determination of something that is only partially determined, even if in this latter case what comes to be progressively determined are collective powers/capacities and aims. It is precisely the idea that social struggle represents a process by which previously suppressed collective aims and power/capacities come to be articulated what characterizes Dewey's understanding of the different stages of the learning process of the oppressed.

HERMENEUTICAL INJUSTICE

As Pierre Bourdieu argues in *La misère du monde* (1993), social groups living under relations of domination are very often unable to articulate their experiences of social suffering in a way that can become publicly visible and politically mobilized. Members of these groups often lack the necessary symbolic resources or categories for developing a collective voice capable of reflecting their own social experience. In her recent book, *Epistemic Injustice* (2007), Miranda Fricker has provided a new, normative perspective to this situation of a lack of "symbolic means" in terms of "hermeneutical injustice." Fricker characterizes hermeneutical injustice by pointing to the existence of gaps in what she calls the shared hermeneutical resource, that is, the spectrum of concepts to which members of a social group have access in order to describe and understand their own (social) experiences. As an example of these gaps, Fricker mentions the inability of women to adequately describe the situations of sexual harassment at the work place until the very concept of "sexual harassment" became available to them. As such, in many cases hermeneutical injustice represents what we could call a second-order injustice: the injustice of not being able to articulate one's own social situation as involving an injustice (of first order).

How can we account for the existence of such conceptual or symbolic gaps? And to which extent do they constitute an hermeneutical injustice and not a mere case of epistemic bad luck? In order to answer these questions, Fricker mobilizes some essential social-theoretical premises. According to her view, in all societies we can identify privileged loci for the generation of socially legitimate meanings. These loci are characterized by the social prestige attached to them: talking from a position of symbolic power such as journalists or a lawyers do, those social groups that have a easy access to those positions are able to impose on the rest of society the social categories by which they are able to make sense of their own experience. In so doing, they render invisible the experiences of the members of those groups who have no proper representation in these privileged loci. The central question then becomes who occupies these positions of symbolic power: in most Western societies, it is white, heterosexual males, at the expense of other groups, such as women or members of other minority groups. As a result, the spectrum of symbolic resources accessible to the members of society is restricted to those concepts that best describe the way members of dominant groups experience the world. This situation is normatively problematic—constituting a genuine injustice as opposed to merely a case of "epistemic bad luck"—to the extent that gaps in the hermeneutical resource are due to the systematic, socially coerced marginalization of members of nondominant groups from those privileged positions of symbolic production.

Based on this explanation of the origin of hermeneutical injustice, we can draw the following conclusion: only those social orders that provide equal access to privileged positions of legitimate symbolic production are capable to adequately articulate the situated experiences of injustice of these groups. Hence, an emancipatory project aiming at overcoming epistemic injustice would need to inquire into the mechanisms generating inequality of access and promote forms of inclusion. However, as the history of many social movements in the last century shows, the abolition of barriers to equal access to social positions of symbolic power has rarely been a direct way in which existing hermeneutical injustices have been overcome. In historical analysis, what we can observe is that gaps in the general hermeneutical resource have come to be "filled" due to the epistemic work of particular social struggles involving the political mobilization of oppressed groups such as women, homosexuals, workers, and so on. Among many other social and political effects, social movements like those fighting for the rights of women have been able to both generate and expand the use of new concepts such as "sexual harassment" or "post-natal depression." But—to put a question that has been central for the present study—how did actually such new, counter-hegemonic notions come into existence? What processes are responsible for their generation and confirmation as notions with sufficient symbolic force to account for women's everyday experiences? By appealing to the narrations provided by Carmita Wood, Fricker analyzes the internal dynamics of new communicative settings such as "consciousness-raising" meetings and speak-outs in the context of second-wave feminism, which can be taken as paradigmatic for this kind of innovative symbolic work.

In her characterization of these innovative forms of organization and communication, Fricker explores only shortly the conditions involved in the emergence of these new concepts as they arise within the context of political mobilization. These conditions concern mainly the reinforcement of what she calls the "epistemic self-confidence" of those women participating in the process of collective sharing and interpretation of their own individual experiences. "Epistemic confidence" refers, according to Fricker, to the self-relation of individuals concerning their capacity as "knowers." It has to do with the individual's capacity to understand her contributions to any collective inquiry as valuable. Epistemic confidence is usually hindered in a larger context of the set of social relations which normally govern the ordinary lives of the members of oppressed groups. As Fricker shows, consciousness-raising groups are paradigmatic forms of communicative organization which involve a transformation of relations among participants that reinforce their epistemic confidence, promoting the communication of experiences and collective reinterpretation of these experiences. Hermeneutical innovation is hence possible within the context of what she later calls an "inclusive hermeneutical climate" (Fricker 2007: 170), one in which similarly situated individuals are able to share their experiences and mutually reinforce their confidence as "knowers" and interpreters of the world.

I contend, however, that even if Fricker's analysis sheds light upon the epistemic processes leading to the building of an oppositional consciousness, her analysis concerning both the causes and the ways of overcoming hermeneutical injustice can be complemented by our experimentalist approach. In particular, Fricker's analysis needs to be completed by dealing with two major difficulties: on the one hand, Fricker seems to assume that dominant groups are able to generate their conceptual resources in a nonproblematic way, that is, without taking into consideration that communicative pathologies affecting dominant groups might generate, among other things, symbolic gaps that negatively affect the ability of their members to make sense of their own experiences. On the other hand, Fricker does not take into account the fact that the epistemic self-confidence of those who participate in communicative settings such as consciousness-raising groups might be a necessary but not sufficient condition for counter-hegemonic conceptual innovations. Hence, social movements can experience obstructions on their way to conceptual innovation even when an inclusive hermeneutical climate promoting epistemic confidence is generated. As a result, movements may still run the risk of reproducing the ideological perspectives of the dominant groups and fail to account for their own experiences. Indeed, movements might employ hegemonic logical operations that impede the revision of concepts in the light of new experiences made visible by people's testimonies, for example, as they are expressed in "consciousness-raising" meetings and other communicative settings. In previous chapters I have characterized these logical operations as "pathologies" of public life. To reformulate the previous ideas: we can only account for the processes leading to innovative perspective if we see groups as able to overcome—or at least immunize against—pathologies of public life. As a result, describing the conditions of conceptual and symbolic innovation in such communicative settings necessarily involves taking the quality and transformative possibilities of these operations into account.

In other words, Fricker assumes that individuals can adequately account for their individual experiences in a context where mutual recognition of epistemic authority—and hence the possibility for epistemic confidence—is equally provided to all participants in communication. However, we fail to give a satisfactory social-critical account of the conditions for overcoming epistemic injustices if we do not take into account the epistemic quality of the communicative processes by which individual experiences are collectively shared and elaborated. In my view, John Dewey's theory of inquiry can provide a compelling account of the communicative difficulties concerning the possibility of overcoming hermeneutical injustice in the context of social mobilization. With Fricker—and contrary to Bourdieu's well-known prioritization of the critical-hermeneutical role of intellectuals—Dewey's position is that social analysis must direct its attention to the conditions under which social agents themselves are able to articulate their own experiences. Dewey's analysis of these conditions, however, goes beyond Fricker's in that it concerns itself with the epistemic culture in which individuals are able to account for the way they experience the (social) world as well as their possible transformation.

OVERCOMING PATHOLOGIES IN CULTURAL LIFE

In different places in his work, Dewey demonstrates his awareness of the problems affecting what he calls the "cultural life" of groups, which he understands as the set of practices and symbolic resources of groups living under relations of domination. These problems concern both dominant and dominated groups, albeit in different ways. As he puts it in Democracy and Education:

A separation into a privileged and a subject-class prevents social endosmosis. The evils thereby affecting the superior class are less material and less perceptible, but equally real. Their culture tends to be sterile, to be turned back to feed on itself; their art becomes a showy display and artificial; their wealth luxurious; their knowledge overspecialized; their manners fastidious rather than humane. (MW 9: 90)

And he goes on:

Lack of the free and equitable intercourse with springs from a variety of shared interest makes intellectual stimulation unbalanced. Diversity of stimulation means novelty, and novelty means challenge to thought. The more activity is restricted to a few definite lines—as it is when there are rigid class lines preventing adequate interplay of experiences—the more action needs to become routine on the part of the class at disadvantage, and capricious, aimless, and explosive on the part of the class having the materially fortunate positions. (MW 9: 90)

Due to a lack of "free and equitable intercourse" among them, both dominant and dominated groups experience important difficulties in their relation to their own cultural life and products. While the lack of social contact on equal terms has a certain effect on the dominated group—Dewey speaks of "routinization" in the fragment just quoted—from the position of the dominant we observe different pathological phenomena that are characteristic of its particular social position. For example, rigidification, lack of reflectivity and of the capacity for stimulation are, for Dewey, problems that affect those who find themselves in dominant social positions. Under these conditions, the culture of the dominant tends to "turn back to feed for itself." Reformulating this idea in Fricker's terms, we can say that these pathologies concern the capacity of the shared hermeneutical resource to (re-)connect its symbolic resources to the experiences of the individuals for whom it should presumably be working as an adequate means of articulation. In other words, under conditions of domination, dominant groups become incapable of establishing an appropriative relation to their very own cultural products: their culture becomes "autonomous" and hence, detached from the experiences their members make in their everyday life. As such, it appears Fricker's implicit assumption that dominant social groups are able to impose the hermeneutical resources that best fit their own experience should be conditioned (or modified) by the threat of cultural pathologies that may affect the members of the dominant group in their isolation from other groups.

Furthermore, Dewey was also aware of the pathologies in cultural life that can be identified by the oppressed themselves. As we just saw, in

Democracy and Education Dewey speaks in terms of the "routinization" of the intellectual activity of the oppressed. In his China lectures of 1919–1920, he characterized the oppressed as "the subdued, depressed, comparatively dumb group" (Dewey 2015: 20), who tends to share the way members of the dominant group describe their world. Thus, the hermeneutical disadvantage affecting members of the oppressed group should not be only seen as the result of hermeneutical marginalization (as being marginalized from privileged social spaces of symbolic production), but also as the product of the pathologies that affect their cultural life of the oppressed—insofar as they are situated in a subordinate position. Thus, for collective emancipation to be possible in an epistemic sense, the pathologies affecting the possibility of connecting hermeneutical resources to individual and collective experiences must be overcome. In this context, social mobilization is seen by Dewey as a process in which the conditions for a necessary renewal of the cultural life of groups in the sense just stated are progressively embedded within a collective dynamics, which affect both sides of the relation of domination and can be understood as a "learning process."

In fact, Dewey does not immediately identify group mobilization with the establishment of a nonpathological cultural life. On the contrary, pathologies can be also identifiable in those moments in which the oppressed have collectively organized in struggles against domination. In these cases, they become obstacles in the incipient process of the articulation of a collective voice that involves struggling against injustice. In many cases, these pathologies are constitutive of the very process of mobilization of the oppressed. According to Dewey, the first steps out of a situation of acceptance of the (unjust) status quo are characterized by a radical reaction against it as well as social reality in general, which are seen as fundamentally unjust:

> This is the period of marked "individualism" of revolt against authority and established institutions, a feeling that they are [either] merely conventional, or else positively oppressive and to be destroyed in the interest of individual freedom, which is negatively viewed [as] absence of restraint doing as one pleases etc. (Dewey 2015: 23)

And it is precisely in this radical rejection that we can once again identify the origin of pathologies concerning the possibility of cultural self-appropriation: by radically rejecting social reality, "rebels" block access to the individual and collective experiences that are produced in social life, and, therefore, the possibilities for the flexibilization of shared symbolic resources that would allow for collective self-appropriation.

In other words, for Dewey, the active negation of the social world—which, as we saw, is seen as a mere obstacle for the realization of freedom—that is involved in the explosive attitude of the rebels implies a negation of the Weltbezüglichkeit inherent to processes of collective self-comprehension. As I will show in the next chapter, this situation of experiential obstruction of the oppressed can be overcome only in a context where the members of the oppressed group learn to see social reality as a resource—and not as a mere obstacle—for action. This learning process might be fostered by the interplay of factors such as increasing recognition by other social groups, widening of the opportunities for participation in social life, or experiences of defeat linked to the consequences of "explosive" forms of action.

In light of the above, we must conclude that Fricker's analysis of the factors involved in the generation and overcoming of hermeneutical injustice—inclusive hermeneutical climate promoting cognitive self-confidence—is incomplete. This becomes clear when we accept the possibility of pathologies in both the dominant and dominated group's cultural life, such as rigidification and autonomization of their respective cultures. In general, these pathologies involve a disconnection of culture from experience in which cultural transformation is not stimulated by the experiences of individuals and, therefore, becomes unable to provide the resources to make sense of them. Pathologies do not only affect groups living in relations of domination, but they also can affect groups when they mobilize in struggle against injustice, in so far as they react against the status quo through an abstract rejection of social reality as means to the realization of collective aims. Thus, we need to describe the emergence of powerful, innovative, counter-hegemonic communicative settings such as "consciousness-raising" meetings as involving a learning process of collective self-appropriation by which groups have overcome cultural pathologies or have immunized themselves against them.

To recall, according to Dewey, inquiry involves action in the world. For him it does not make sense to talk about knowledge or truth without the implementation of our hypothesis in empirical settings and checking out the consequences of implementation. Within the different phases of experimentalist inquiry, our ideas, categories, or understandings acquire "a directive function in control of observation and ultimate transformation of antecedent phenomena [and] are tested and continually revised on the ground of the consequences they produce in existential application" (LW 12: 499). In other words, in experiment, our ideas, categories, and understandings are both mobilized in giving direction to experimental transformation of the world and revised on the ground of new observations that result from the controlled and observed change. By seeing the development of experimentalist habits as the reverse of the overcoming of cultural pathologies, it becomes possible to grasp transformations in epistemic practice as the result of a collective learning process. In fact, Dewey's view allows to see experimentalism precisely as the series of fundamental operations that are involved in the (re-)connection of culture and experience, namely, as those operations implied by an existential attitude that takes the (social) world both as obstacle and as resource for action. Here, experimentalism could be seen as a method that is contrary to other forms of existential attitude, such as "explosivism" or conservatism. If—against the "explosive" attitude we have described in previous section—by experiencing the (social) world as a means or resource for action, collectives also learn to perceive it as an obstacle, then we are to expect that they mobilize old experiences of obstacle-overcoming as resources for actions in the light of concrete problems they deal with. If—against a conservative attitude—by experiencing the (social) world as an obstacle, we learn to consider it also as a resource for action, then observation of consequences plays not a self-satisfying, but a revisionist role for our ideas and understandings, which must be seen now in light of these consequences (LW 1, Chap. 6). Hence, though experimentalism cannot be reduced to an exercise of hermeneutics, the latter seems to be implied in the former: it is our cultural background or matrix that is mobilized in experiment and it is through a experimentalist attitude that we become able to reconstitute this background.

CONCLUDING REMARKS

Arriving at a self-appropriative cultural life of groups goes hand in hand with developing a experimentalist attitude toward the (social) world, one that is reflected in the emergence of new operations in epistemic practice with counter-hegemonic potential. Hence, as a condition for conceptual innovation that satisfies the hermeneutical needs of members suffering from epistemic disadvantage, groups must have developed collective habits of experimental operation that (re)-connect ideas and experiences. Insofar as we can speak, as Fricker does, of the cognitive achievements of the oppressed, we should see collective mobilizations as loci for the generation of an experimentalist culture of inquiry: one by which groups have learned to experience the categories they mobilize in their self-understanding as hypotheses to be implemented and tested. Both the obstructions affecting these local developments—and the possible mechanisms of collective regression—as well as the influence of these local developments in the larger political culture(s) of their time are phenomena yet to be explored.

Chapter 8

Articulating a Sense of Powers

An Expressivist Reading of Dewey's Theory of Social Struggles

In the series of lectures he delivered during the two years he spent in China, John Dewey provided the most complete version of his theory of social conflict and struggle. The two textual sources from this time we have at our disposal—the doubly translated lectures published in *Honolulu* (1973) and Dewey's original notes recently published under the name of *Lectures in Social and Political Philosophy* (2015)—outline an original understanding of social conflict as taking place between groups with different interests, aims, and powers. After formulating a programmatic account of the nature and the tasks of social philosophy, Dewey devoted one of his lectures to the exploration of society's tendencies to generate disparities in the realization of what he called "social interests," interests which are embodied by different social groups living in relations of both cooperation and domination. In the following lecture, Dewey outlined a general theory of social struggle between dominant and oppressed groups as arising from this initial situation of social imbalance—a situation that he characterized as "one sided" mode of social life (Dewey 2015: 17)—leading to a transformed social order in which the interests of oppressed groups come to be recognized by the wider society.

Dewey's China lectures clearly represent a valuable resource for those scholars interested in understanding the evolution of Dewey's thought, especially concerning the role he gave to social philosophy at this stage of his intellectual life. Recently, scholars have also approached the lectures as providing valuable insights on current problems in political and social philosophy, especially concentrating on the central notions of "social conflict," "recognition," and "social interest" (Särkelä 2013, Frega 2015). The aim of this chapter is to provide an interpretation of Dewey's theory of social struggles that brings its epistemic and normative elements to the foreground of analysis. More concretely, I aim to show that the transformations experimented by three of its constitutive elements—collective self-understandings, frames of injustice, and methods of inquiry—are better understood from the perspective of what I will call an "expressivist reading," which draws on the Deweyan notion of "act of expression," as it is developed in the famous work *Art and Experience* (1934). According to this reading, Dewey describes struggles as involving a learning process on the side of the oppressed that consists in the development of expressive abilities, that is, abilities to self-reflectively articulate collective interests and aims through the mediating role of an active confrontation with external conditions. Hence, this learning process should be seen as providing the foundation of the dynamics of struggle, allowing us to analyze the factors involved in struggle from the point of view of their contribution to the collective development of expressive abilities. The expressivist interpretation not only sheds some light on Dewey's own conception of social struggle, but also provides valuable insights on the extent to which a pragmatist approach can contribute to the study of social movements from a contemporary perspective.

In order to lay the foundations for my expressivist reading, in the first section of the chapter, I will provide a reconstruction of John Dewey's theory of social struggle as a three-stage process leading from a situation of accepted or unperceived domination to one of social recognition, taking into special consideration the normative and epistemic elements that concern the members of the oppressed group. In the second section, I will provide a reconstruction of Dewey's reflections on the concept of "act of expression" that distinguishes two different, though interrelated processes: first, the progressive determination of aims out of primary nondirected impulsion through the mediation of the environmental conditions; second, the process through which individuals—or groups—acquire the ability to "express" themselves instead of being guided by their nonreflected impulsion. In the third section, I will explore the transformations concerning the normative and epistemic dynamics of social struggle by concentrating on the mediating function played by the learning process leading to the development of expressive capacities. Finally, I will conclude by pointing to some important consequences of my reading for current debates on the value and meaning of social struggles.

JOHN DEWEY'S THREE-STAGE THEORY OF SOCIAL STRUGGLE—EPISTEMIC AND NORMATIVE DIMENSIONS

According to Dewey, social struggle can be described as a three-stage process in which different groups progressively develop and transform their collective self-understandings. On the side of the oppressed groups, struggles involve different steps of a learning process that goes from a lack of collective self-awareness to the self-reflected assertion of their practical stance toward larger society. Thus, self-understandings are not normatively neutral, but rather are inscribed within more general evaluative frames on the basis of which groups assess the normative quality of the relation of domination in which they are involved. These frames define what sort of harm is done in the relation of domination, allow for the identification of the agent and victim of such harm, and determine the ways groups can project a transformation of the situation (Renault 2004). Finally, within social struggle, we can also identify an ongoing transformation of the methods of inquiry put to work by the oppressed in the realization of their own interests and aims, as well as in the communications with other, opposing groups. As will be shown later, these changes in method concern most notably the epistemic role played by facts—and more specifically, social facts—as constitutive elements of operations of inquiry.

It is now time to analyze the three stages of social struggle in detail, placing special attention on the changes experienced by each of the three factors I just described, namely, collective self-understandings, frames of injustice, and methods of inquiry. Dewey describes the first, initial phase of struggle as one in which "one set of persons represents and embodies the dominant, law interpreting group and other persons the subdued, depressed, comparatively dumb group. The former have the authority, the prestige of custom, to back them," (Dewey 2015, 20) while on the other side, "[t]he persons who represent the relatively suppressed group will appear to behave socially, to be actuated by social motives just as long as they accept the existing state of things and conform to its traditional prescriptions" (Dewey 2015: 20). Dewey's depiction of this phase clearly shows the extent to which the position of domination and oppression is intertwined with the existing recognitional order in society. The imposition of one group over another is sustained by the recognition of the dominant group as the one representing the interests of society as a whole, interests which are most notably embodied by custom and tradition. In this context, any attempt to innovate in a way that challenges social custom is either seen as a threat to be eradicated or is displaced through cultural mechanisms into the field of fantasy and thereby politically neutralized.

Concerning the epistemic and normative features of this initial phase—one that, properly speaking, precedes mobilization—and concentrating on the way oppressed groups experience existing relations of domination, Dewey's lectures seem to imply that, at this stage, no collective self-understanding, frame of injustice, or method of inquiry capable of decoupling itself from the epistemic and normative position of the dominant group has still emerged. Hence, at this initial stage "there is such an equilibrium that the suppressed

group or lass is not aware of its suppression, or takes it as part of the established and necessary order of things. There are no opportunities to suggest
the idea of a different state of things, and hence no idea of an effort to bring
about change" (Dewey 2015: 23).

This first state of equilibrium contrasts with the second stage of struggle,
one of protest and revolt on the part of the oppressed group:

> This is the period of marked *"individualism"* of revolt against authority and
> established institutions, a feeling that they are [either] merely conventional, or
> else positively oppressive and to be destroyed in the interests of the individual
> freedom, which is negatively viewed [as] *absence of restrain* doing as one
> pleases etc. (Dewey 2015: 23, author's emphasis)

The actual struggle of the oppressed against domination starts at this second phase. But here its central normative and epistemic elements take a
preliminary form that radically diverges from that of the dominant group
and which will itself be transformed during struggle. During this phase,
oppressed groups come to see themselves as "rebels against society" fighting for freedom in its negative sense, that is, fighting for the "absence
of restraint" in their actions. As we can see in the quotation above, this
phase is marked, on the side of the oppressed group, by a rejection of
existing social institutions as invalid forms of social order. Furthermore,
Dewey affirms that this attitude of rejection often does not only concern
actual existing institutions, but the very institutional nature of society as
intrinsically oppressing. In their defense of their negative freedom, social
institutions in general are seen by the oppressed merely as obstacles for
the realization of their aims, activities, and powers. Hence, the realization
of the group's characteristic and usually suppressed powers are thought
to imply a destruction of existing institutions, which excludes any further
consideration of the positive institutional transformations that their very
revolt might bring about.

According to Dewey, in the first phase of struggle, the existing institutional
order is either not perceived as dominating or it is naturalized, and, therefore,
a recognition of any conflict of interests between the oppressed and the rest
of society is missing. Now, in correspondence with its new collective self-
understanding, the oppressed group frames the relation of domination, as well
as its struggle against it, in the following terms:

> a movement of revolt, of emancipation, of claims for personal rights, and enjoy-
> ments. Natural, inalienable rights to life, liberty and the pursuit of happiness
> residing in the individual irrespective of social consideration. (Dewey 2015: 24)

We seem thereby justified to identify a normative positioning on the side of the oppressed that can be seen as a preliminary stage in framing the relation of domination as unjust. According to this initial "frame of injustice," the situation of domination generates (normatively unacceptable) harm by blocking the realization of individual liberties. From the perspective of this initial frame, existing institutions and even society—independently of its particular institutional forms—are seen as the perpetrating agents of harm against individuals, understood in an atomized way, that is, in their independence from social relations.

Finally, it is possible to understand Dewey's critical characterization of a method of inquiry involving "the method of opinion, dogmatic assertion, bitter recriminations and disparaging name calling, epithets of abuse" (Dewey 2015: 25) as referring to this initial collective self-understanding and frame of injustice. This method contrasts with the one Dewey later attributes to the third stage of struggle, which he describes as "an appeal to intelligence." In this context, it should be noted that Dewey's attribution of the "method of opinion" to the second stage of struggle does not only concern the revolting group but it also concerns the "despotic reactionary" position of the dominant group and describes the nature of the communication that takes place between both. As such, framing domination and struggles in terms of an abstract opposition between atomized individuals and institutional reality contributes to "the formation of opposed groups based on emotion, prejudice and vested rights and wrongs, and stimulates resort to the method of dispute, recrimination and even physical force" (Dewey 2015: 24).

Communication between groups that takes the form of cooperative inquiry is all the more difficult in a context where both the oppressed and the dominant groups similarly adopt an epistemically problematic approach toward those conditions that constitute the existential matrix for their activities—what Dewey calls "facts" of two kinds: "facts of history, existing facts and conditions [and] new facts, facts to be brought in" (Dewey 2015: 25).

Thus, at this stage of the struggle, both in their approach to the existential conditions which constitute their context of action (facts of history) and to the kinds of new social realities they commit themselves to bringing about (new facts), oppressed groups adopt what we could call a "dismissive attitude." This attitude contrasts with the conservatism of the dominant group, whose members take facts of history "too much" into account, thereby blocking an open interplay between facts and ideas that would allow for an intelligent attitude toward the reform of social institutions. According to the former, existing conditions are seen as mere obstacles to get rid of instead of as useful instruments for the generation of new social realities. At the same time, the realization of the group's aims is not taken to imply a careful consideration of the changes and innovations that are necessarily involved in their activities. Consequently, Dewey also characterizes this doubly dismissive approach to facts—as existing conditions or as future realities—as "destructive."

Finally, we come to the third and final stage of social struggle, which involves a progressive change that goes from the oppressed group's realization of the social value of its "suppressed interest" to its final recognition by the dominant group and wider society. At this stage, we first observe that the oppressed group has abandoned its former collective self-understanding. It sees itself no longer as the defender of an individualistic interest but has learned to see how a full realization of its suppressed powers can contribute to the well-being of society at large: *"the demand ceases to be for individualistic expression, and becomes a demand for a chance to perform a badly needed social function"* (Dewey 2015: 23, author's emphasis). This transformation goes hand in hand with a new normative framing of the relation of domination to which the oppressed group is submitted. In the normatively charged discourse of the oppressed *"The claim shifts from a right* to a *neglected social duty"* (Dewey 2015: 23, author's emphasis). Hence, the injustice of domination is understood in terms of the hindering of a socially valuable activity. This seems to cohere with examples Dewey provides in his lectures, for example, with what he calls the scientific movement against the social dominance of religion. In this case, "the claim of the right to exercise the scientific interest is made in behalf of social need and welfare not in behalf of purely individualistic non-social factors" (Dewey 2015: 24). According to this new frame of injustice, the (normatively problematic) harm perpetrated by the dominant group is not only directed toward the oppressed group but also toward society as a whole, since the "idiosyncratic" activity of the group is now considered to provide a valuable service to society.

Finally, in relation to this new collective self-understanding and its corresponding normative frame, Dewey identifies a shift from the aforementioned "method of opinion" to a *"method of analysis, of taking things in details and discriminating"* (Dewey 2015: 25, author's emphasis). Here it is worth quoting Dewey's description of this new method of inquiry at length:

> The innovator has a case to prove. He is the propounder of a hypothesis that the welfare of society would be promoted by the adoption of a certain change, that if this harms a special class for a time, this loss to the class is in the interest of the community of the whole, and is the measure of justice to some other class now suffering from inadequate social recognition. [. . .] His claim that certain defects exist, and that they may be remedied by the adoption of certain proposed measures of change are propositions to be examined in the light of facts. (Dewey 2015: 25)

As mentioned earlier, in the context of Dewey's analysis, changes in the methods of collective inquiry basically concern the epistemic status of social facts. At this final stage, the oppressed group has abandoned its dismissive attitude. It has learned to see facts not only as obstacles but also as necessary conditions—as "resources" for action—as well as relevant factors for the evaluation of its aims, activities, and measures (see Bohman 2004). In other words, it has become "experimental" and "intelligent."

Moreover, this evolution into intelligent inquiry also affects the quality of political communication between the oppressed and the dominated group: here, the "the innovator has a case to prove," not to impose. The oppressed thus put themselves in a position of cooperative inquiry with the group hitherto seen as its enemy, which has a positive effect on the quality of intergroup communication: "[i]f the people on one side of an issue adopt an attitude of calm inquiry, it becomes less difficult for those who hold opposing view to adopt a rational approach to the problem" (Dewey 1973: 80).

THE ACT OF EXPRESSION

In the previous section I have outlined the main epistemic and normative traits of each of the stages of social struggle of oppressed groups: these concern both the group (self-) understanding (from rebels against society to contributors to the social), the frames of injustice (from injustice to an atomized individual to injustice to a "social individual" as well as to society at large), and their method of inquiry (from "method of opinion" to intelligent, cooperative inquiry). The description provided, however, remains only partial if we do not also account for the process of transformation which leads from one phase of the struggle to the next. As a result, one still may want to ask the following questions: How is the emergence of a collective spirit of revolt from a situation of lack of perception and naturalization possible? And how should we account for the transformation of this spirit of revolt into a sense of contribution to society at large? As I will show in the next section, these two sets of changes seem to be mediated by a learning process of collective self-articulation through which the group first gains what he calls "a sense of powers" and becomes progressively capable of an intelligent determination of its collective aims. In order to better understand this process of collective articulation as well as its mediatory function in struggle, I will draw upon Dewey's notion of "act of expression" as outlined in *Art as Experience* (1934).

With the notion of "act of expression" Dewey aims at capturing the internal dynamics of an "integral human experience" (LW 10: 70), one which is lived in its unity and completeness. According to Dewey, it represents the process through which the different elements of an experience are integrated into a unified whole, which involves different stages of growth within experience: "inception, development and fulfillment" (LW 10: 62). Hence, an experience always starts "as impulsion," which represents its organic "initial state" and ends, if it is to be seen as unitary and complete, in the transformation of impulsions into "contrived undertakings" (LW 10: 65). Contrary to specialized impulses, which are fixedly directed toward particular objects, an impulsion is a reaction of the organism that does not have a definite direction at its initial stage, but which is directed within experience. Dewey mentions two factors involved in this process in which impulsions "gain form and solidity" (LW 10: 66): the work of environmental conditions and the deposited "working capital" that individuals have "in virtue of prior experiences" (LW 10: 66).

Regarding environmental conditions, Dewey holds that "it is the fate of a living creature [. . .] that it cannot secure what belongs to it without an adventure in a world that as a whole it does not own and to which it has no native title" (LW 10: 65). This condition should not be regretted as representing an obstacle for the realization of our impulsions, since it is the very condition of possibility for the internal dynamics that Dewey calls an act of expression: "In the process of converting these obstacles and neutral conditions into favoring agencies, the live creature becomes aware of the intent implicit in its impulsion. The self, whether it succeeds or fail, does not merely restore itself or its former state. Blind surge has changed into a purpose" (LW 10: 65). In this context, two important aspects are worth underlining. First, confrontation with environmental conditions fosters a self-reflective attitude on the side of the individual: "nor without resistance from surroundings would the self become aware of itself; it would have neither feeling nor interest, neither fear nor hope" (LW 10: 65). Second, in the experience with environmental conditions, we do not become aware of what our intentions were about from the outset. On the contrary, our intentions are formed—we could also say "progressively determined"—within the process of confrontation with the external world. In other words, expression as transformation from raw impulse to intentional activity is mediated by the necessary confrontation with environmental conditions in a way that fosters self-awareness and intentional self-articulation. Most importantly, this mediating function is only possible when conditions are such that two extremes can be avoided, viz. the role of "mere smooth channels or else blind obstructions" (LW 10: 66) in the realization of our impulsive energy. On the one extreme, uniformly favorable conditions would not allow for self-reflective and hence, intelligent will-formation, since the emergence of these features is essentially linked to the presence of obstacles capable of interrupting activity. On the other, no intelligent determination of intentions can be expected when conditions are such that the realization of impulsions becomes impossible. According to Dewey, in such cases we can only expect a further reproduction of impulsive activity, which takes the general form of rage and destructiveness.

But in his discussion about the act of expression, Dewey is not only concerned about the structure and dynamics of experience in terms of what we could call a microscale learning process that goes from immediate impulsion to intelligently directed aims and emotions but also whose logic constitutes the measure of unity and integrity of all human experience. Rather, Dewey is also concerned about how individuals learn to relate expressively to their intentional and emotional states at the ontogenetic level. Thus, expressive abilities, which concern the individual's capacity to articulate internal intentional or emotional states through the reflected mediation of the environment, are not immediately given, but rather represent a way of relating to one's own mental states that must be progressively acquired and which can be unlearned or forgotten. This learning process is most notably observed in the evolution of the newborn into "higher" stages of will-formation and emotional self-expression:

> At first a babe weeps, just as it turns its head to follow light; there is inner urge but nothing to express. As the infant matures, he learns that particular acts effect different consequences [. . .]. He thus begins to be aware of the meaning of what he does. As he grasps the meaning of an act at first performed from sheer internal pressure, he becomes capable of actors of true expression. (LW 10: 68)

According to this description, active confrontation with environmental conditions is not only a necessary condition for any integral experience to take place, but it is also a necessary factor involved in a larger-scale learning process that concerns the development of our abilities to have experiences in a strong expressivist sense.

In short, the notion of "act of expression" shows how reflected self-articulation can only take place within given existential conditions which work as a medium, that is, as obstacles and resources for the progressive determination of an initially indeterminate impulse. At the same time, it shows that expressive abilities must be learned in a process in which the world is experienced, in its turn, in this double role. In my view, this double sense of the act of expression helps us to understand what I have called the articulatory dimension of social struggle and the mediating role it plays in the progressive transformation of its epistemic and normative elements. According to the expressivist reading I provide in the next section, we should conceive of struggle as multistaged process in which social groups both progressively determine and acquire consciousness of what Dewey calls their own powers and collective aims.

FROM A SENSE OF POWERS TO ARTICULATED AIMS: THE ACT OF EXPRESSION IN SOCIAL STRUGGLE

As mentioned in the first section, Dewey identifies in the first, preliminary phase of social struggle a state of equilibrium in which the existing relations of domination that affect groups representing different social interests are either not perceived as such or merely lived as natural both by the dominant and the oppressed. Dewey points to the fact that the stability of this equilibrium depends most notably on the intensity of the relations of domination pervading society at a given moment: "When slavery is most complete, when government is most successfully despotic there is no thought of slavery or despotism as evils to be protested against." Thinking of slavery or despotism "as evils to be protested against" seems then only possible when some central changes take place, changes that open and expand the opportunities for the oppressed group to perceive itself in a new light. As such, the initial equilibrium might be broken when "conditions are such as to stimulate *a consciousness of powers which are not expressed and satisfied*" (Dewey 2015: 23, author's emphasis). But how should we conceive of these new, stimulating conditions?

As we saw earlier, Dewey provides a short analysis of different social struggles having taken place in the history of both Western and Oriental civilizations that serve to illustrate his more general account. By talking about women's struggle for their right to participate in social and political life, he points to the catalyst effects of a change in life conditions at the origin of their revolt:

> When industrial changes took away from women household activities that had belonged to them previously, there was not only relative loss of activity, but also a leisure for other things. Better education was given. This created a sense of powers that had no outlet and created restlessness and uneasiness which didn't exist as long as women had [been] more completely absorbed in the household life. (Dewey 2015: 23)

In this example, we can observe that the emergence of a collective attitude of revolt from a primary state of equilibrium is mediated by a change in conditions which could be described as an (even minimal) enlargement of the group's opportunities to participate in social life, which results from women's "leisure for other things." It is through such an enlargement of opportunities produced by the change of social conditions that the group seems to become able to perceive itself as having its own powers/abilities suppressed. This is precisely where the notion of expressive act is useful for interpreting Dewey's argument: changes in conditions create the opportunity for at least initial phases of collective self-expression, something Dewey calls a "sense of powers." With the notion of expressive act we are able to stress the fact that the emergence of this "sense of powers" must be related to changes in conditions which involve, at least partially, the opportunity for the groups' powers to confront the environmental conditions for their realization in the new activities those changes have made now possible.

But as we already know, this is in fact only an initial step in the development of the group's capacities for self-expression. In fact, Dewey characterizes the spirit of revolt precisely by the denial of social reality as a valuable resource for the realization of the group's recently discovered powers. Indeed, the attitude of dismissal and destruction seems to resemble more Dewey's view on the outbursts of children than an act of expression in the strong sense, even if we need to assume that something like an act of expression must have taken place such that, at this stage, it stimulates both the determination and self-reflective attitude that allows for the emergence of such a collective self-understanding. Here we can identify what seems to be a paradox within Dewey's argumentation: this self-understanding of revolt against society that corresponds to an individualistic frame of social injustice arises precisely when society starts to provide the group with a larger space for confrontation with environmental conditions and, therefore, for self-expression.

This paradoxical situation takes a second form that concerns what has been called the method of inquiry, which is put to work by the group in revolt: according to Dewey, the "method of opinion" is characterized by the denial of the epistemic status of (social) facts in inquiry. If we take the notion of act of expression into account, however, we see that collective self-articulation can take place only if existential conditions—social facts—begin to be taken into account in their double quality of obstacles and resources for action. As a result, it appears that it is only when social facts start being relevant for the group's own activity, that they can be dismissed as relevant facts for their collective inquiries and activities.

The double paradoxical nature of the second stage of struggle—which expresses the contrast between the constitutive mediation of (social) conditions for the expressive articulation of collective aims and its active rejection—fades away when we consider the two following aspects. First, as we saw in the former section, collective self-expression is something that must be learned in a process that fosters self-reflexivity and self-articulation. However, more than simply a matter of time, this development depends most importantly on how environmental conditions can be experienced by the oppressed: as mere obstructions or as conditions which can be intelligently converted into means for action. Second, at this stage, the way oppressed group's experience of environmental conditions is profoundly marked by the recognitional order that pervades social relations. Hence, within such order at least two factors seem to block the collective learning process of the oppressed: firstly, their collective self-understanding is confirmed and thereby reinforced by the negative perception of the dominant group, who sees them as mere destroyers of customs and tradition. Secondly, even if in some sense they must have worked as such, social institutions can hardly be experienced as resources for action, since the expansion of opportunities for self-expression has not been the product of the collective appropriation of conditions as means for, but has rather depended on other factors that are lived as primarily external to the group. Consequently, we should understand revolt as an intermediary stage where the first steps in self-reflected articulation have taken place, but also where, due most notably to the predominant recognitional order and the institutional obstacles it carries with itself, the group still has not yet been able to learn the very social nature of its surrounding conditions.

As we well know, the development of the epistemic and normative features of the oppressed does not stop at this stage. As a result, we must now address our second question concerning further steps in the dynamics of social struggle: how are we to explain the transformation from a spirit of revolt and destruction into one of contribution to the social and its corresponding frame and method of inquiry? What kind of changes take place in this transformation? And what are the factors involved? Let's shortly recall the features of the third stage of Dewey's theory of social struggle: at this stage, the group understands itself as making a contribution to the well-being of society. The suppression of activities that characterize the situation of domination is framed as one implying a double injustice: toward the group of individuals now understood in their social relations as constitutive of their individuality as well as toward society as a whole. As we saw in the first section, this new form of self-understanding and normative framing corresponds to a new method of inquiry. According to this intelligent method, social conditions or facts become relevant elements within inquiry: they are the factual material upon which both operations with given facts and facts to be brought in rely.

The first thing we need to take into consideration when trying to explain the transformation that takes place within oppressed groups when passing from a spirit of revolt to one of contribution is that—against what some might want to conclude from considerations about the paradox of revolt—changes do not seem to be necessarily produced by a substantial change in the order of social recognition that systematically denies the social value of the activities of the oppressed group. Hence, Dewey argues that the realization of the social value of the activities and powers from the side of the oppressed must often be followed by an inquiry activity led by its members, which aims precisely at changing the existing recognitional order in a more or less radical way (see

Dewey 2015: 24–25). If we accept this fact, however, what further options do we have left in Dewey's account for explaining these epistemic and normative transformations in the sense indicated?

Here again, the notion of act of expression and the learning process related to it seem to offer the necessary resources for thinking about the dynamics of struggle at this stage because Dewey draws a direct connection between the changes taking place within the frame of injustice held and the opportunities left to the group for collective self-articulation. In this line, referring to the third stage in social struggle, Dewey states:

> But as social organization proceeds and the capacities of the submerged group are not merely stimulated and brought to consciousness in an emotional way, but get some definite channel of exercise, *the demand ceases to be for individualistic expression, and becomes a demand for a chance to perform a badly needed social function. The claim shifts from a right to a neglected social duty.*
> (Dewey 2015: 23, emphasis added)

Along these lines we can see how Dewey subtly thinks together two different ideas, whose connection is best shown by the notion of act of expression: due to changes in social organization, groups "get some definite channel of exercise." In other words, they gain a space for the realization of their interests and powers. In the same act, the interests and powers of the subjected group cease to be expressed in an emotional way—like in the case of a newborn's outburst—but rather become "intelligent" in the sense elaborated in the second section. Moreover, this new form of articulation of collective aims goes hand in hand with the realization that the pursuit of collective aims, suppressed until now by domination, has an important social value. We find here again the basic structure of the mediating role of collective expression in struggle, even if now the resulting attitude is different from the progression to its second phase: revolt and destruction have been abandoned and substituted for contribution and reform. How should we explain this difference, since the changes stimulating these new understanding are not substantially different from the ones generating "sense of powers" and its corresponding attitude of revolt?

In fact, Dewey provides us with three different models for explaining this contrast in development. Their differences notwithstanding, all three models concern the basic aspect involved in the notion of an act of expression: the group's opportunity to develop its expressive abilities and the factors involved within this development:

According to the first developmental model, changes in the recognitional order of society are indeed the central factor making possible the group's learning of expressive abilities. This model is best represented by the struggle of scientists against religion as depicted by Dewey. Even though revolt is a necessary step in a struggle that results from an initial reaction of rejection on the side of dominant groups and society at large, it does not seem to play an essential role in the generation of a sense of contribution: revolt is just one phase that is condemned to disappearing as long as larger society learns to recognize the social value of the group's "idiosyncratic" activities and thereby breaking the learning-blockage suffered by the oppressed group.

In the second model, social recognition is to be achieved only once the oppressed group has already developed its expressive abilities. Here, the group is already able to perceive the social value of its own activities, even if it still needs to "prove it" to the dominant group as well as to society at large. Therefore, social recognition of the dominant group and society at large does not seem to be a necessary condition for collective self-expression. According to this model, which is best represented by the feminist movement, what Dewey describes as the extension of channels for social action allows for a quantitatively and qualitatively relevant expansion of the opportunities for confronting the social world. As such, previous revolt plays a more relevant, but still secondary function in the collective learning process: its function seems to consist in opening further channels for social action and for thought and, therefore, to foster the progressive acquisition of expressive abilities on the side of the oppressed by promoting a confrontation with world conditions. Here however, contrary to the initial phases of struggle, changes in conditions leading to this expansion are less probable to be experienced as external to the collective activity of the group, since, at least partly, they can be seen as the result of the very activity of revolt of the oppressed group.

Finally, the third developmental model is illustrated in this very brief passage from the lectures in which Dewey raises the topic of the Russian Revolution:

> If the point of view here urged were generally adopted, it would be recognized that *institutions, conventions, modes of social control* that direct the thoughts and acts of the members of society *are bound to grow up*; they are *inevitable*; it is impossible to get rid of them—to destroy them is only to set up another—as [if] may be seen in the rule of the Bolskeviki after destroying that of the Czars. (Dewey 2015: 14, author's emphasis)

In this example, revolt is taken to bear a certain experience, namely, that it is "impossible to get rid of" the institutional nature of society; that to destroy institutions "is only to set up another." In this case, the learning process leading to collective self-expression is a direct consequence that follows from the collective experience of revolt, more concretely, from its failure as merely an antisocial project. In Dewey's exposition, the three developmental models are not mutually exclusive. On the contrary, they merely exemplify cases where one of the three central factors involved has played a stronger role than the other two. In any case, all three factors—recognition, expansion of social opportunities, and revolt—are thought as promoting the oppressed group's possibility of reflexive self-articulation through confrontation with social conditions. These three coexisting models help us to understand them as factors involved in the epistemic and normative learning process of the oppressed.

CONCLUDING REMARKS: LEARNING FROM THE LEARNING PROCESS OF THE OPPRESSED

If the expressivist interpretation proposed here is sound, Dewey understands social conflict as an ontologically open learning process involving central epistemic and normative dimensions, a view from which we can gain valuable insights for current debates on the meaning and value of social mobilization. As such, it is worth ending this chapter with two lessons that emerge from the expressivist interpretation. First, Dewey teaches us also in this context that from the pragmatist perspective, struggles for recognition should be seen as essentially articulatory and, therefore, fundamentally open concerning the "object" of struggle and recognition. In other words, what society is meant to recognize as the result of a struggle cannot be seen as ontologically pregiven, but rather as something progressively determined in part, at least, through the process of struggle.

Second, understanding struggles as involving a multidimensional learning process on the side of the oppressed helps to revise our understanding of the moral and political value of social mobilizations: if, from a pragmatist point of view, we consider that social progress is linked to the essential work of social struggles, then we need to see progress as involving not only normative learning—concerning normative changes that promote greater social and political inclusion—but also epistemic learning—concerning changes in the epistemic quality of established forms of social and political communication. Hence, as we saw, developing the ability of collective self-articulation means adopting a new relation toward (social) facts out of the various situations in which groups experience learning blockages. From a Deweyan perspective, this new, appropriative relation to facts has its counterpart in the evolution of the methods employed by the dominant and the oppressed group as well as in the communication taking place between both. Cooperative inquiry and the development of an experimentalist attitude in social matters thus seem to be stimulated within struggle, thereby transforming established methods of inquiry into social problems which tend to reproduce exclusion and other forms of learning blockage. As such, a Deweyan conception of social movements points to collective ways of overcoming these blockages and stimulates further research on the epistemic features of democratic problem-solving.

Conclusion

The present book has developed an epistemic approach to the positive contribution social movements can make to democracy, one that gives plausibility to the idea that their collective efforts to provide counter-hegemonic accounts of social reality go hand in hand with their capacity to deepen our understanding of democracy. Dewey's idea of experimental inquiry has played a major role in the argument deployed, since it grounds the idea that any attempt to challenge hegemonic views on social problems by experimentalist means on the side of social movements must go hand in hand with the implementation of deeply democratic mechanisms of cooperation. In other words, the book has attempted to present experimentalism as a plausible candidate for explaining why social movements are often able to challenge both, our view on the social world, and our understanding of what it means to participate in democratic life.

Certainly, I have not shown that experimentalism is in a better position than other alternative epistemic methods in accounting for the epistemic success of the oppressed in accounting for their own experiences and building an oppositional consciousness. However, I hope to have grounded the thesis that it represents a plausible account of what happens in many cases, as when feminist women try to find a term that best describes the suffering produced by male domination, when victims of a dictatorship try to find the adequate categories to express the nature of the crimes committed, when those participating in an environmentalist assembly try to figure out the best path of action without hurting the sensibility of a minority group, or when workers try to articulate the moral wrong embodied in the dismissal of security measures at the workplace. As we saw, some of these epistemic practices have been approached in fact by sociologists and movement theorists as putting at work experimentalist features such as the willingness to test and revise ideas, giving a central role to imagination and innovation, and so on. All these analysis contribute to making more plausible the central role experimentalism might have played (and can play) in struggles against injustice.

But, as we well know now, this is not the end of the story. Hence, my aim has also been to show that experimentalism is able to explain why in many of these historical cases something like an advancement in democracy and democratic practice has also taken place. Hence, by putting in practice experimental inquiries these movements have in some cases developed new forms of democratic practice like, for example, story-telling or collective experimentation. Other times they have fostered inclusion of social groups that were previously excluded from legitimate political participation, like undocumented immigrant women in the case of the struggle against evictions in Spain. In other cases, movements have called the attention on the political nature of certain practices that were until then considered to be external to the sphere of legitimate democratic decision-making. In order to show how all these democratic advancements can be connected to the struggle against injustice, I have drawn on a Deweyan epistemic justification of democracy, according to which, the capacity of experimental practices to effectively articulate injustices and propose solutions that constitute moral advancements is linked to the deepening of democratic norms of inclusion and participation.

This was, in short, the core argument of the book, which I presented in part II. However, in order to fully develop these ideas, I have followed several steps. The book began with a discussion concerning current debates on the epistemology of democracy. This was necessary in order to develop what I called an exploration of the political potential of democracy's epistemic value. Under this expression I understood the capacity of the epistemic justification of democracy to promote new, deeper understandings of democratic practice than those which are hegemonic at a certain moment in a democratic society. Since very few consensus exists about the very role democracy's epistemic justification should play for a theory of democracy, chapter 1 started by providing an overview of the different positions existing in current debate on the relation between democracy's intrinsic and epistemic values. Next to an incompatibilist view, according to which, both kinds of values are in potential contradiction—that is, the realization of fundamental intrinsic democratic values such as self-determination and its derivative norms such as inclusion or participatory equality might require practices of decision-making that are incompatible with the prospect of reaching the best possible outcomes—we can find compatibilist views, for whom the realization of democratic intrinsic values represents a necessary condition for the epistemic success of a decision-making process. However, I proposed to distinguish two main ways of understanding this idea. According to the first version of compatibilism, democratic institutions and practices can be justified simultaneously from an intrinsic and epistemic point of view. Since both sets of democratic values, epistemic and intrinsic, seem to justify democratic norms in the same way, I have called this position one of convergence. According to the second, "integrative" version, which draws from Fabienne Peter's work on epistemic democracy, both forms of justification are in a dynamic relation where epistemic values may promote the realization of deeper understandings of democracy's intrinsic values by disclosing new ways in which we can understand the values.

In order to develop the idea that democracy's epistemic values contribute to advancing democracy's intrinsic values I have endeavored to reconstruct the democratic theories of Axel Honneth and John Dewey as providing different mixed models of democratic justification: convergent and integrative. In my analysis I put special emphasis in their accounts of democratic practice and its transformations. Even if I have drawn on Honneth's notion of social freedom in order to account for what it means that intrinsic values are deepened, I have also shown that Honneth fails to provide the theoretical means for a full understanding of the political potential of democracy's epistemic value. Hence, while he characterizes democratic practices as a cooperative problem-solving activity, he subsumes the historical process of political-normative learning to a dynamics fully mediated by people's struggle for (political forms of) recognition. As I have aimed at showing, people's efforts to frame and solve injustices can be by themselves at the very root of the transformation of practices that challenge not only established understandings of political norms, but also even go beyond the reach of our current political imagination. This does not mean that we should deny the priority of the development of democracy's intrinsic values such as social freedom when identifying progress in political life. Hence, the last word about what constitutes a political progress must be left to people's ability to appropriate the new meanings given to political norms in a process such as the one Honneth describes in his methodological texts. However, these new meanings are sometimes disclosed by an epistemic dynamics that Honneth does not seem to take into account. In contrast to Honneth's view, John Dewey sees in democracy's epistemic value an independent social force that is responsible for the concretion, maintenance, and further development of democracy's intrinsic values. Drawing partially on Fabienne Peter, I have understood this relation of cooperation as the capacity of an autonomous epistemic normativity to promote the reinterpretation of political-ethical norms by making of this (re-)interpretation a functional requirement of problems of justice.

This exercise of explication of the political potential of democracy's epistemic dimension represents a necessary task providing the framework for a more specific question of this book, namely, that of the political contribution social movements can make in modern democratic societies. This is so because in many cases, social movements do not directly struggle for democracy, nor is democratization their central political concern. However, as feminists, ecologists, and antiracist protests of recent times have shown, movements struggling against injustice and for just social relations have also historically contributed to the advancement of democracy in a variety of ways. That the latter can be due to the adoption of experimentalism as a way of articulating injustice and searching for just social relations is the thesis I have attempted to substantiate in part II.

Finally, in part III I have developed further some of the consequences of my epistemic approach for an analysis of social movements. Firstly, I have shown that this approach complements the analysis of the counter-hegemonic practices of feminist movements provided by Miranda Fricker in her book on epistemic injustices. Hence, even if the power of consciousness-raising meetings to generate new categories such as "sexual harassment" is partly due to generation of conditions promoting the cognitive self-confidence of participants, our analysis has also to look at the fundamental epistemic operations that make possible the (re-)definition of categories, the generation of innovative hypotheses, and so on. Secondly, my expressivist approach to inquiry, which sees it essentially as a multidimensional process of articulation, has been shown to be able to account for certain aspects constitutive of the dynamics of social movements. Dewey's theory of social mobilization, as he formulated it in his Lectures in China, is able to grasp social mobilization from the perspective of the evolution of political claims raised by those suffering from oppression. As we saw, he provides a phenomenological approach to mobilization that divides any social struggle in three stages: a situation of blind acceptance of the situation of domination, the emergence of individualistic claims for freedom and finally, the emergence of a sense of contribution to the social whole. By understanding this three-stage process as one of collective self-articulation I hope to have shown that the way social movements raise their claims very much depends on the range of opportunities, given their members to participate and contribute to social life.

The present book should be understood as a reaction to the social, economic, and political developments that followed from the Lehman Brothers crash in 2008 and whose consequences are still visible in many parts of the world. The new cycle of protests that came into being after the effects of the 2008 economic crisis came to be felt almost all over the world was characterized by the generalization and radicalization of democratic claims (Ogien & Laugier 2014). This process took the form either of struggles for democracy tout court, particularly in those countries governed by authoritarian regimes, and of struggles for further democratization or democratic deepening in more or less consolidated democratic political systems. For many, however, the new cycle of protest contributed both in institutional and in more subtle ways—which usually remain unseen by political theorists—to a radical transformation of hegemonic understandings of democracy, concerning its institutional organization as well as its more or less formalized forms of political practice. In this context, authors like Albert Ogien and Sandra Laugier (2014) in France, drawing on central Deweyan insights, saw in those movements democratizing potential condensed from a learning process that had to do with an intensification of our moral sensibility.

The present account aims at providing a complementary interpretation to what Ogien and Laugier provided in 2014. In my view, the deepening of democratic understandings that came to be seen as condition for the solution of the problem of massive is only one example among many others. In Brazil, enormous protests aiming at further democratization had their local origin in the problems of public transportation and the more general problems afflicting the country, such as corruption and violence. In Turkey, protests in Taksim Square started with the privatization and construction plans of Gezi Park. In Greece, the effects of the economic crisis were dramatic and for many the radicalization of principles of political participation came to represent the only "method" to counteract both the deep causes and the dramatic consequences of the actions of the Greek government and the Troika. It would certainly be naive to reduce these dynamics from local problems to democratization to pure epistemic terms and abstract from the power of the ideas and the political cultures that the protesters brought with them into the streets. However, the link between local problem-solving and democratization seems undeniable. These forms of articulation of claims for a deepening of democracy and the particular struggle for justice, which is not unique to our time but which became particularly relevant in this preceding cycle of social protest, represent the particular reality the present study aims to account for.

Bibliography

Adorno, T. W. (2010). *Einführung in die Dialektik*. (1958). Berlin: Suhrkamp.

Almeida P. & Johnston, D. H. (2006). *Latin American Social Movements: Globalization, Democratization, and Transnational Networks*. Lanham, Md: Rowman & Littefield Publishers.

Anderson, E. (2006). The Epistemology of Democracy. *Episteme*, 3(1–2), 8–22.

Anderson, E. (2014). Social Movements, Experiments in Living, and Moral Progress: Case Studies from Britain's Abolition of Slavery. *The Lindley Lecture*. University of Kansas.

Anderson, E. (2015). Moral Bias and Corrective Practices: A Pragmatist Perspective. *Proceedings and Addresses of the APA*, 89, 21–47.

Anderson, E. (2016). The Social Epistemology of Morality: Learning from the Forgotten History of the Abolition of Slavery. In M. Brady & M. Fricker (eds.), *The Epistemic Life of Groups: Essays in Collective Epistemology*. Oxford: Oxford University Press, 75–94.

Ansell, C. (2011). *Pragmatist Democracy: Evolutionary Learning as Public Philosophy*. Oxford: Oxford University Press.

Antic, A. (2016). John Dewey's Philosophical Legacy for the Global Access to Knowledge Movement in the Digital Age. *Kinesis*, 41(1), 6–16.

Arendt, H. (1967). Truth and Politics. *The New Yorker*, Feb 25, 49–88.

Arendt, H. (2006). *On Revolution*. London: Penguin.

Arneson, R. (2004). Democracy Is Not Intrinsically Just. In K. Dowding, R. E. Goodin, & C. Pateman (eds.), *Justice and Democracy: Essays for Brian Barry*. Cambridge, UK: Cambridge University Press, 40–58.

Arribas Lozano, A. (2018). Knowledge Co-production with Social Movement Networks. Redefining Grassroots Politics, Rethinking Research. *Social Movement Studies*, 17(4), 451–463.

Aya, R. (2006). Theory, Fact, and Logic. In Goodin, R.E. & Ch. Tilly, *The Oxford Handbook of Contextual Political Analysis*, Oxford: Oxford University Press. 114–128.

Balibar, E. (2014). *Equaliberty: Political Essays*. Durham: Duke University Press.

Beverly, J. (2004). *Testimonio: The Politics of Truth*. Minneapolis: University of Minnesota Press.

Bohman, J. (1998). *Public Deliberation. Pluralism, Complexity and Democracy*. Cambridge, MA: MIT Press.

Bohman, J. (1999). Democracy as Inquiry, Inquiry as Democratic: Pragmatism, Social Science, and the Cognitive Division of Labor. *American Journal of Political Science*, 43(2), 590–607.

Bohman, J. (2004). Realizing Deliberative Democracy as a Mode of Inquiry: Pragmatism, Social Facts, and Normative Theory. *The Journal of Speculative Philosophy*, 18(1), 23–43.

Borio, G., F. Pozzi, & G. Roggero. (2007). Conricerca as Political Action. In M. Coté, R. J. F. Day, & G. de Pauter (eds.), *Utopian Pedagogy*. Toronto: University of Toronto Press. 163–185.

Bourdieu, P. (1979). *La Distinction*. Paris: Editions de Minuit.

Bourdieu, P. (1993). *La misère du monde*. Paris: Editions du Seuil.

Bourdieu, P. (2001). *Masculine Domination*. Stanford: Stanford University Press.

Brandom, R. B. (2019). *A Spirit of Trust: A Reading of Hegel's Phenomenology*. Cambridge, MA: Harvard University Press.

Brunkhorst, H. (1998). Demokratischer Experimentalismus. In H. Brunkhorst (ed.), *Demokratischer Experimentalismus: Politik in der komplexen Gesellschaft*. Frankfurt am Main: Suhrkamp, 7–12.

Casas-Cortés, M., M. Osterweil, & D. E. Powell (2008). Blurring Boundaries: Recognizing Knowledge-Practices in the Study of Social Movements. *Anthropological Quarterly*, 8(1), 17–58.

Casals, M. & Perry, M. (2020). De la democracia revolucionaria a la democracia posible. Trayectorias políticas y conceptuales de la democracia en la izquierda marxista chilena, c.1950-c. 1990. *Historia*, 56(1), 11–44.

Castoriadis, C., E. Escobar, M. Gondicas, & P. Vernay. (2013a). *Quelle démocratie?* Vol. 1. Paris: Sandre.

Castoriadis, C., E. Escobar, M. Gondicas, & P. Vernay. (2013b). *Quelle démocratie?* Vol. 2. Paris: Sandre.

Cefaï, D. (2001). Les cadres de l'action collective. Definitions et problèmes. In D. Cefai & D. Trom (eds.), *Les formes de l'action collective. Mobilisations dans les arènes publiques*. Paris: Editions de l'EHESS, 51–98.

Cefaï, D. (2007). *Pourquoi se mobilise-t-on? Les théories de l'action collective*. Paris: La Découverte.

Cefaï, D. (2016). Publics, problèmes publics, arènes publiques . . . Que nous apprend le pragmatisme ? *Questions de communication*, 30, 25–64.

Cefaï, D., & C. Lafaye. (2001). Lieux et moments d'une mobilisation collective. Le cas d'une as sociation de quartier. In D. Cefai & D. Trom (eds.), *Les formes de l'action collective. Mobilisations dans les arènes publiques*. Paris: Editions de l'EHESS, 195–228.

Cefaï, D., & C. Terzi (ed.) (2012). Présentation. In *L'expérience des problèmes publics*. Paris: Editions de l'EHESS. 9–47.

Celikates, R. (2009). *Kritik als soziale Praxis*. Frankfurt am Main: Campus Verlag.

Celikates, R. (2015). Digital Publics. Digital Contestation: A New Structural Transformation of the Public Sphere? In R. Celikates, R. Kreide, & T. Wesche (eds.), *Transformations of Democracy: Crisis, Protest and Legitimation*. London: Rowman & Littlefield Publishers. 159–175.

Celikates, R. (2018). *Critique as Social Practice: Critical Theory and Social Self-Understanding*. London: Rowman & Littlefield.

Chesters, G., & I. Welsh. (2010). *Social Movements: the Key Concepts*. London and New York: Routledge.

Christiano, Th. (1996). *The Rule of the Many. Fundamental Issues in Democratic Theory*. Boulder, CO: Westview Press.

Cohen, J. (1986). An Epistemic Conception of Democracy. *Ethics*, 97(1), 26–38.

Colau, A., & A. Alemany. (2013). *¡Sí se puede!: Crónica de una pequeña gran victoria*. Barcelona: Planeta.

Cox, L., (2014). Movements Making Knowledge: A New Wave of Inspiration for Sociology?. *Sociology*, 48(5), 954–971.

Dahlgren, P. (2005). The Internet, Public Spheres, and Political Communication: Dispersion and Deliberation. *Political Communication*, 22(2), 147–162.

De la Dehesa, R. (2010). *Queering the Public Sphere in Mexico and Brazil*. Durham: Duke University Press.

Della Porta, D. (2009). *Democracy in Social Movements*. New York: Palgrave Macmillan.

Della Porta, D. (2013). *Can Democracy be Saved?* Cambridge, MA: Polity Press.

Della Porta, D. (2017). Progressive and Regressive Politics in Late Liberalism. In H. Geiselberger (ed.), *The Great Regression*. Cambridge, UK: Polity Press. 26–29.

Della Porta, D., & E. Palava. (2017). Repertoires of Knowledge Practices: Social Movements in Times of Crisis. *Qualitative Research in Organizations and Management: An International Journal*, 12(4), 297–314.

Demirović, Alex. 1989. *Demokratie, Ökologie, ökologische Demokratie: Demokratievorstellungen und -konzepte der neuen sozialen Bewegungen und der Partei 'Die Grünen'*. Berlin: IKO-Verlag für Interkulturelle Kommunikation.

De Sousa Santos, B. (2005). *Democratizing Democracy: Beyond the Liberal Democratic Canon*. London: Verso.

De Sousa Santos, B. (2009). *Una epistemología del sur: la reinvención del conocimiento y la emancipación social*. Barcelona: Siglo XXI.

Dewey, J. (1916). *Democracy and Education. The Middle Works, 1899–1924*. Vol. 9. Carbondale: Southern Illinois University Press.

Dewey, J. (1925). *Experience and Nature. The Latter Works, 1925–1953*. Vol. 1. Carbondale: Southern Illinois University Press.

Dewey, J. (1927). *The Public and Its Problems. The Later Works, 1925–1953*. Vol. 2. Carbondale: Southern Illinois University Press.

Dewey, J. (1929). *The Quest for Certainty. The Later Works, 1925–1953*. Vol. 4. Carbondale: Southern Illinois University Press.

Dewey, J. (1930). *Individualism Old and New. The Later Works, 1925–1953*. Vol. 5. Carbondale: Southern Illinois University Press. 42–124.

Dewey, J. (1934). *Art as Experience. The Later Works, 1925–1953.* Vol. 10. Carbondale: Southern Illinois University Press.

Dewey, J. (1935). *Liberalism and Social Action. The Later Works, 1925–1953.* Vol. 11. Carbondale: Southern Illinois University Press. 1–65.

Dewey, J. (1938). *Logic: The Theory of Inquiry. The Later Works, 1925–1953.* Vol. 12. Carbondale: Southern Illinois University Press.

Dewey, J. (1939b). *Freedom and Culture. The Later Works, 1925–1953.* Vol. 13. Carbondale: Southern Illinois University Press.

Dewey, J. (1973). *Lectures in China 1919–1920.* Honolulu: The University Press of Hawaii.

Dewey, J. (2015). Lectures in Social and Political Philosophy. *European Journal of Pragmatism and American Philosophy*, 7(2), 7–44.

Dewey, J., & J. Tufts. (1932). *Ethics. The Later Works, 1925–1953.* Vol. 14. Carbondale: Southern Illinois University Press.

Diaz, P. (2012). D'une verité à l'autre sur les crimes du passé. Le cas de Chili. In D. Cefaï & C. Terzi (eds.), *L'expérience des problèmes publics*, 221–350.

Dorf, M. (2012). Could Occupy Wall Street Become the Realization of Democratic Experimentalism's Aspiration for Pragmatic Politics? *Contemporary Pragmatism*, 9(2), 263–271.

Dorf, M., & C. Sabel. (1998). Constitution of Democratic Experimentalism. *Columbia Law Review*, 98(2), 267–473.

Dryzek, J. (2000). *Deliberative Democracy and Beyond: Liberals, Critics, Contestations.* Oxford: Oxford University Press.

Estalella, A., & A. Corsín. (2013). Assambleas populares: el ritmo urbano de una política de la experimentación. In M. Cruells & P. Ibarra (eds.), *La democracia del futuro. Del 15M a la emergencia de una sociedad civil viva.* Barcelona: Icaria, 61–80.

Estlund, D. (2008). *Democratic Authority. A Philosophical Framework.* Princeton: Princeton University Press.

Fairfield, P. (2013). *Philosophical Hermeneutics Reinterpreted. Dialogues with Existentialism, Pragmatism, Critical Theory and Postmodernism.* London & New York: Bloomsbury.

Festenstein, M. (1997). *Pragmatism & Political Theory.* Cambridge: Polity Press.

Festenstein, M. (2004). Deliberative Democracy and Two Models of Pragmatism. *European Journal of Social Theory*, 7(3), 291–306.

Festenstein, M. (2018). Does Dewey Have an "Epistemic Argument" for Democracy? *Contemporary Pragmatism*, 16(2–3), 217–241.

Fraser, N. (1992). Rethinking the Public Sphere: A Contribution to the Critique of the Actually Existing Democracies. In C. Calhoun (ed.), *Habermas and the Public Sphere*. Cambridge, MA: The MIT Press.

Frega, R. (2006). *John Dewey et la philosophie comme épistémologie de la pratique.* Paris: l'Harmattan.

Frega, R. (2010). What Pragmatism Means by Public Reason. *Ethics & Politics*, 12(1), 28–51.

Frega, R. (2014). Between Pragmatism and Critical Theory: Social Philosophy Today. *Human Studies*, 37(1), 57–82.

Frega, R. (2015a). John Dewey's Social Philosophy: A Restatement. *European Journal of Pragmatism and American Philosophy*, 7(2), 98–127.

Frega, R. (2015b). Beyond Morality and Ethical Life: Pragmatism and Critical Theory Cross Path. *Journal of Philosophical Research*, 40, 63–96.

Frega, R. (2016). Pragmatizing Critical Theory's Province. *Dewey Studies*, 1(2), 4–47.

Frega, R. (2019). *Pragmatism and the Wide View of Democracy*. Berlin: Springer.

Fricker, M. (2007). *Epistemic Injustice*. Oxford: Oxford University Press.

Fung, A., & E. O. Wright. (2003). *Deepening Democracy. Institutional Innovations in Empowered Participatory Governance*. London: Verso.

Ghis Malfilatre, M. (2017a). The Impossible Confinement of Nuclear Work: Professional and Family Experiences of Subcontracted Workers Exposed to Radioactivity. *Travail et emploi*, Hors-série, 5, 103–125.

Ghis Malfilatre, M. (2017b). La CGT face au problème de la sous-traitance nucléaire. Le cas de la mobilisation de Chinon (1987–1997). *Sociologie du travail*, 59(1). Available at https://journals.openedition.org/sdt/570, accessed March 08, 2021.

Graeber, D. (2013). *The Democracy Project: A History, a Crisis, a Movement*. London: Penguin.

Guzman-Concha, C. (2012). The Students' Rebellion in Chile: Occupy Protest or Classic Social Movement? *Social Movement Studies*, 11(3–4), 408–415.

Habermas, J. (1991). *The Structural Transformation of the Public Sphere: An Inquiry into a Category of Bourgeois Society*. Cambridge, MA: The MIT Press.

Habermas, J. (1998a). On the Internal Relation Between the Rule of Law and Democracy. In J. Habermas (ed.), *The Inclusion of the Other*. Cambridge, MA: MIT Press.

Habermas, J. (1998b). *Between Facts and Norms: Contributions to a Discourse Theory of Law and Democracy*. Cambridge, MA: MIT Pr.

Habermas, J. (2003). *Truth and Justification*. Oxford: Polity.

Hartmann, M. (2003). *Die Kreativität der Gewohnheit: Grundzüge einer pragmatistischen Demokratietheorie*. Frankfurt am Main: Campus Verlag.

Hirschman, A. O. (1977). *The Passions and the Interests. Political Arguments for Capitalism Before Its Triumph*. Princeton, NJ: Princeton University Press.

Honneth, A. (1995). Moral Consciousness and Class Domination: Some Problems in the Analysis of Hidden Morality. In *The Fragmented World of the Social*. Albany: State University of New York Press. 207–219.

Honneth, A. (1998). Democracy as Reflexive Cooperation. John Dewey and the Theory of Democracy Today. *Political Theory*, 26(6), 763–783.

Honneth, A. (2014a). *Freedom's Right: The Social Foundations of Democratic Life*. Cambridge, UK: Polity Press.

Honneth, A. (2014b). The Normativity of Ethical Life. *Philosophy and Social Criticism*, 40(8), 817–826.

Honneth, A. (2015). *The Struggle for Recognition: The Moral Grammar of Social Conflicts*. John Wiley & Sons.

Honneth, A. (2017a). Three, Not Two, Concepts of Liberty: A Proposal to Enlarge Our Moral Self-Understanding. In R. Zuckert & j. Kreines (Eds.), *Hegel on Philosophy in History*. Cambridge: Cambridge University Press, 177–192.

Honneth, A. (2017b). *The Idea of Socialism. Towards a Renewal.* Cambridge, UK: Polity Press.

Honneth, A., & F. Sütterluty. (2011). Normative Paradoxien der Gegenwart. *Westend,* 8(1), 67–85.

Hunyadi, M. (ed.) (2014). *Axel Honneth: de la reconaissance à la liberté.* Paris: Le Bord de l 'Eau.

Jaeggi, Rahel. (2014). *Alienation.* Columbia University Press.

Jamison, A. (2001). *The Making of Green Knowledge: Environmental Politics and Cultural Transformation.* Cambridge: Cambridge University Press.

Jung, M. (2009). *Der bewusste Ausdruck: Anthropologie der Artikulation.* Berlin, New York: de Gruyter.

Kadlec, A. (2007). *Dewey's Critical Pragmatism.* Lanham, MD: Lexington Books.

Kettner, M. (2015). John Deweys demokratische Experimentiergemeinschaft. In *De mok ratischer Experimentalismus. Politik in der Komplexen Gesellschaft.*

Kitcher, Ph. (2001). *Science, Truth and Democracy.* Oxford: Oxford University Press.

Laclau, E. (2005). *On Populist Reason.* London & New York: Verso Books.

Levi, I. (2011). Dewey's Logic of Inquiry. In M. Cochran (ed.), *The Cambridge Companion to Dewey.* Cambridge: Cambridge University Press.

Longino, H. (2002). *The Fate of Knowledge.* Princeton: Princeton University Press.

Maeckelbergh, M. (2009). *The Will of the Many: How the Alterglobalisation Movement is Changing the Face of Democracy.* London & New York: Pluto Press.

Mansbridge, J. (1998). Feminism and Democracy. In Phillips, A. (ed.), *Feminism and Politics.* Oxford University Press. 142–160.

Mansbridge, J. (2001a). The Making of Oppositional Consciousness. In J. Mansbridge & A. Morris (ed.), *Oppositional Consciousness: The Subjective Roots of Social Protest.* Chicago & London: The University of Chicago Press. 1–19.

Mansbridge, J. (2001b). Complicating Oppositional Consciousness. In J. Mansbridge, & A. Morris (ed.), *Oppositional Consciousness: The Subjective Roots of Social Protest.* Chicago & London: The University of Chicago Press. 238–264.

Martí, J. L. (2017). Democracy, Indignados, and the Republican Tradition in Spain. In J. Muñoz-Bassols, L. Lonsdale & M. Delgado Morales (eds.), *The Routledge Companion to Iberian Studies.* Abingdon: Routledge. 558–569.

McAdam, D., McCarthy, J. & M. Zald (1996). Opportunity Mobilizing and Framing Processes—Toward a Synthetic, Comparative Perspetive on Social Movements. In D. McAdam, J. McCarthy & M. Zald (eds.), *Comparative Perspective on Social Movements.* Cambridge: Cambridge University Press, 1–20.

Medina, J. (2012). *The Epistemology of Resistance.* Oxford: Oxford University Press.

Mills, Ch. W. (1998). *Blackness Visible. Essays on Philosophy and Race.* Ithaca, London: Cornell University Press.

Mir Garcia, J. (2016). *A Democratic Revolution Underway in Barcelona.* Near Futures Online 1 "Europe at a Crossroads."

Negt, O., & A. Kluge. (1972). *Öffentlichkeit und Erfahrung. Zur Organisationsanalyse von bürgerlicher und proletarischer Öffentlichkeit.* Frankfurt am Main: Suhrkamp.

Ogien, A., & S. Laugier. (2014). *Le principe démocratie. Enquête sur les nouvelles formes du politique.* Paris: La Découverte.

Orellana, P., & E. Q. Hutchison. (1991). *El Movimiento de Derechos Humanos en Chile 1973–1990.* Santiago de Chile: CEPLA.

Pappas, G. (2016). ILA AND JOHN MELLOW PRIZE: The Pragmatist's Approach to Injustice. *The Pluralist,* 11(1), 58–77.

Peter, F. (2009). *Democratic Legitimacy.* London and New York: Routledge.

Peters, B. (2001). Deliberative Öffentlichkeit. In L. Wingert and K. Günther (eds.), *Die Öffentlichkeit der Vernunft und die Vernunft der Öffentlichkeit. Festschrift für Jürgen Habermas.* Frankfurt am Main: Suhrkamp, 655–677.

Polletta, F. (2004). *Freedom Is an Endless Meeting: Democracy in American Social Movements.* University of Chicago Press.

Putnam, H. (1990). A Reconsideration of Deweyan Democracy. *Southern California Law Review,* 63, 1671–1697.

Putnam, H. (2002). *The Collapse of the Fact/Value Dichotomy and Other Essays.* Cambridge, MA: Harvard University Press.

Queré, L. (2012). Le travail des émotions dnas l'expérience publique. Marées vertes en Bretagne. In D. Cefaï & C. Terzi (eds.) *L'expérience des problèmes publics* Paris: Editions de l'EHESS, 135–163.

Renault, E. (2008). *Souffrances sociales : Philosophie, psychologie et politique.* Paris: Editions La Découverte.

Renault, E. (2019). *The Experience of Injustice: A Theory of Recognition.* New York: Columbia University Press.

Rheinberger, H-J. (1997). *Toward a History of Epistemic Things: Synthesizing Proteins in the Test Tube.* Stanford, CA: Stanford University Press.

Richter, E. (2008). *Die Wurzeln der Demokratie.* Weilerswist: Velbrueck.

Rogers, M. L. (2009). Dewey, Pluralism and Democracy. Response to Robert Talisse. *Transactions of the Charles S. Peirce Society,* 45(1), 75–79.

Roggero, G. (2011). *The Production of Living Knowledge: The Crisis of the University and the Transformation of Labor in Europe and North America.* Philadelphia: Temple University Press.

Sabel, Ch. (2012). Dewey, Democray, and Democratic Experimentalism, *Contemporary Pragmatism,* 9(2), 35–55.

Santarelli, M. & Serrano Zamora, J. (2020). The Affective Side of Political Identities: Between Pragmatism and European Social Theory. In Festl, M. (ed.), *Pragmatism and Social Philosophy: Exploring a Stream of Ideas from America to Europe,* New York & London: Routledge. 248–264.

Särkelä, A. (2013). Ein Drama in Drei Akten. *Deutsche Zeitschrift für Philosophie,* 61(5–6), 681–696.

Särkelä, A. (2020). American Pragmatism and Frankfurt School Critical Theory: A Family Drama. In M. Festl (ed.), *Pragmatism and Social Philosophy: Exploring a Stream of Ideas from America to Europe.* New York & London: Routledge, 145–162.

Särkelä, A., & J. Serrano Zamora. (2017). John Dewey and Social Criticism: An Introduction. *Journal of Speculative Philosophy,* 31(2), 213–217.

Seigfried, C. H. (1996). *Pragmatism and Feminism: Reweaving the Social Fabric.* Chicago: University of Chicago Press.

Serrano Zamora, J. (in preparation). Articulating the Social: An Expressivist Approach to Dewey's Epistemic Argument for Democracy.

Serrano Zamora, J., & L. Herzog. (under review). A Real Epistemic Utopia? Epistemic Practices in a Climate Camp.

Serrano Zamora, J., & M. Santarelli. (2020). Populism or Pragmatism: Two Ways of Under-standing Political Articulation. *Constellations: An International Journal of Critical and Democratic Theory*, 1–15.

Smith, K. (1998). Storytelling, Sympathy and Moral Judgment in American Abolitionism. *Journal of Political Philosophy*, 6(4), 356–377.

Stahl, T. (2013). *Immanente Kritik. Elemente einer Theorie sozialer Praktiken*. Frankfurt am Main, New York: Campus Verlag.

Stråth, B., & P. Wagner. (2017). *European Modernity: A Global Approach*. London & Oxford: Bloomsbury Publishing.

Suárez, M. (2014). Movimientos Sociales y Buen Vivir: Ecuatorianos en la lucha por la vivienda en la plataforma de afectados por la hipoteca (PAH). *Revista de Antropología Experimental*, 14(6), 71–89.

Taylor. Ch. (1977). *Hegel*. Cambridge: Cambridge University Press.

Taylor, Ch. (1985). *Philosophical Papers I: Human Agency and Language*. Cambridge: Cambridge University Press.

Taylor, Ch. (1989). *Sources of the Self: The Making of the Modern Identity*. Cambridge: Cambridge University Press.

Testa, I. (2017). The Authority of Life. The Critical Task of Dewey's Social Ontology. *Journal of Speculative Philosophy*, 31(2), 231–244.

Tilly, C., & L. J. Wood. (2016). *Social Movements 1768–2012*. London & New York: Routledge.

Tully, J. (1995). *Strange Multiplicity: Constitutionalism in an Age of Diversity*. Cambridge: Cambridge University Press.

Trom, D. & B. Zimmerman. (2001). Cadres et institutions des problèmes publics. Le cas du chomage et du paysage. In Cefaï, D. & Trom, D., *Formes de mobilisation collective. Mobilisations dans les arènes publiques*. Paris: EHESS. 281–315.

Von Eschen, P. M. (1997). *Race Against Empire: Black Americans and Anticolonialism, 1937–1957*. Ithaca & London: Cornell University Press.

Young, I. M. (2001). *Inclusion and Democracy*. Oxford: Oxford University Press.

Wagner, P. (2016). *Progress: A Reconstruction*. Cambridge: Polity Press.

Westbrook, R. (1991). *John Dewey and American Democracy*. Ithaca: Cornell University Press.

Index

act of expression, 166–67, 176, 181–87
Adorno, Theodor W., xvii–xviiin29,
    135–39
Anderson, Elizabeth: on epistemic
    democracy, xv, 7, 23, 127, 131; on
    social movements, xxii, 82, 88–89,
    94–95, 99
Arendt, Hanna: on politics and truth,
    65–70; on the value of democracy,
    5–6, 15, 27–30
Arneson, Richard J., 5
assemblies, 13, 15, 111–12, 118–19,
    146, 157–58, 191
autonomy: of the individual, 47, 49,
    59–60, 80–82; political, 58–59, 61,
    80–82; private. *See* autonomy of the
    individual

Balibar, Etienne, xiin21
Bohman, James, 82–83, 95–100, 131
Bourdieu, Pierre, 30, 150, 167, 170
Brandom, Robert, 128
Brunkhorst, Hauke, 126

Cefaï, Daniel, xin13, xiin17
Celikates, Robin, xin16
Chilean dictatorship, 150–52
climate camp, 106, 157–58
Cohen, Joshua, xv, xvin26, 81

collective aims, 167, 173, 181–87
collective learning, x, 12, 77, 117, 157,
    165–66, 173, 186, 188
conricerca, xxi, 153–56

democracy: advancing, xix, 4, 10–11,
    13, 16–17, 39, 64–65, 70–71,
    79, 107, 144, 192–94. *See also*
    deepening democracy; crisis of, 49,
    52, 54–56; deepening, ix–xxii, 8,
    15–17, 38, 42–45, 55–56, 60, 75, 79,
    113–14, 130–36, 145, 148–50, 158–
    59, 191–95; epistemic dimension of.
    See epistemic value of democracy;
    epistemic value of, xv–xx, 3–14, 16,
    19, 26, 39, 41, 57, 68–71, 80, 105,
    109, 130, 152, 156, 192–93; intrinsic
    value of, xiv, xvii, xx, 3–17, 19, 26,
    36, 39, 41, 48, 57, 71, 75, 84, 86,
    91, 94, 109, 130, 153, 161, 192–93;
    Jeffersonian, 50–51, 54; radical, 27,
    158
Dewey, John: and Adorno, xvii–
    xviiin29, 136–39; on articulation,
    xviii, 109, 128–30, 166–67, 175–90.
    See also act of expression; on
    dominant groups, 76, 170–72, 177–
    81, 186–90; on epistemic practices.
    See Dewey on experimental inquiry;

www.ingramcontent.com/pod-product-compliance
Lightning Source LLC
Chambersburg PA
CBHW022311280326
41932CB00010B/1061